THE MANGA
COOKBOOK

Japanese Bento Boxes, Main Dishes and More!

Critical acclaim for
The Manga Cookbook

"When I first spotted *The Manga Cookbook* I just loved the concept. It was the perfect combination of my two newfound hobbies, cooking and reading comics."
Esther Keller, *School Library Journal*

"The book is so popular that it's outselling weighty tomes written by stars of the Japanese TV show *Iron Chef.*"
Lynn Andriani, *Gourmet Magazine*

"After many of the recipes is additional information, often quite fascinating, about the dishes and ingredients. You will learn plenty of Japanese culinary terms as well as elements of Japanese culture."
Richard Auffrey, *The Passionate Foodie*

"Any kid who likes comics will love this book — and may be inspired to head to the kitchen to do a little cooking."
Jolene Thym, *Oakland Tribune*

"A lovely little collection of Japanese recipes."
Brigid Alverson, *Graphic Novel Reporter*

"Top 10 Popular Paperbacks" selection for 2011
American Library Association / Young Adult Library Services Association

"Quick Pick for Reluctant Young Adult Readers" selection for 2009
American Library Association / Young Adult Library Services Association

THE MANGA
COOKBOOK

Japanese Bento Boxes, Main Dishes and More!

Presented by the Manga University Culinary Institute

Illustrated by Chihiro Hattori

Japanime

TOKYO   SAN FRANCISCO

The Manga Cookbook:
Japanese Bento Boxes, Main Dishes and More!
Presented by the Manga University Culinary Institute
Featuring recipes by Yoko Ishihara
Illustrated by Chihiro Hattori

Published by Manga University under the auspices of Japanime Co. Ltd.,
3-31-18 Nishi-Kawaguchi, Kawaguchi-shi, Saitama 332-0021, Japan.

www.mangauniversity.com

A sweet thing is another belly.

ISBN: 978-4-921205-07-2
eISBN: 978-4-921205-59-1 (ebook)

26 25 24 23 22   y 25 24 23 22 21

Printed in the U.S.A.

 # FOREWORD

Your favorite Japanese comic books frequently show the characters eating unusual things. Triangles of rice wrapped in seaweed. Tiny sausages shaped like octopuses. Pastries filled with ... *beans?!*

Don't laugh. Japanese food may seem a bit strange at first, but it's actually very tasty, relatively easy to make, and not that unusual at all. In fact, around the world, people hoping to eat better are looking toward Japan and its famously healthy cuisine. And Japanese food is more than just restaurant staples like sushi and tempura. In fact, Japanese meals have a dimension to them that go far beyond the mere ingredients of each dish.

The Japanese use the word *mitateru* to describe the appearance of their food — and more specifically, food that's been arranged to look like something else. Apples shaped like rabbits. Box lunches laid out like flower gardens. The possibilities are endless.

By the time you're done with this book, you'll be a mitateru master. This alone won't ensure a tasty meal, raise its nutritional value or even guarantee that the picky eater in your house will try it. But it will help fill your stomach, and your heart, with *omotenashi* — a concept that simultaneously means hospitality, entertainment and service. In other words, by giving your food a unique and creative look, the overall experience of eating it is more pleasurable because it's surprising and fun.

And if you follow our recipes, you'll soon be eating like a manga character, too!

Cast of Characters

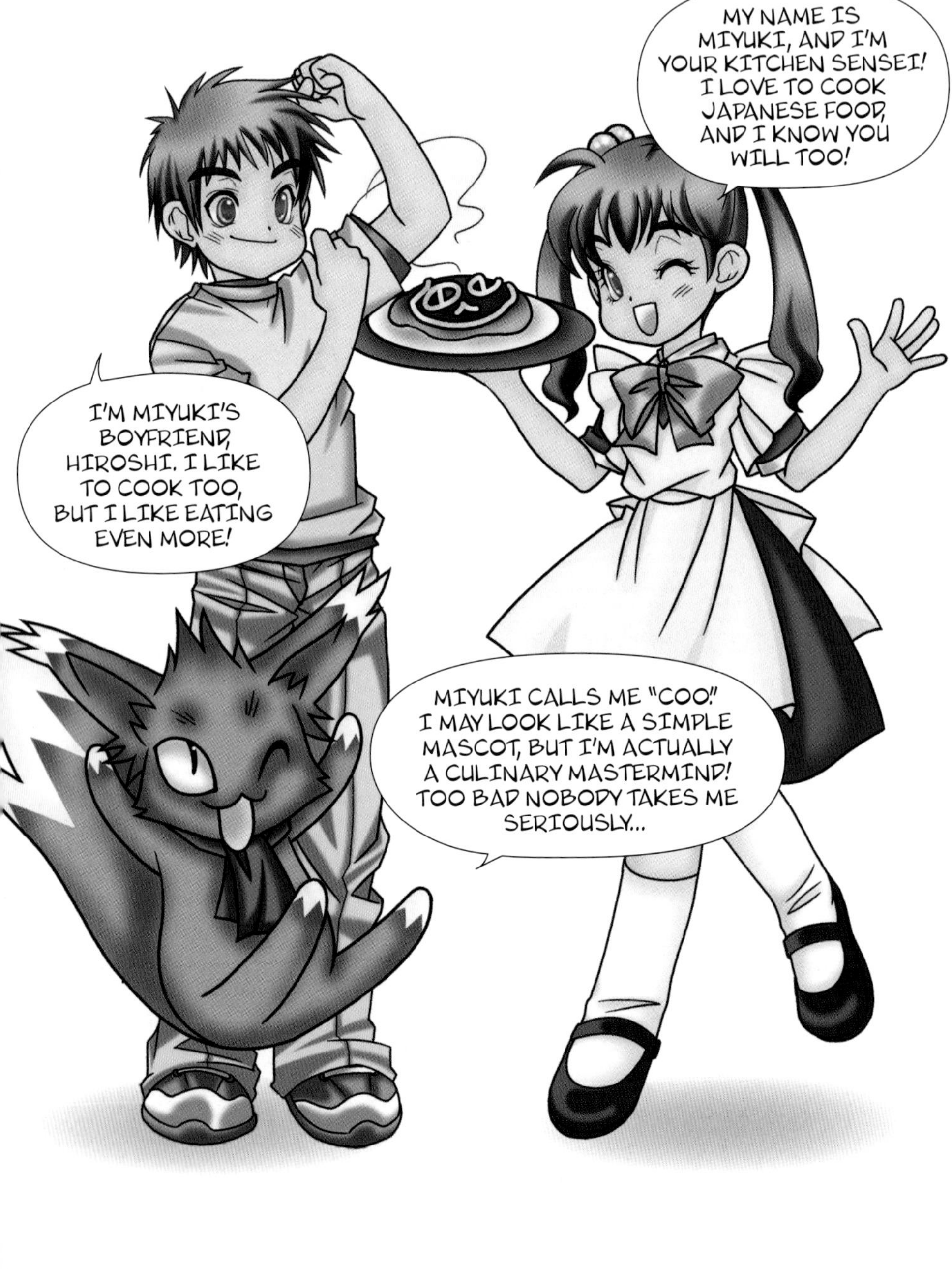
MY NAME IS MIYUKI, AND I'M YOUR KITCHEN SENSEI! I LOVE TO COOK JAPANESE FOOD, AND I KNOW YOU WILL TOO!
I'M MIYUKI'S BOYFRIEND, HIROSHI. I LIKE TO COOK TOO, BUT I LIKE EATING EVEN MORE!
MIYUKI CALLS ME "COO!" I MAY LOOK LIKE A SIMPLE MASCOT, BUT I'M ACTUALLY A CULINARY MASTERMIND! TOO BAD NOBODY TAKES ME SERIOUSLY...

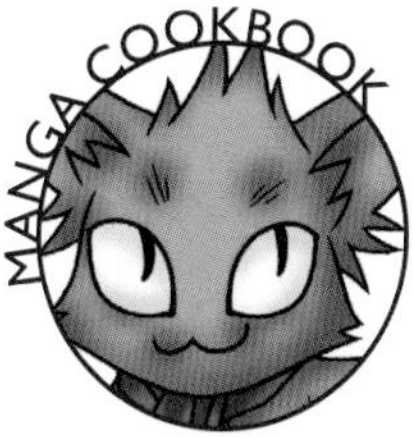
MANGA COOKBOOK

TABLE OF CONTENTS

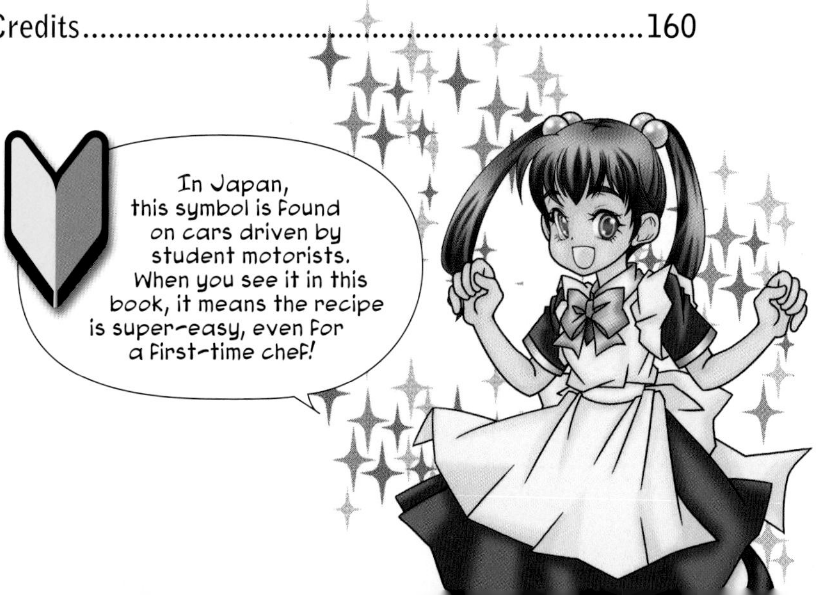
In Japan, this symbol is found on cars driven by student motorists. When you see it in this book, it means the recipe is super-easy, even for a first-time chef!

How to Use Chopsticks

Chopsticks, or *hashi*, are the primary eating utensils of Japan and other parts of Asia. Disposable wooden chopsticks called *waribashi* are commonly found in restaurants, while the ones used at home are made of plastic or lacquerware.

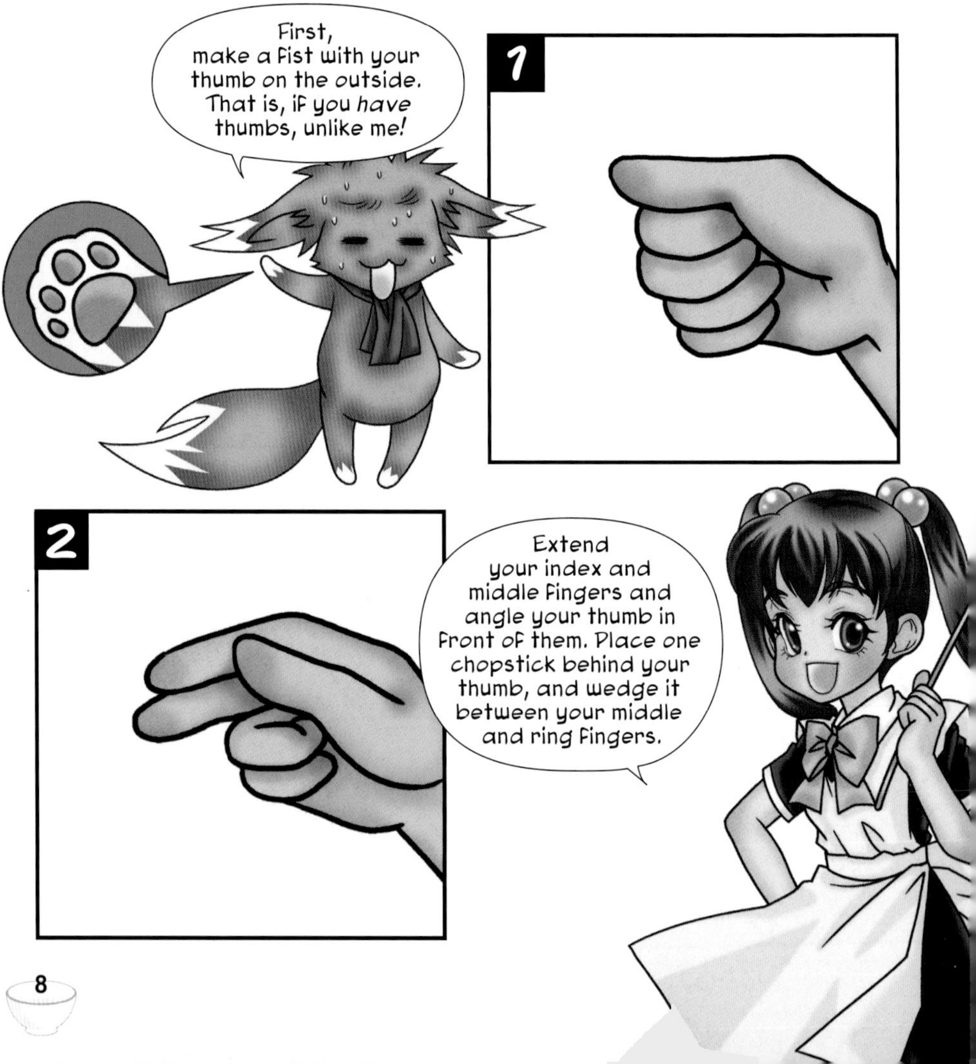
First, make a fist with your thumb on the outside. That is, if you *have* thumbs, unlike me!
1
2
Extend your index and middle fingers and angle your thumb in front of them. Place one chopstick behind your thumb, and wedge it between your middle and ring fingers.

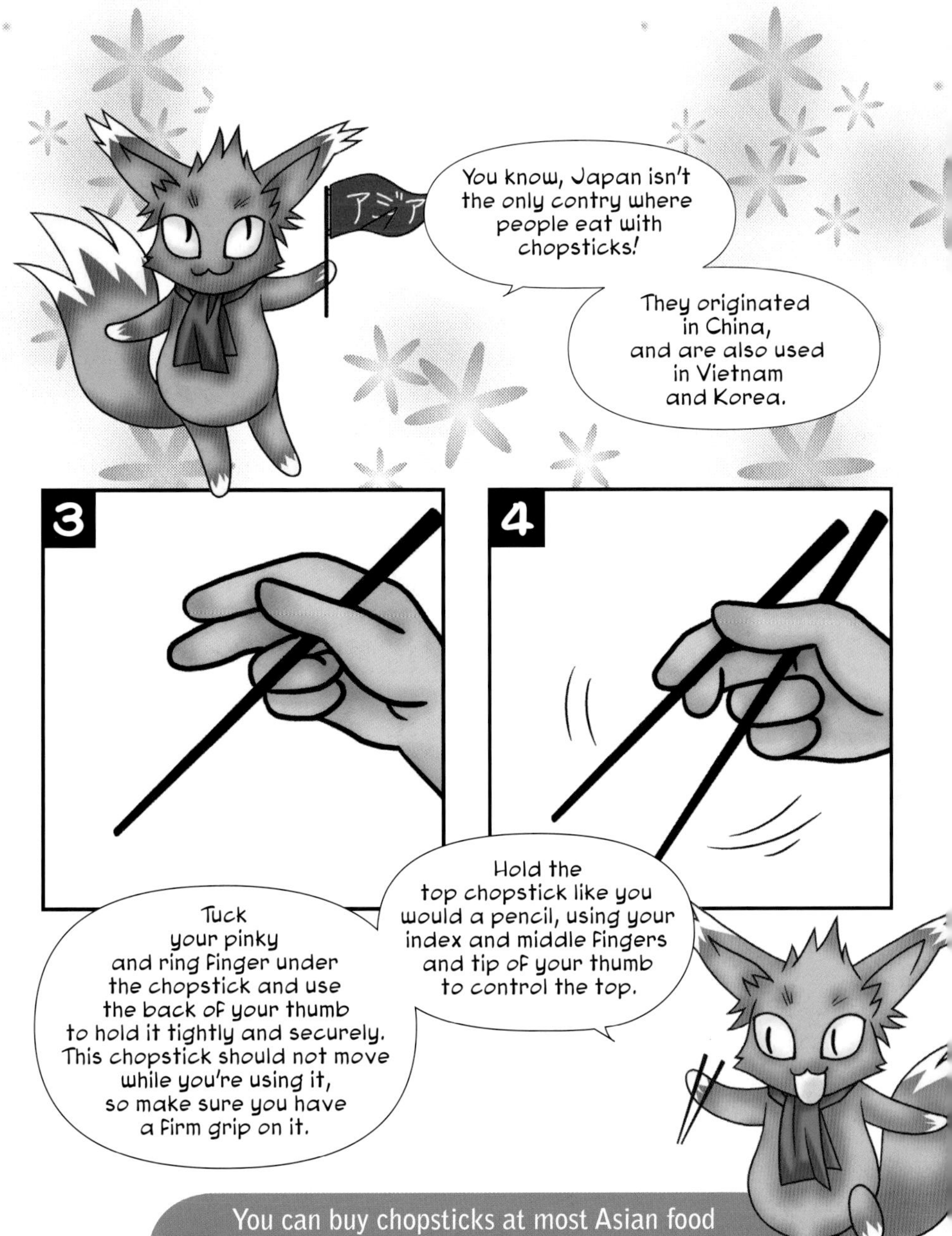
アジア
You know, Japan isn't the only contry where people eat with chopsticks!
They originated in China, and are also used in Vietnam and Korea.
3
4
Tuck your pinky and ring finger under the chopstick and use the back of your thumb to hold it tightly and securely. This chopstick should not move while you're using it, so make sure you have a firm grip on it.
Hold the top chopstick like you would a pencil, using your index and middle fingers and tip of your thumb to control the top.

You can buy chopsticks at most Asian food and gift shops. Or, the next time you go to a Japanese or Chinese restaurant, ask the server for an extra pair that you can take home for practice.

Appealing Appetizers

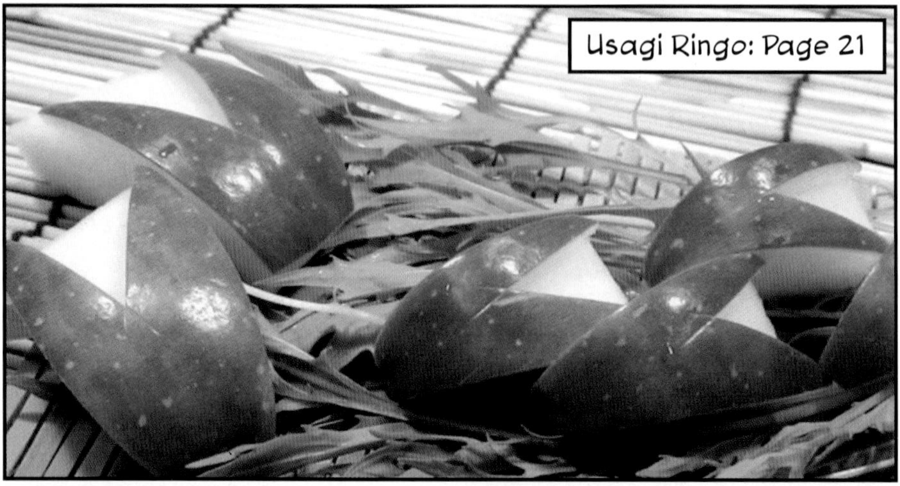
Usagi Ringo: Page 21

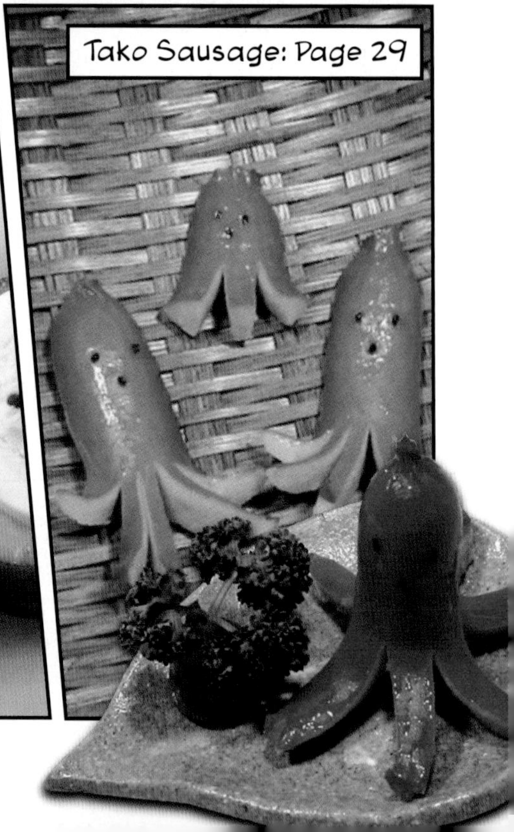
Tako Sausage: Page 29

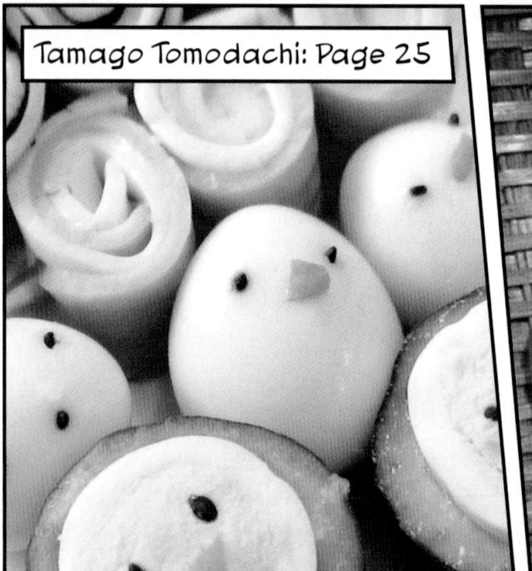
Tamago Tomodachi: Page 25

Bento Basics

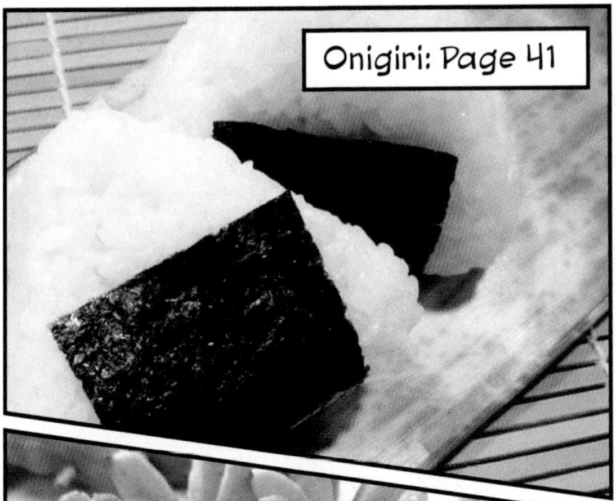

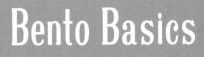

Onigiri: Page 41

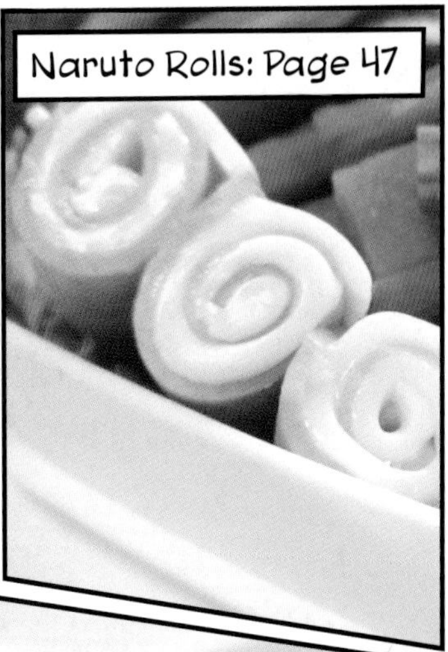

Naruto Rolls: Page 47

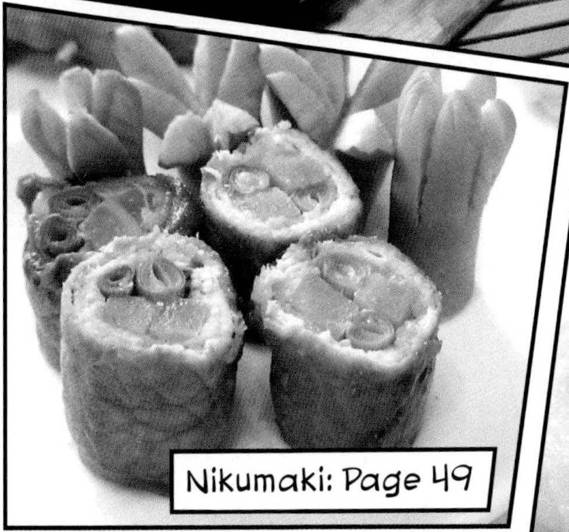

Nikumaki: Page 49

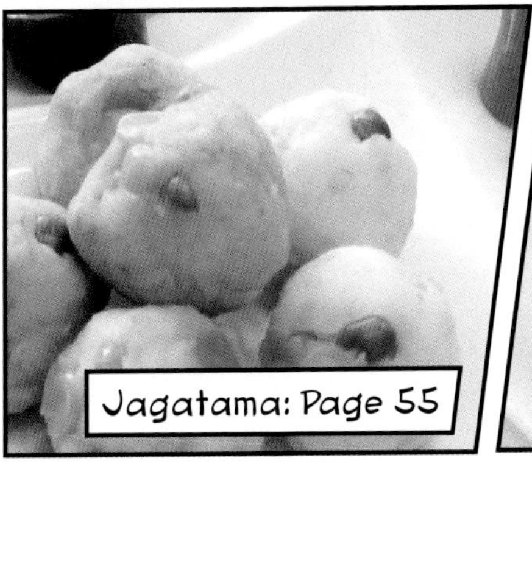

Jagatama: Page 55

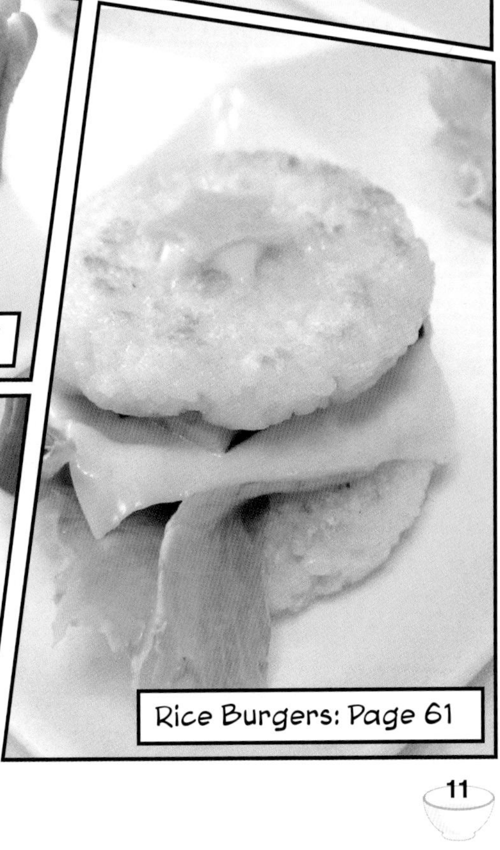

Rice Burgers: Page 61

Bento Basics

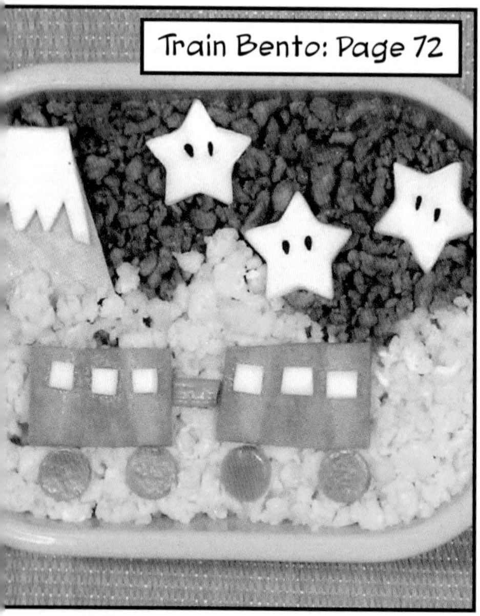

Train Bento: Page 72

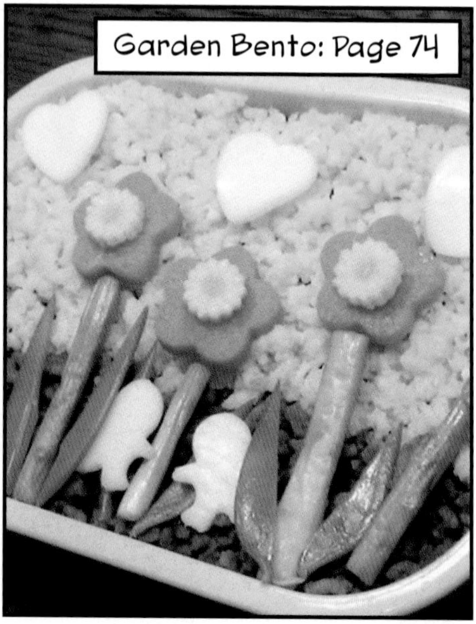

Garden Bento: Page 74

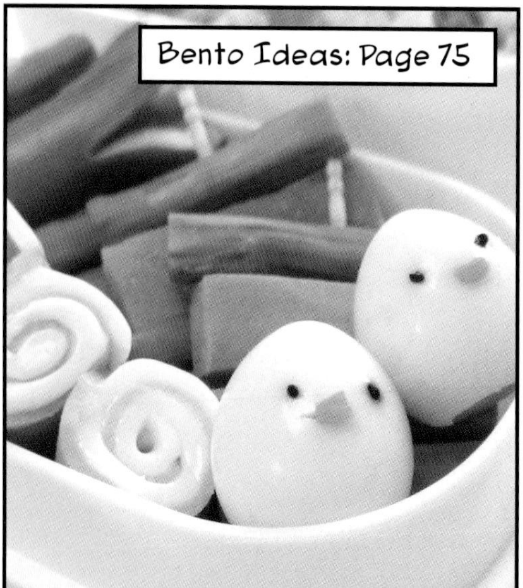

Bento Ideas: Page 75

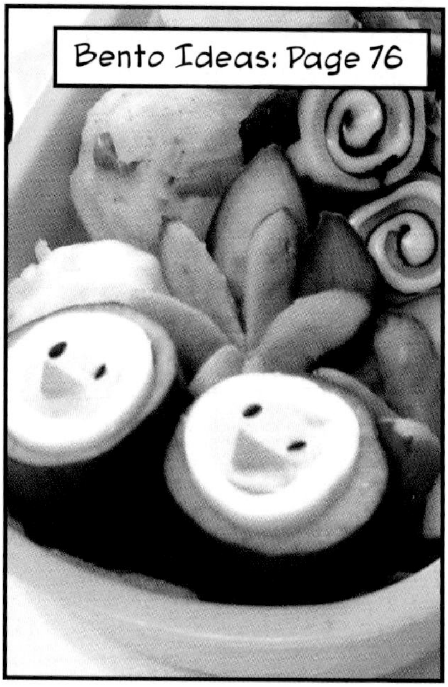

Bento Ideas: Page 76

The Main Course

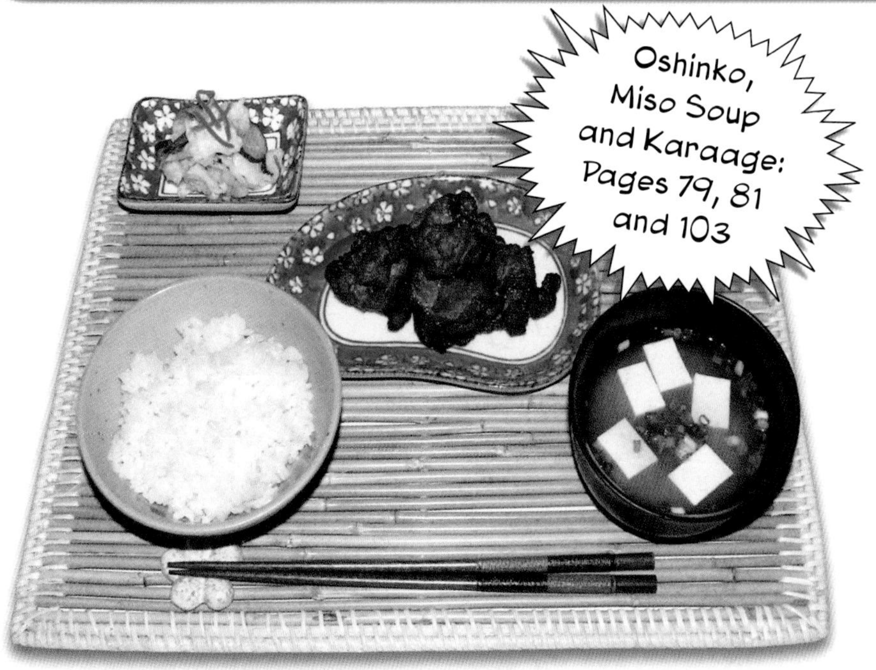
Oshinko, Miso Soup and Karaage: Pages 79, 81 and 103

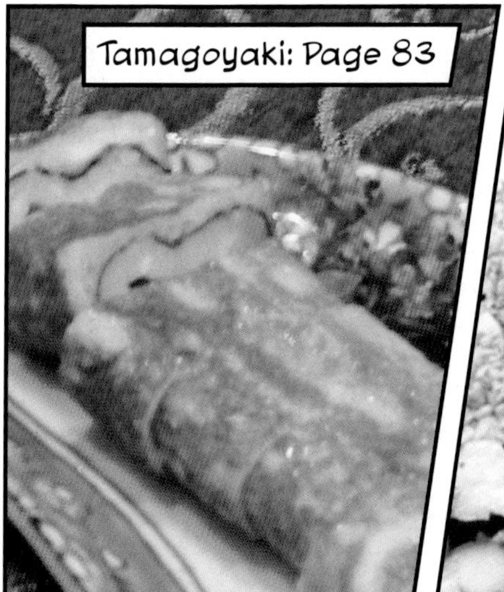
Tamagoyaki: Page 83

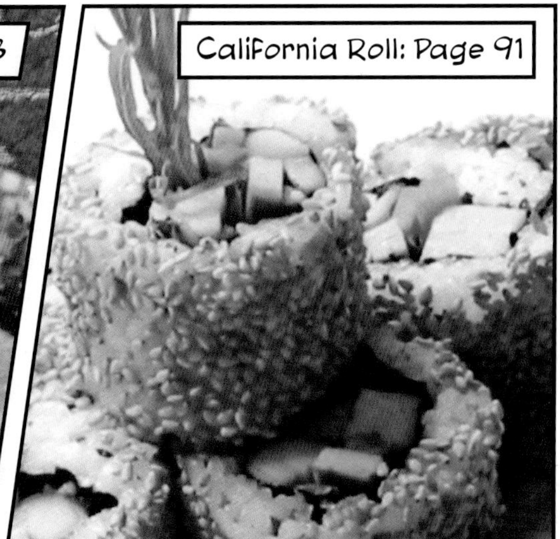
California Roll: Page 91

The Main Course

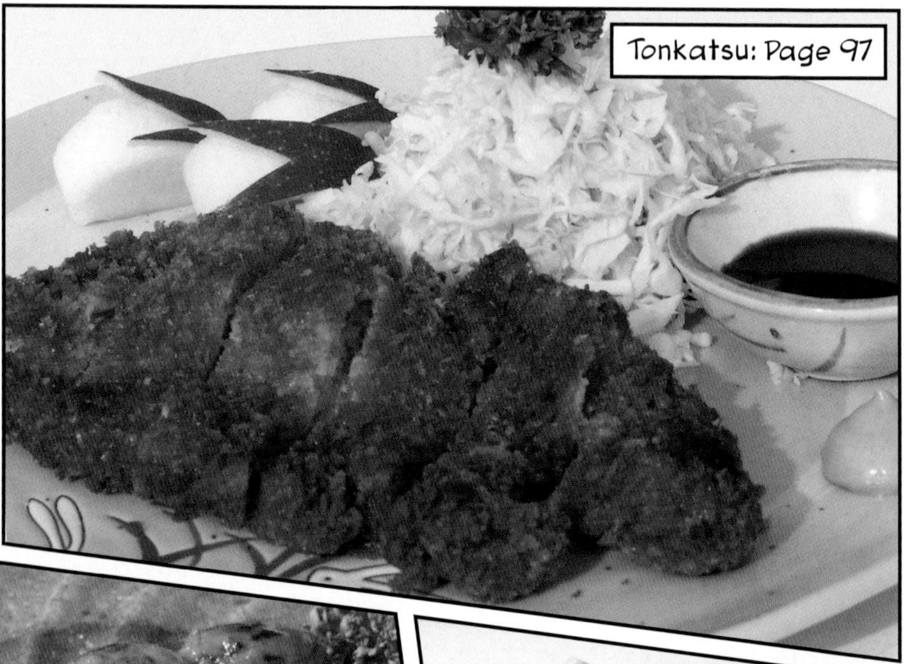

Tonkatsu: Page 97

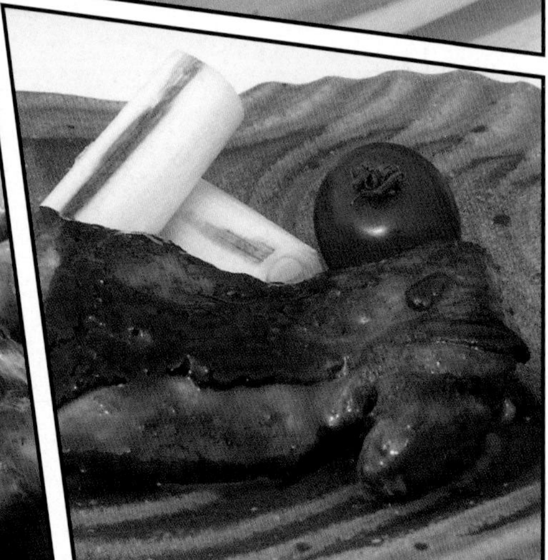

Teriyaki Chicken: Page 111

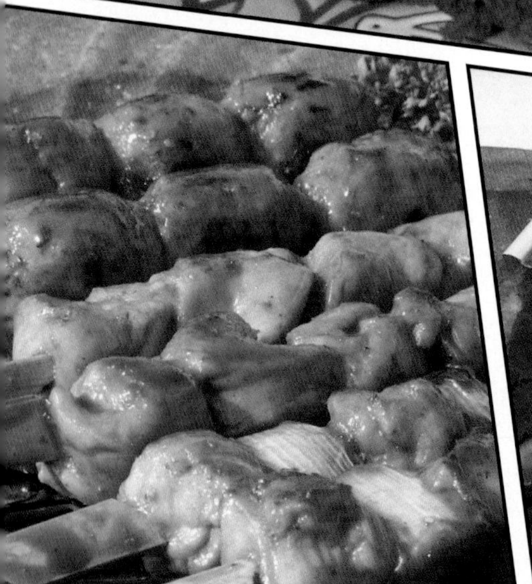

Yakitori: Page 113

The Main Course

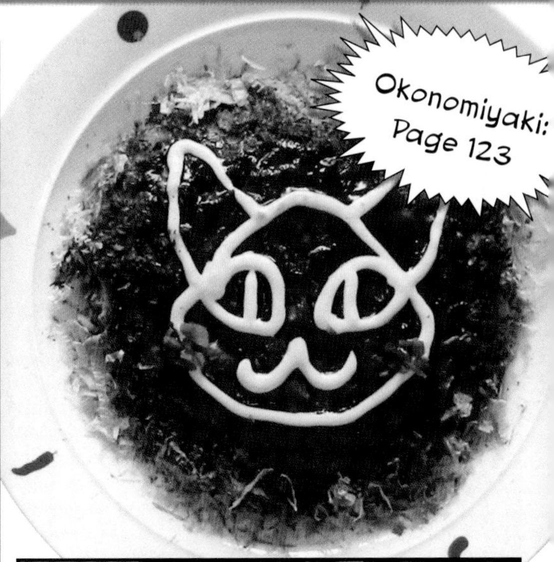
Okonomiyaki: Page 123

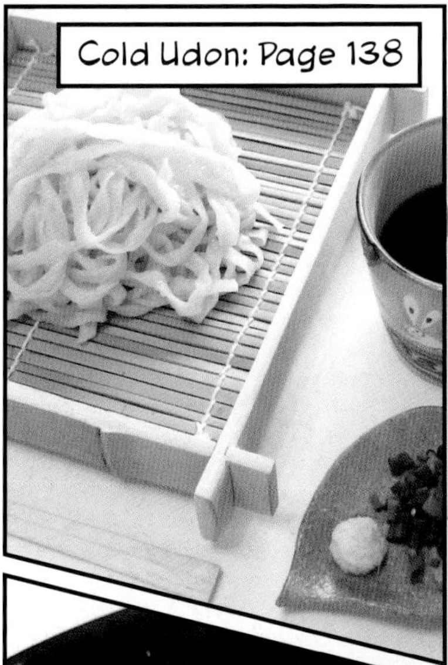
Cold Udon: Page 138

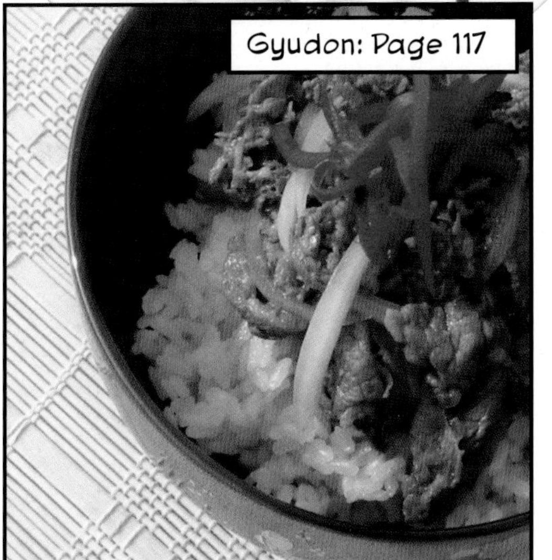
Gyudon: Page 117

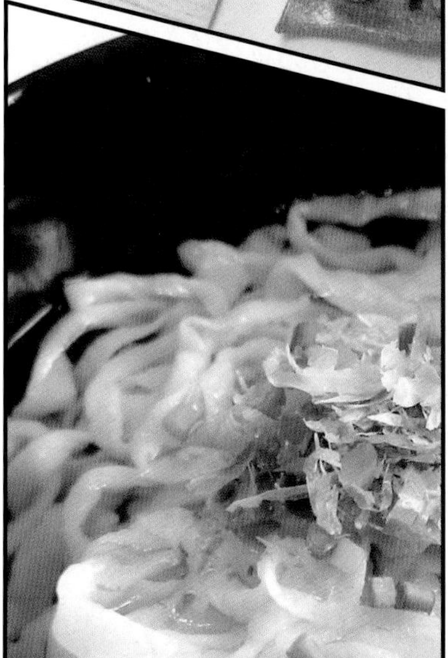
Hot Udon: Page 140

Welcome to Wagashi

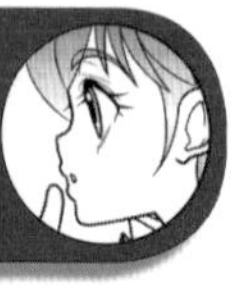

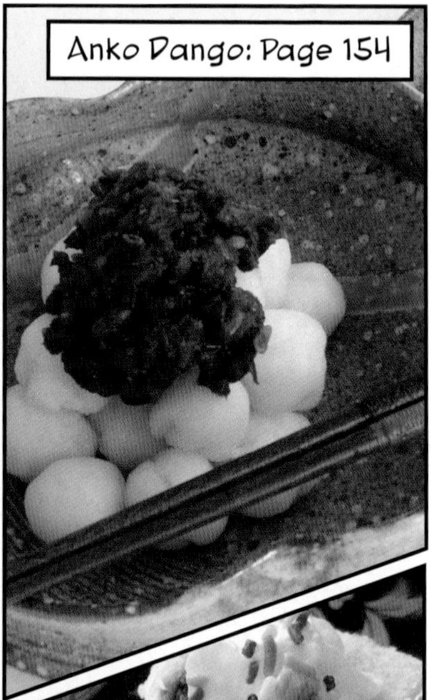

Anko Dango: Page 154

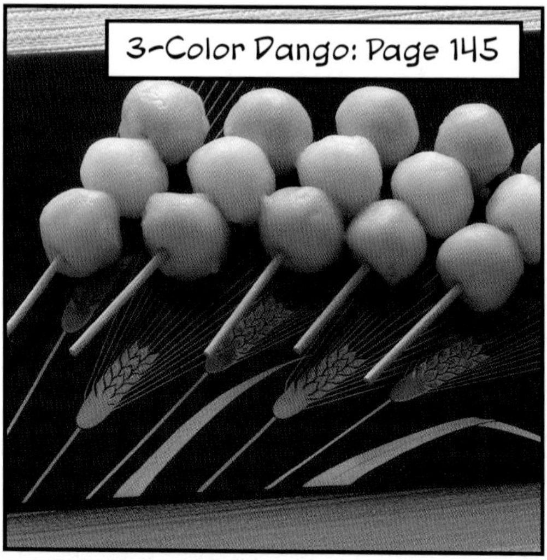

3-Color Dango: Page 145

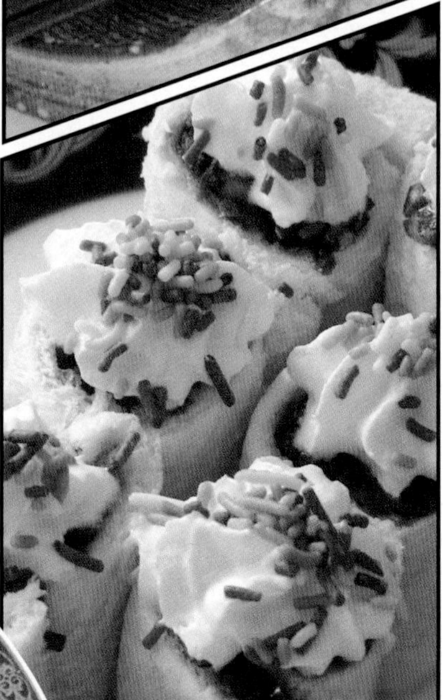

Anko Cake: Page 155

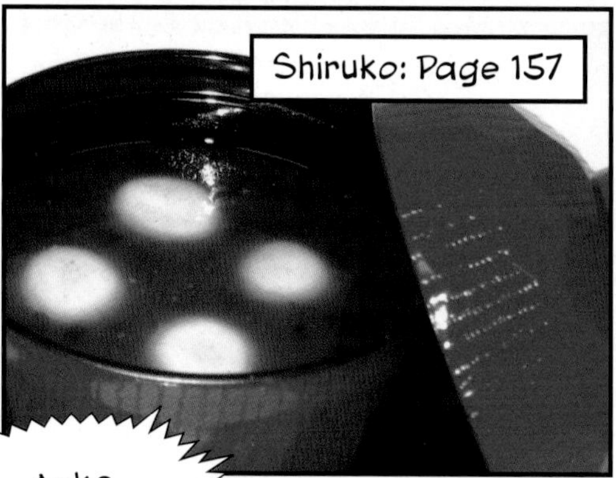

Shiruko: Page 157

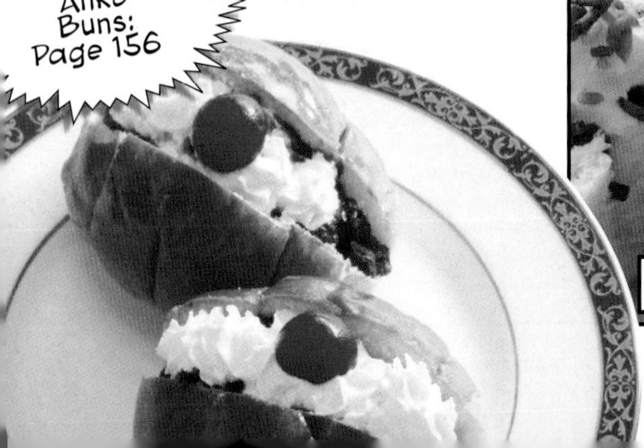

Anko Buns: Page 156

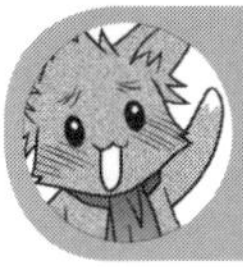

Setting the Table

In Japanese, *ichijuusansai* refers to a meal consisting of soup, three side dishes and rice. This is the traditional way meals are served in Japan.

❶Steamed rice or rice dish
Served with every meal
❷Soup
Typically miso with tofu
❸Mukouzuke
Pickled vegetables, cooked vegetables or small pieces of fish
❹Boiled vegetables
Served in their broth
❺Meat
Grilled fish, tempura, teriyaki chicken, etc.

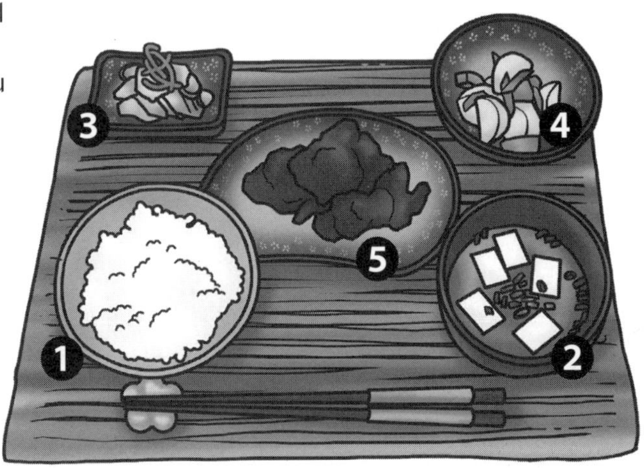
3
4
5
1
2

Nutrition Information

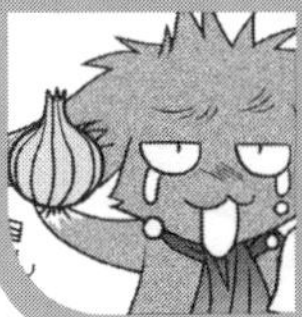

Japanese food is rich in both flavor and nutrition. You'll get carbohydrates from rice dishes, protein from meats and tofu, and your vitamins and minerals will come from cooked or pickled vegetables. And with flavors ranging from sweet to sour to salty and beyond, you'll also get a meal that won't be dull.

The Purpose of Ichijyuusansai

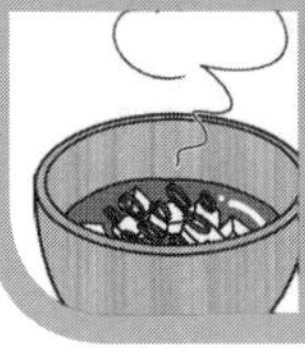

By arranging the various foods on separate plates, you can take your time eating and savor each dish. Eating slowly is also good for digestion and can help with dieting. You will discover new tastes, and your stomach is guaranteed to feel just as satisified as if you'd gobbled down everything all at once!

Before Cooking...

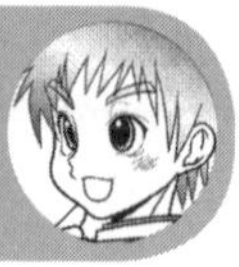

Wash Your Hands!

- Cleanliness is the first ingredient to good cooking!
Be sure to wash your hands thoroughly before working with any food, and always scrub up after handling raw meat or eggs.
- It's also a good idea to keep cutting boards and utensils in a separate working area if you're using them to prepare raw meat or eggs.

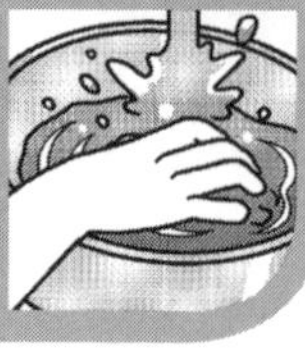

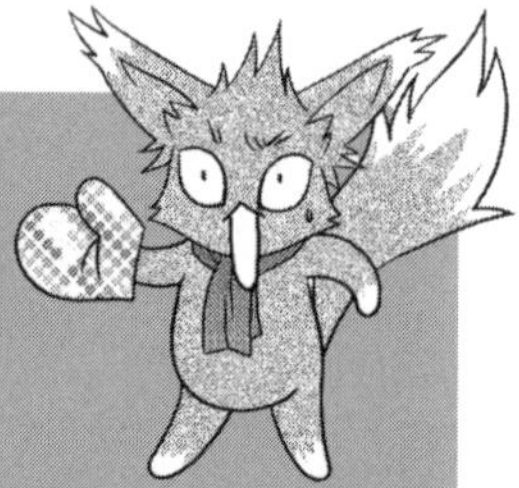

Turning Up the Heat

- Most stovetops have settings for high, medium and low heat, so the recipes in this book use those same conventions. For reference: low heat is usually between 300 and 320 degrees Fahrenheit; medium heat is around 340-355 degrees, and high heat is between 360-390.
- When using a gas stove, always make sure the flame is properly lit before cooking, and allow electric stoves ample time to heat up or cool down to the desired temperature.
- Also, before you do any cooking, it's important to make sure you are well-informed about fire safety. If you don't know what to do in the event of a fire, ask an adult before taking on any recipe that uses the stovetop.

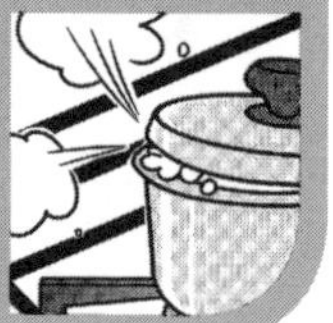

Cut Like a Pro!

- When you're slicing and dicing with a sharp knife, always do so on a clean cutting board, and curl your fingers away from the blade while holding down the food.

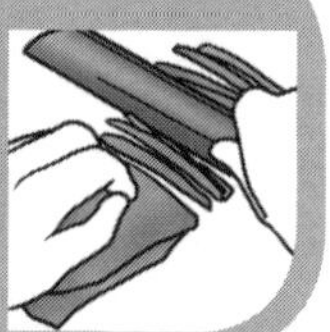

About Ingredients...

About Ingredients

- The ingredients of each recipe in this book are measured for two servings. So if, for example, you are cooking for four people, just double the amount of each ingredient.

There are a few ingredients in this book that might be a little uncommon in both Western kitchens and in Western markets. Here's some information about those ingredients, and a few substitutions if you can't find them.

- **Rice:** Japan doesn't export rice to the West, but you can find Japanese-style white rice under a number of brand names at most supermarkets.

- **Nori:** These are thin sheets of dry seaweed that are used to make sushi and rice balls, and can be boiled in soup or used as a topping on all sorts of food. Nori can be found in the Asian section of most supermarkets.

- **Mirin:** This is a sweet rice wine. It can usually be found in the Asian section of a supermarket, but if you can't find it, you can make a pretty good substitution by combining cooking sake with sugar. Just add 1 teaspoon of sugar for every tablespoon of sake.

- **Miso:** This paste is made out of soybeans and primarily used for soups. You can get it almost everywhere, and it usually comes in a tub or a plastic bag. If your market has a good selection there may be different types available, but the choice is yours, as any kind of miso paste will work in our recipes.

- **Kamaboko:** This is a kind of imitation crabmeat that's actually made out of whitefish. In Japan you can buy it in all sorts of different shapes, sizes and colors, but in the West the most common form is a stick shape that's made just for sushi, and you can find it at almost any supermarket.

- **Tofu:** A curd made from mashed soybeans, tofu is a popular ingredient in vegetarian cooking, and widely available in the West.

About Ingredients...

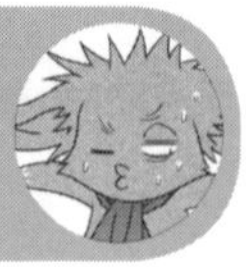

About Ingredients

- **Dashi:** This is made from the shavings of the bonito fish and a kind of edible kelp called kombu. In Japan, most people use packs of instant dashi powder. Usually the packs are pre-measured, but since you can buy jars of instant dashi as well, this book measures it in tablespoons. If you can't buy dashi locally, then use ½ tablespoon of bonito flakes and 1 inch of kombu for each cup of water called for in the recipe, and do the following:
  1. Pour ¾ the amount of water called for in the recipe into a pot and add the kombu. (If you do not have kombu, skip steps 2 and 3 and simply bring the water to a boil.)
  2. Cook on high for 10 minutes but don't boil the water. If it boils, add ¼ cup cold water.
  3. Remove the kombu and boil the stock.
  4. Add the remaining ¼ cup of water (cold) and the bonito flakes. Bring to a boil without stirring the flakes.
  5. Once the flakes settle in the bottom of the pan, turn off the heat and strain through a sieve. You can use this dashi for any recipe that calls for it.

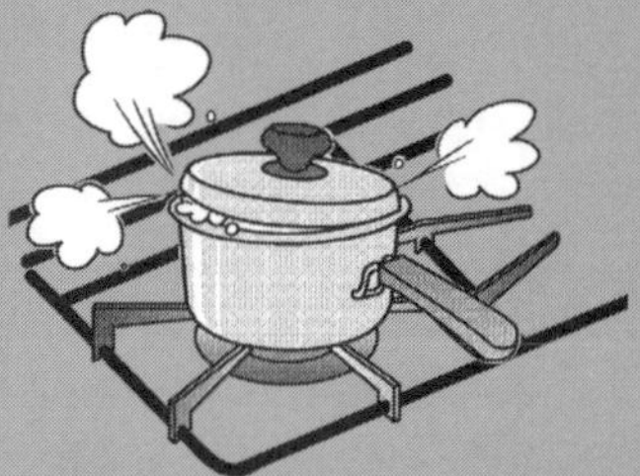

- **Panko:** These are small, Japanese-style breadcrumbs used for breading and frying meats and vegetables. If your local supermarket only has larger breadcrumbs or croutons, buy those and crush them before cooking.
- **Joshinko and Shiratamako:** These are different kinds of rice flour that are sometimes difficult to find outside of Japanese markets. You can often find them at Asian grocery stores, where they are usually called *rice flour* and *glutinous rice flour*, respectively. If you can find mochiko, another kind of rice flour, you can substitute it for both joshinko and shiratamako.
- **Powdered Matcha:** This is simply powdered green tea. If you can't find it, just use 1 drop of green food coloring in the dango recipe. If you do have it, try adding some hot water to make tea — it's really tasty!
- **Adzuki Beans:** These are small, dark red-colored beans that are used in Japanese desserts. You can find them dry in the bulk bins at almost any supermarket.

Appealing Appetizers

MANGA COOKBOOK

Usagi Ringo 兎りんご

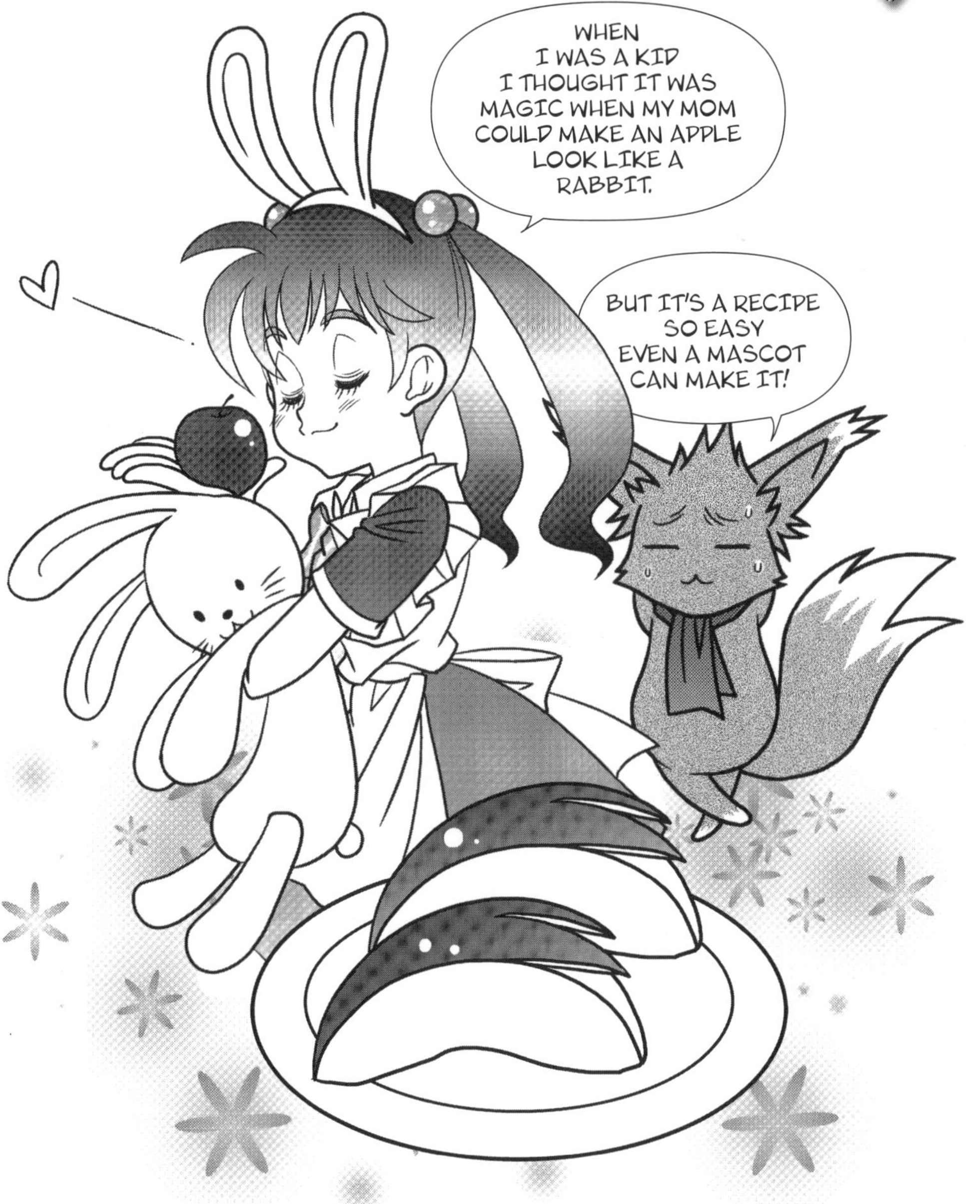
WHEN I WAS A KID I THOUGHT IT WAS MAGIC WHEN MY MOM COULD MAKE AN APPLE LOOK LIKE A RABBIT.
BUT IT'S A RECIPE SO EASY EVEN A MASCOT CAN MAKE IT!

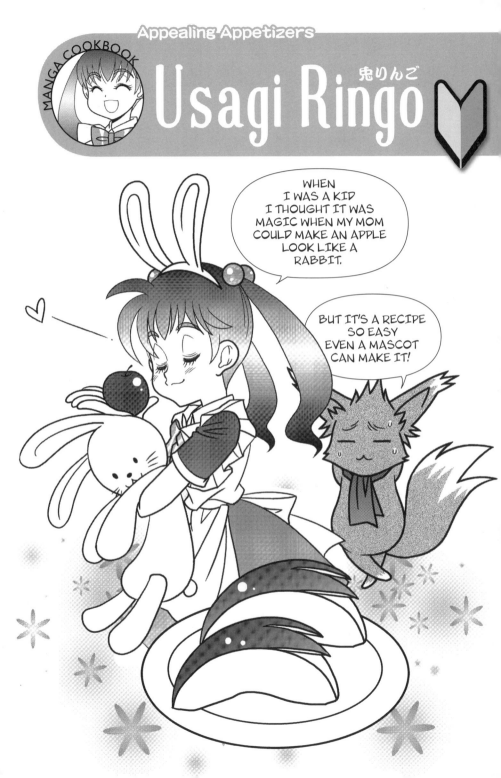

Usagi Ringo (rabbit-shaped apple slices)

About 80 calories
(per large apple)

Any number of apples (1 sliced apple makes about 8 "rabbits")

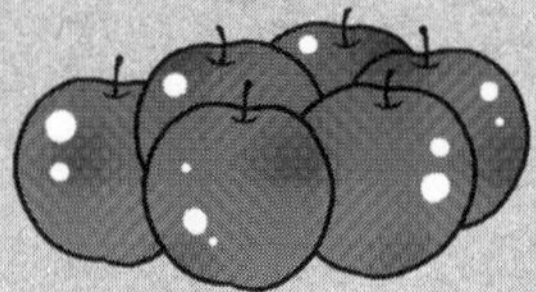

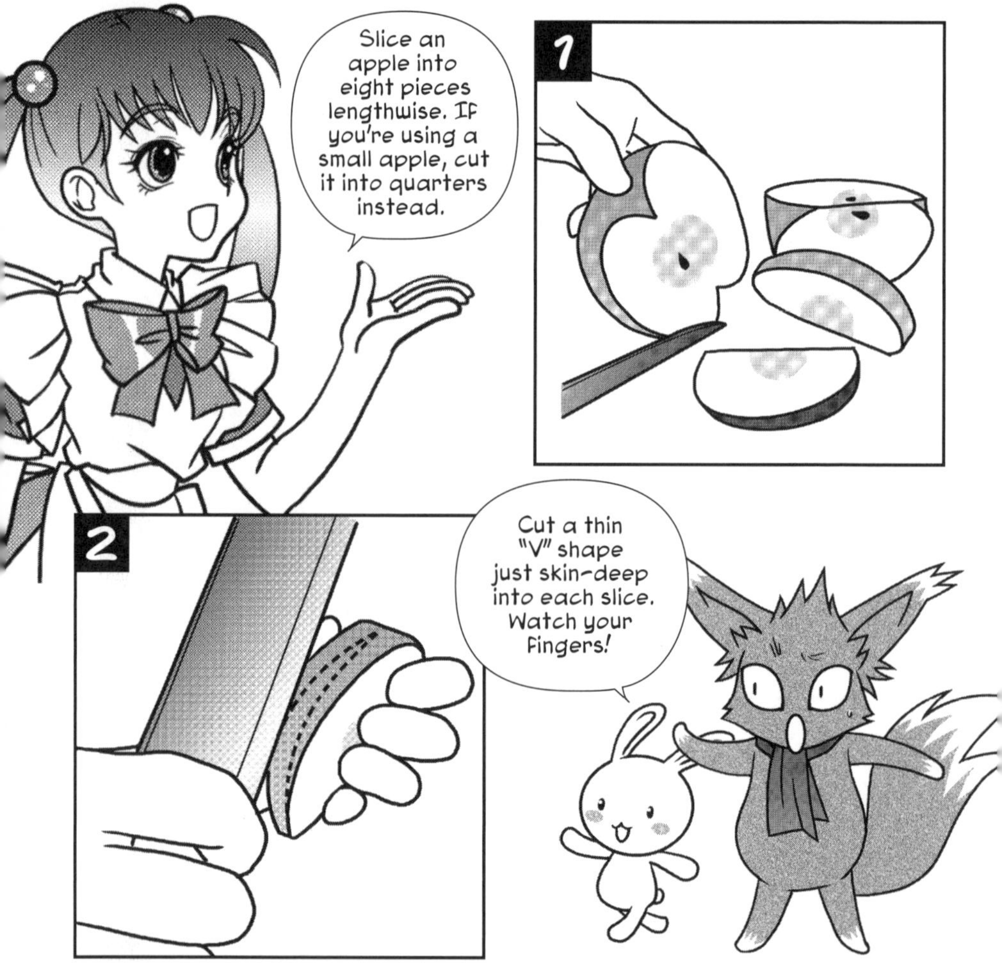

Slice an apple into eight pieces lengthwise. If you're using a small apple, cut it into quarters instead.
1
2
Cut a thin "V" shape just skin-deep into each slice. Watch your fingers!

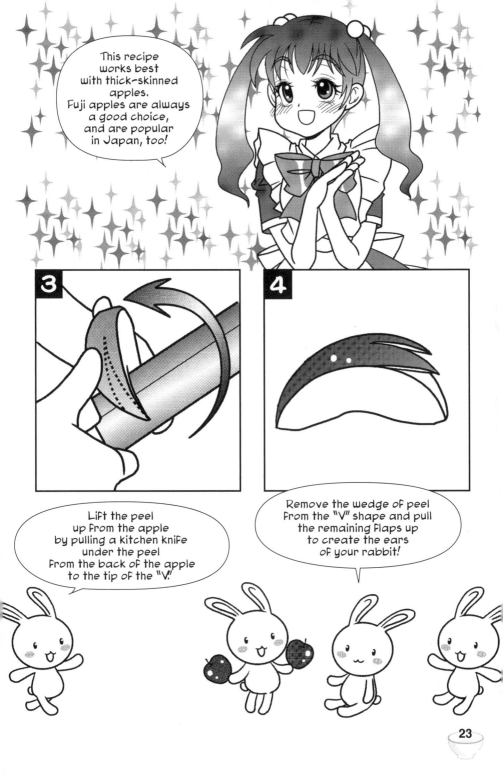

This recipe works best with thick-skinned apples. Fuji apples are always a good choice, and are popular in Japan, too!

③

④

Lift the peel up from the apple by pulling a kitchen knife under the peel from the back of the apple to the tip of the "V!"

Remove the wedge of peel from the "V" shape and pull the remaining flaps up to create the ears of your rabbit!

Miyuki's Notes on Apples

In case you didn't know, "usagi" is the Japanese word for rabbit, and "ringo" means apple. Usagi also happens to be the name of the main character in one of my favorite manga series, "Sailor Moon"!

In the West, most apples are small enough to be eaten whole with lunch or as a snack, but in Japan the typical apple is too large to bite into. There are many varieties available, and each one differs in flavor and consistency.

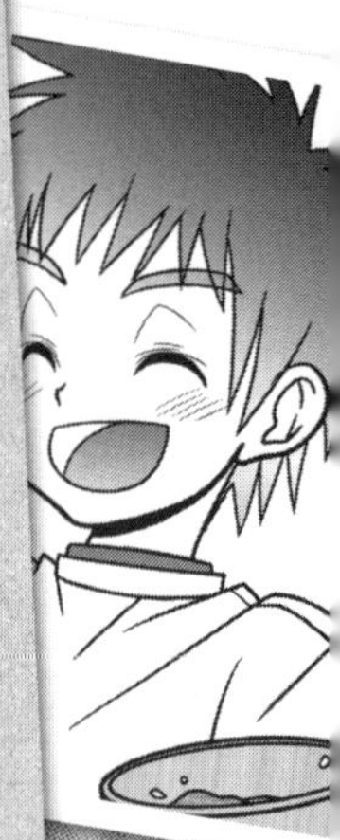

Once you peel an apple's skin, the flesh will start to turn brown. However, if you dip the slices into diluted saltwater, they won't discolor as quickly. I always do this if I'm not going to serve my Usagi Ringo right away.

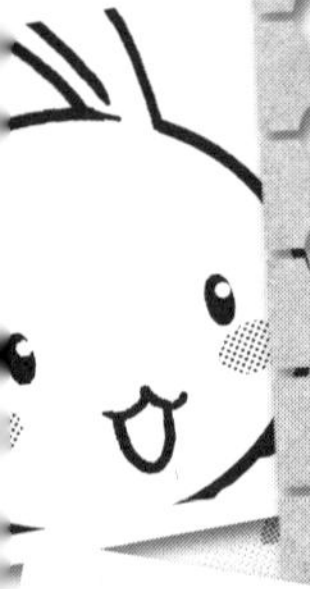

The next time you slice some apples, try this Usagi Ringo recipe – and maybe you'll be inspired to come up with some interesting shapes on your own!

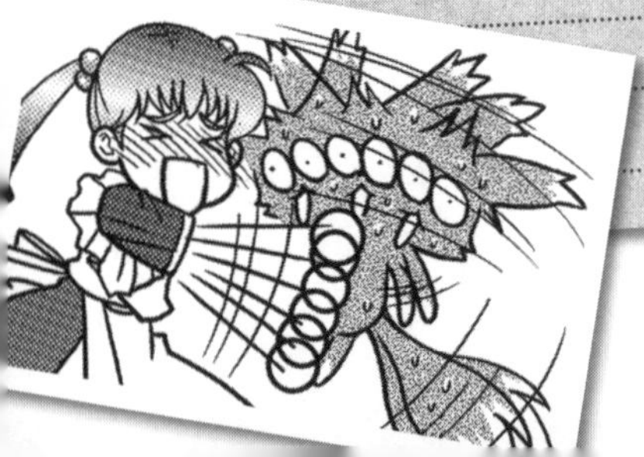

MANGA COOKBOOK

たまご友達 Tamago Tomodachi

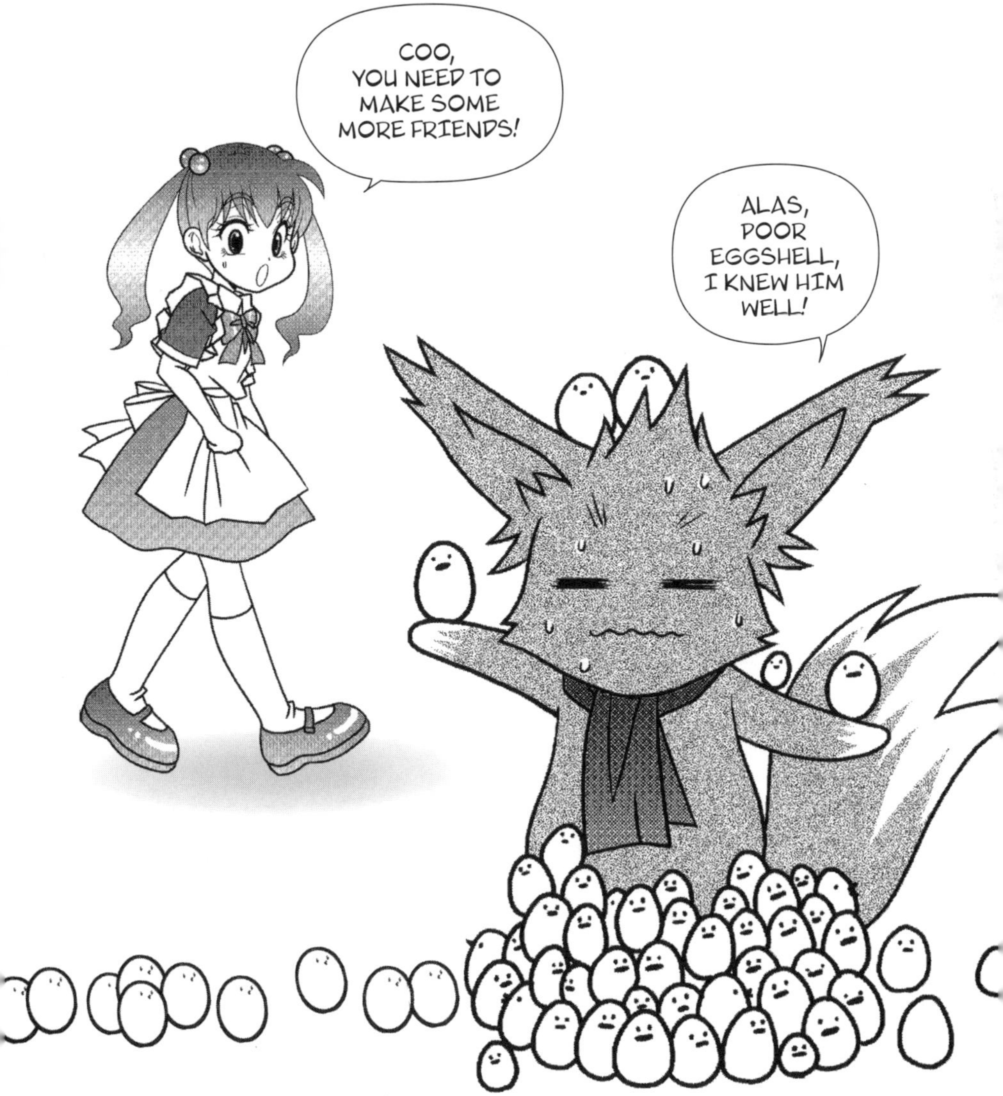
COO, YOU NEED TO MAKE SOME MORE FRIENDS!
ALAS, POOR EGGSHELL, I KNEW HIM WELL!

Tamago Tomodachi ("egg buddies")

76 calories
(per serving)

Any number of small eggs
1 cucumber
1 carrot
Black sesame seeds (regular sesame seeds if you can't find black ones)

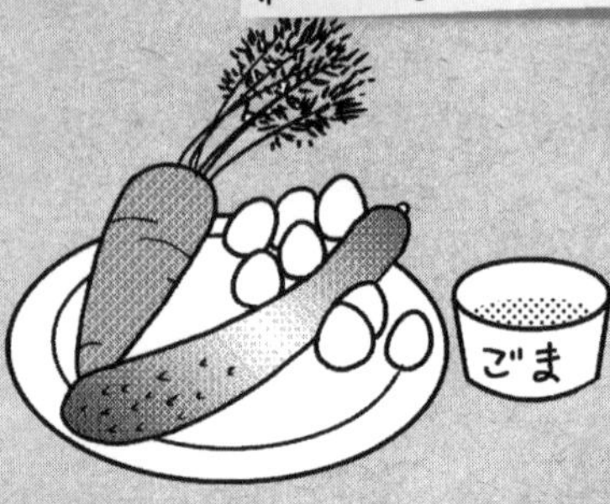
ごま

1

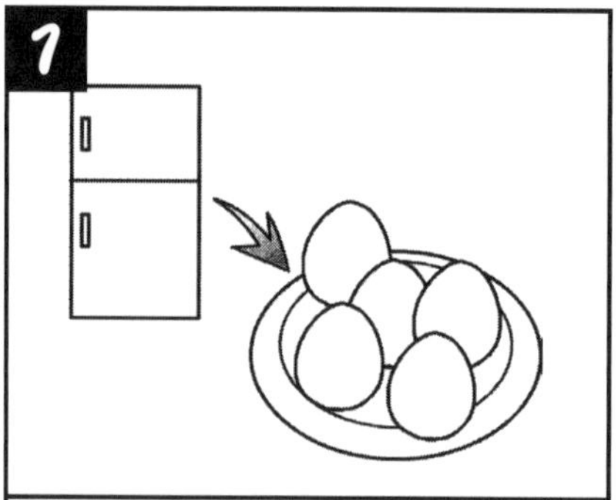

Remove eggs from the fridge 20 minutes ahead of time. Eggs boil better at room temperature.

2

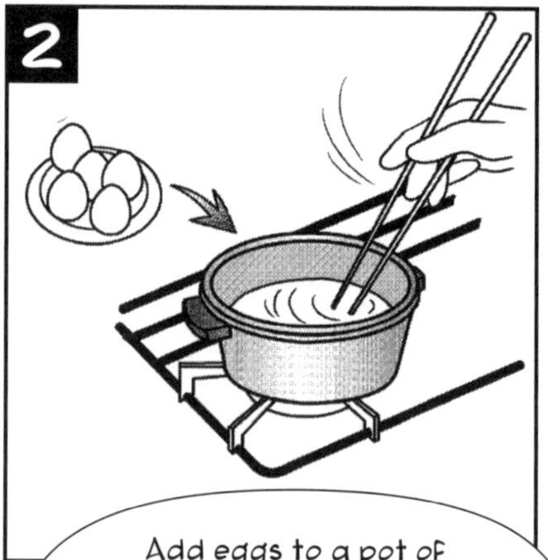

Add eggs to a pot of boiling water and stir them until the water begins to boil again. This will keep the yolk in the center of the eggs. Once the water is boiling again, cook for 10-12 minutes on low heat.

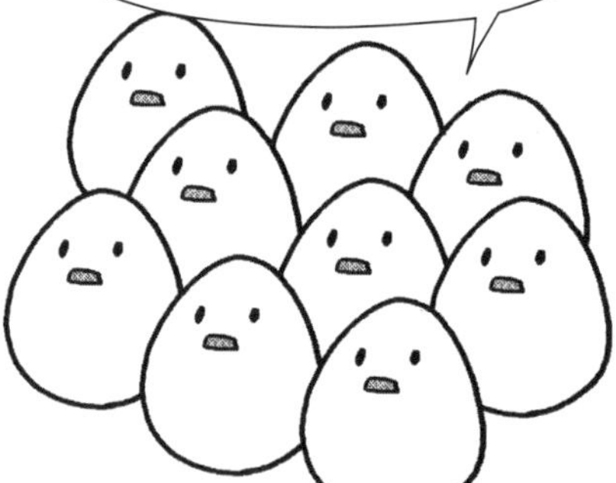

3

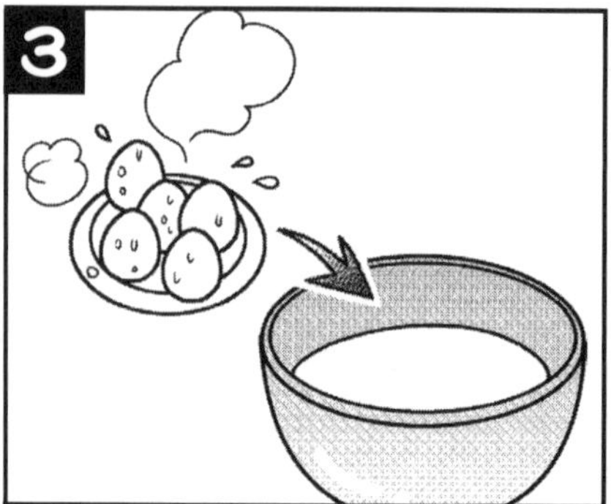

Cool the eggs in a bowl of cold water before removing the shells.

Hiyoko (chick)

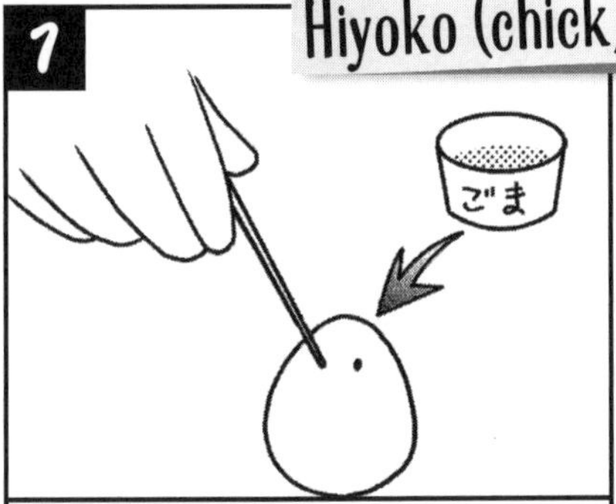
1
ごま

With the shell removed, poke two holes into the egg with a toothpick, then insert sesame seeds for the eyes.

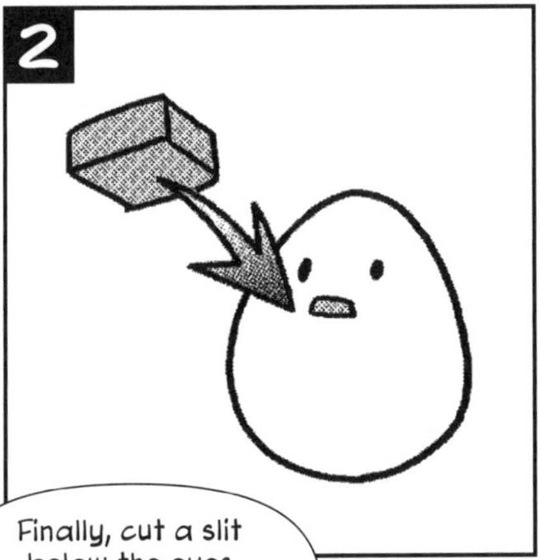
2

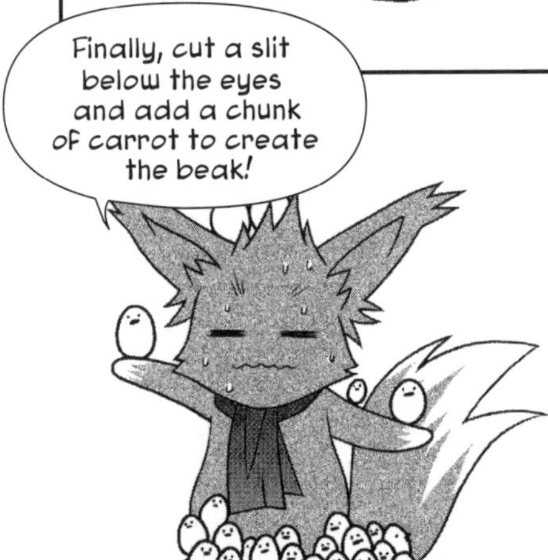
Finally, cut a slit below the eyes and add a chunk of carrot to create the beak!

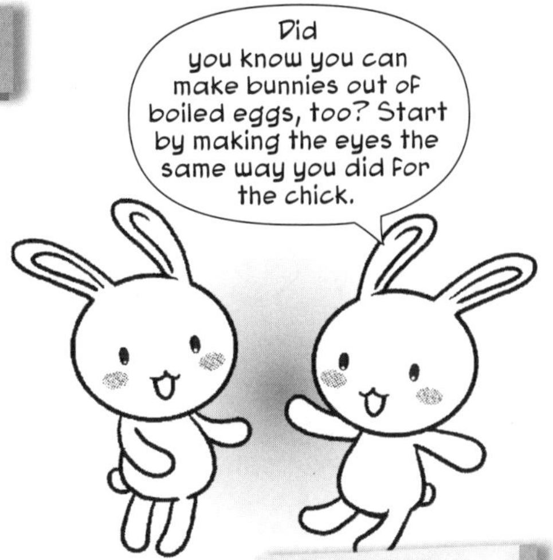
Did you know you can make bunnies out of boiled eggs, too? Start by making the eyes the same way you did for the chick.

Usagi (rabbit)

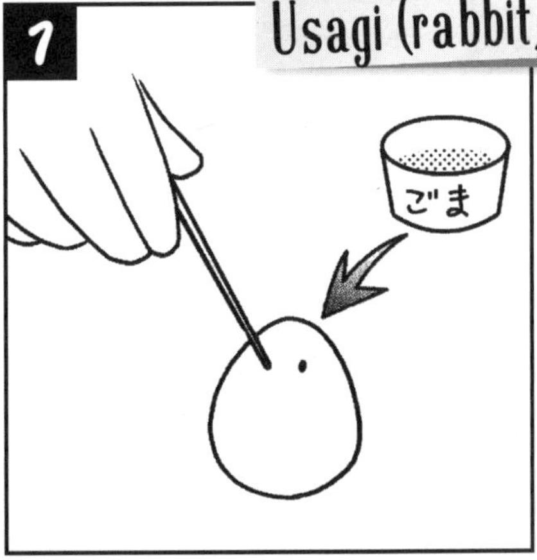
1
ごま

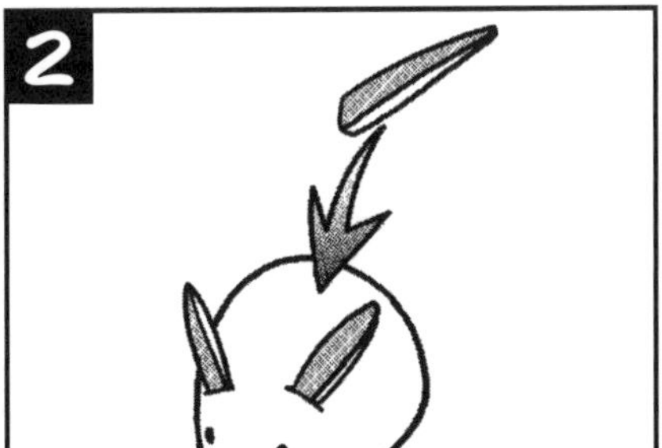
2

Turn the egg over, cut two slits into the top and insert thin cucumber slices to make the rabbit's ears.

Hatchlings

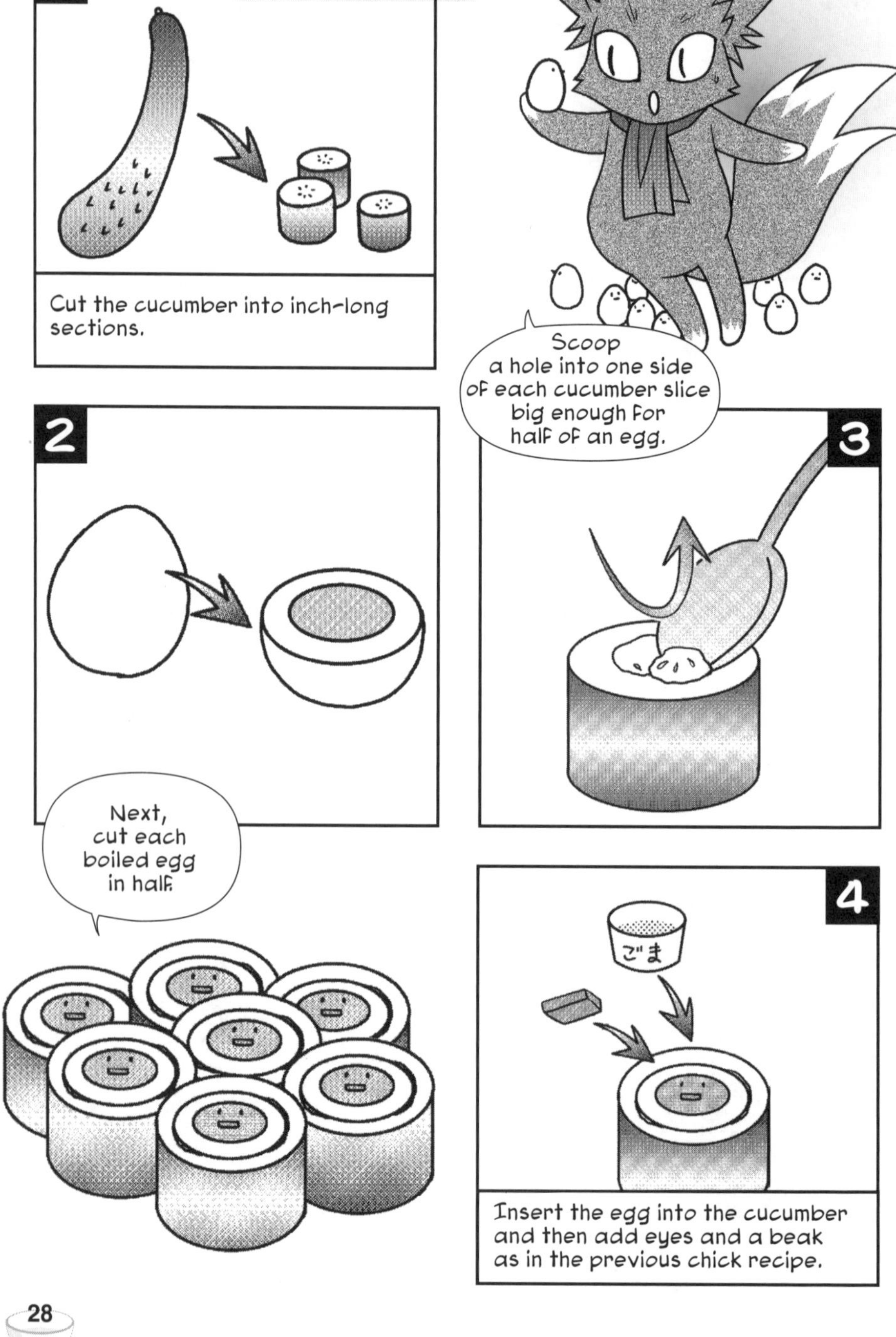

1
Cut the cucumber into inch-long sections.
2
Next, cut each boiled egg in half.
3
Scoop a hole into one side of each cucumber slice big enough for half of an egg.
4
ごま
Insert the egg into the cucumber and then add eyes and a beak as in the previous chick recipe.

Appealing Appetizers

MANGA COOKBOOK

Tako Sausage たこソーセージ

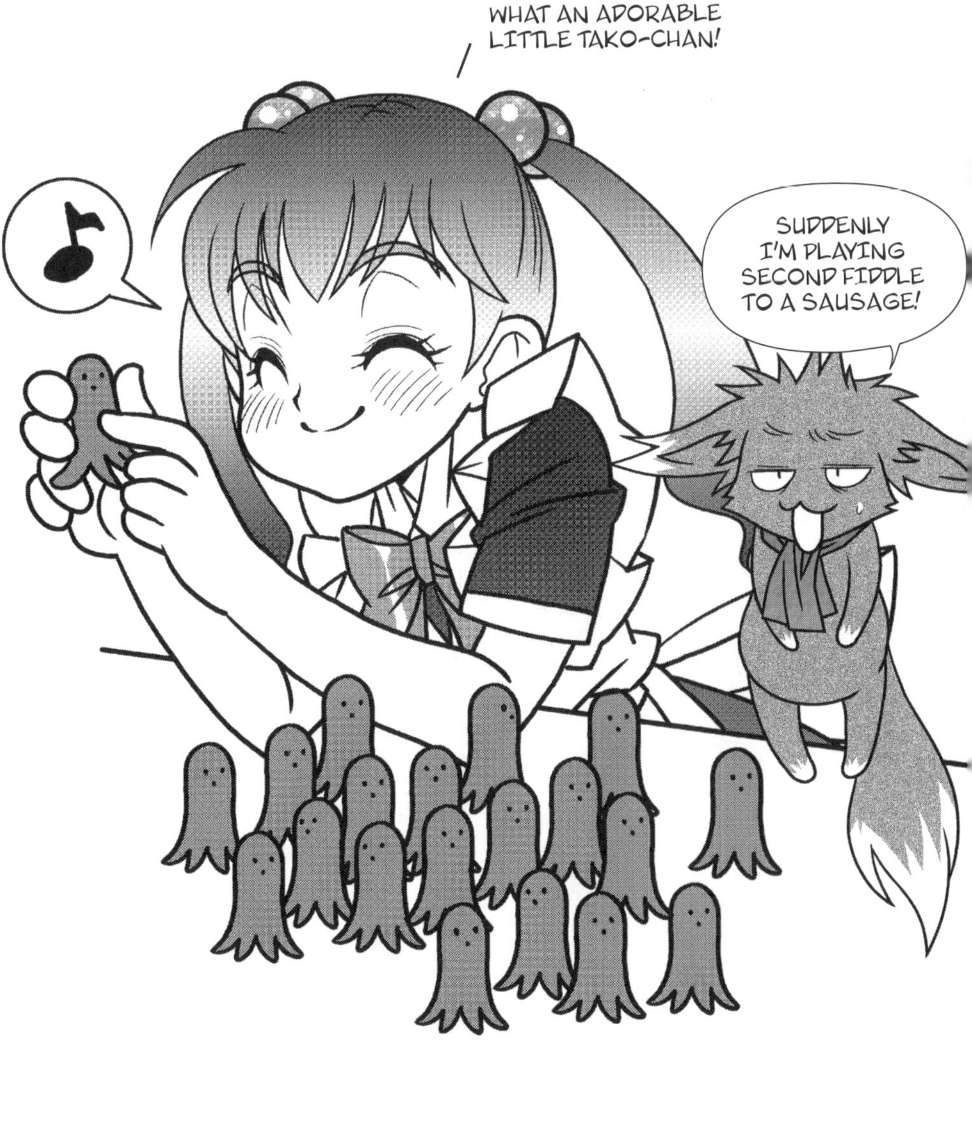
WHAT AN ADORABLE LITTLE TAKO-CHAN!
SUDDENLY I'M PLAYING SECOND FIDDLE TO A SAUSAGE!

Tako Sausage (and more!)

About 60 calories
(per wiener)

Any number of cocktail wieners.................................

or other small sausages...

1 tablespoon vegetable oil...

Black sesame seeds (optional)..................................

....

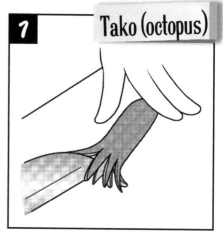

Tako (octopus)

1

Slice the bottom third of each wiener vertically, then rotate the wiener and make another vertical slice across the first one, creating four "legs." Rotate and cut two more times to create all eight legs.

2

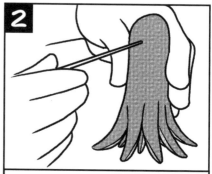

Poke three holes into the top of each wiener, two for the eyes and one for the mouth.

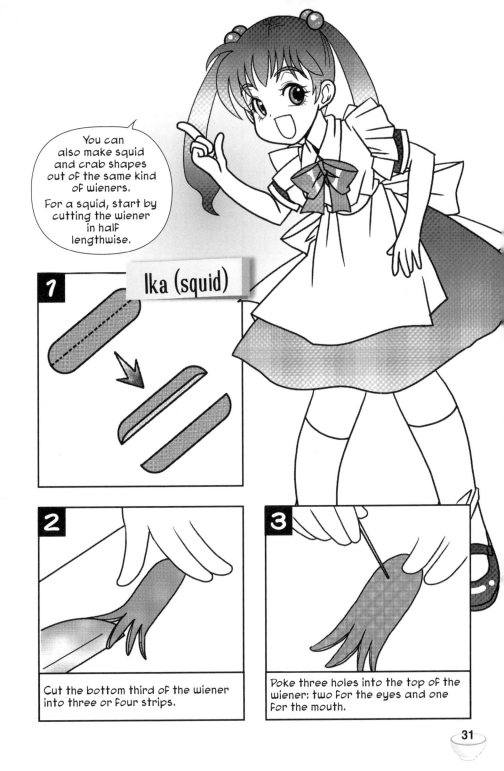

You can also make squid and crab shapes out of the same kind of wieners.

For a squid, start by cutting the wiener in half lengthwise.

Ika (squid)

1

2

Cut the bottom third of the wiener into three or four strips.

3

Poke three holes into the top of the wiener: two for the eyes and one for the mouth.

Kani (crab)

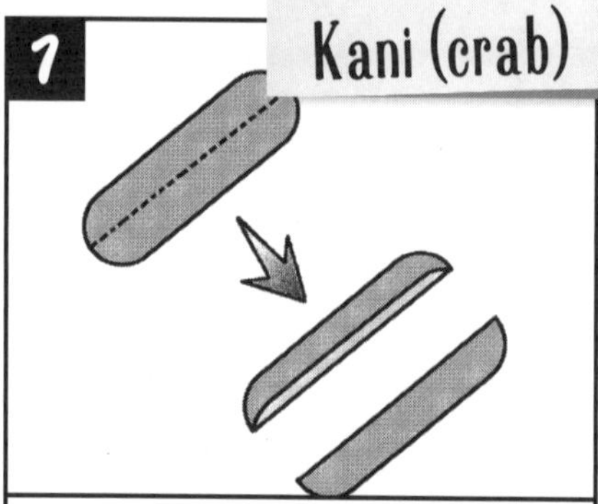

Cut the wiener in half lengthwise. the same way you did for the squid.

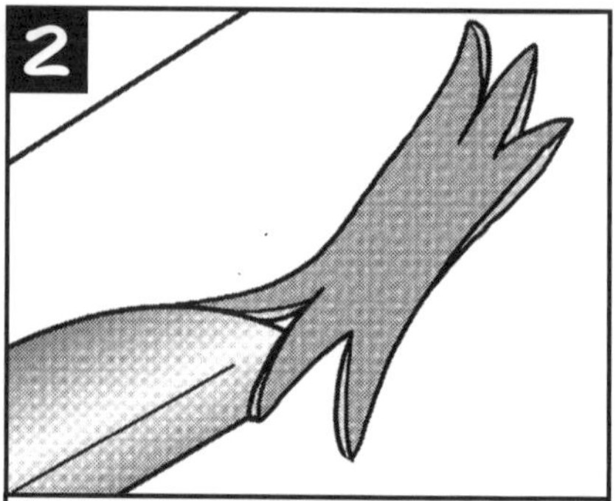

Slice each end of the wiener twice so there are three legs on both the left and right sides.

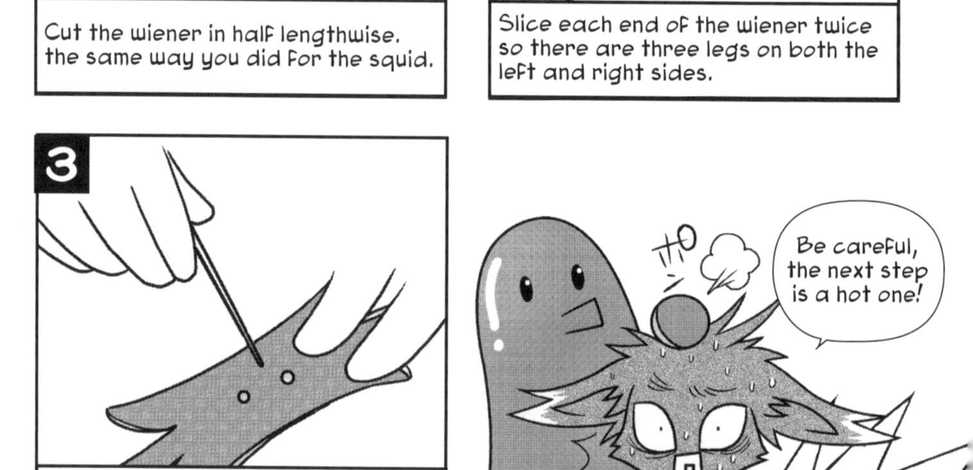

Poke two holes for eyes, and one for the mouth.

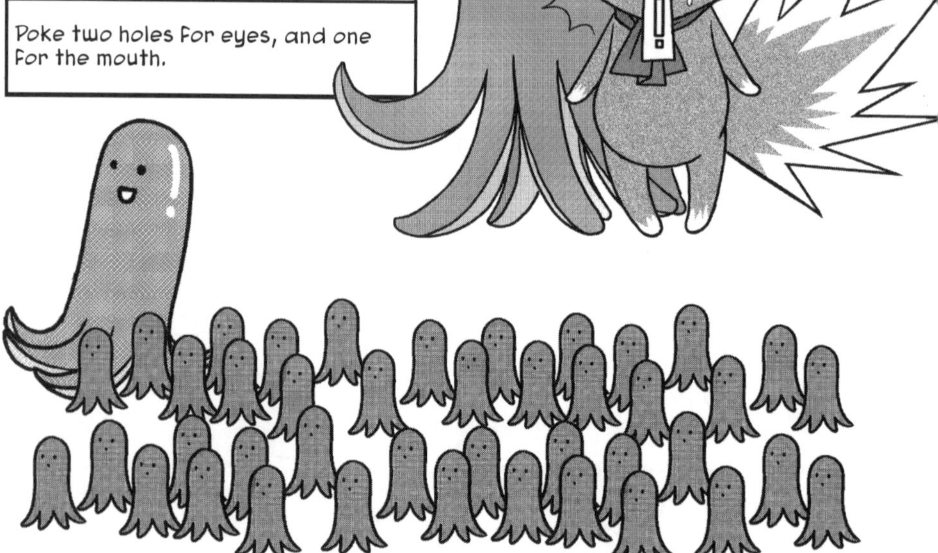
Be careful, the next step is a hot one!

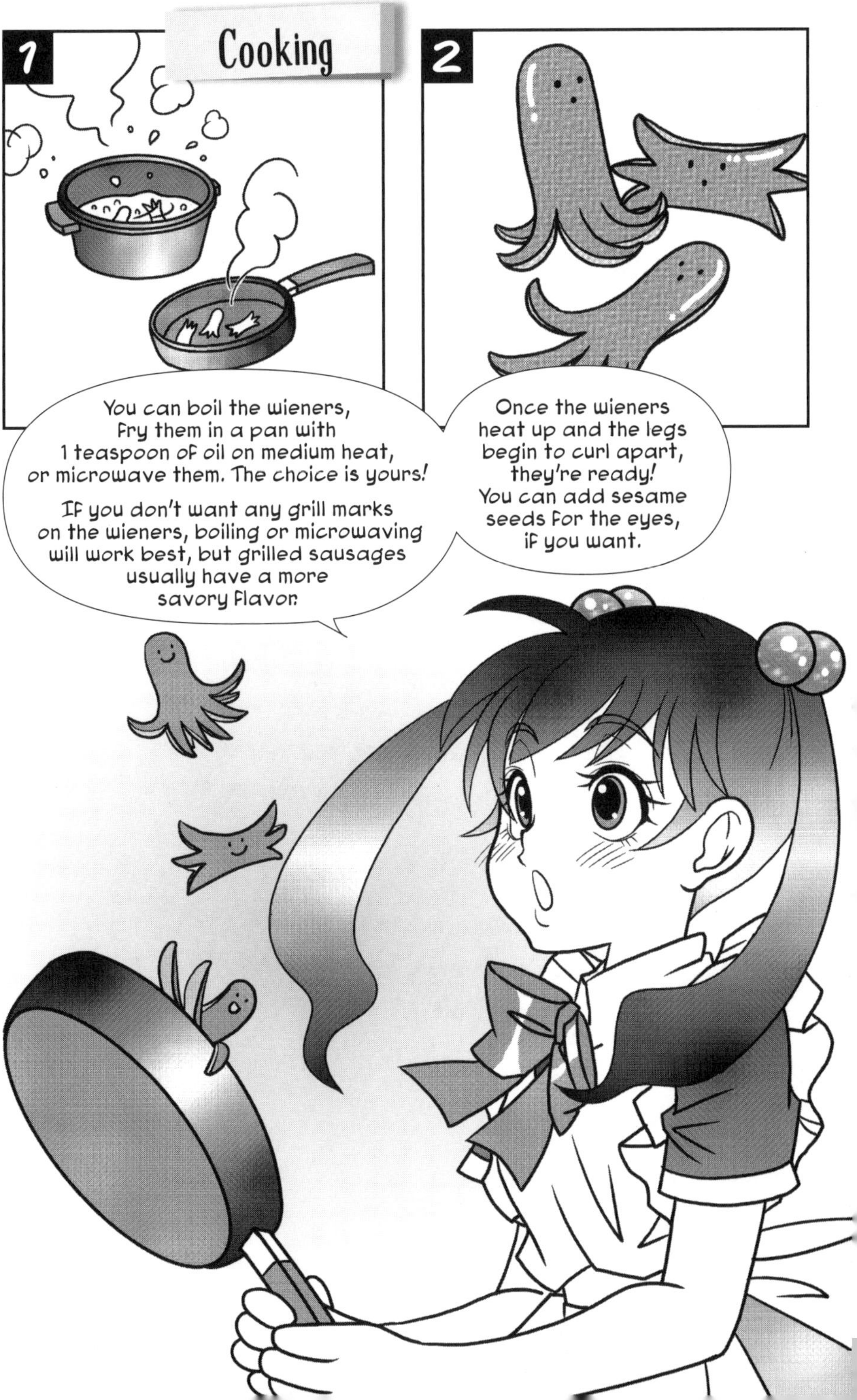
Cooking
1
2
You can boil the wieners, fry them in a pan with 1 teaspoon of oil on medium heat, or microwave them. The choice is yours! If you don't want any grill marks on the wieners, boiling or microwaving will work best, but grilled sausages usually have a more savory flavor.
Once the wieners heat up and the legs begin to curl apart, they're ready! You can add sesame seeds for the eyes, if you want.

Miyuki's Notes on Appetizers

In Japan there's a long tradition of trying to make food as beautiful as it is delicious. Especially with children's lunches — if the food isn't cute, kids just won't eat it!

Of course, the appetizers in this book aren't just for kids. Serve them as hors d'oeuvres the next time you and your friends get together to watch anime, or include them in a "bento," or boxed-lunch. These and other finger foods can be arranged together, sometimes even creating a scene with foods that resemble characters, and placed into a special plastic or laquerware box. When I was in elementary school, I carried my old-fashioned bento box to class tied in a handkerchief so the box wouldn't come apart on the way. Today, we can buy snap-top bento boxes as well.

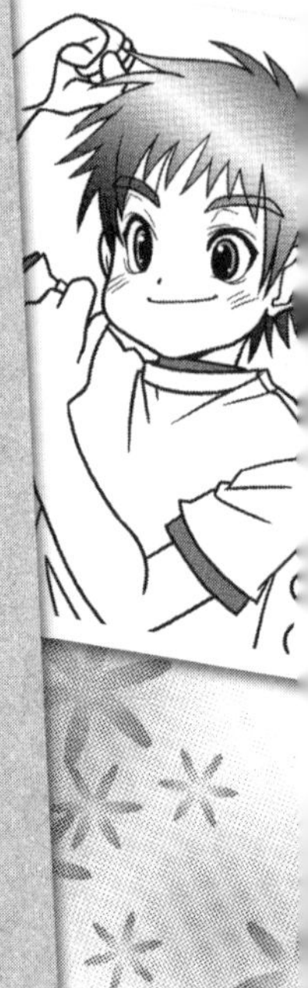

No school-themed manga or anime would be complete without bento, and in one of my favorites, the adorable "Azumanga Daioh," there's a scene where the main characters trade items from their bento. Now, that's fun!

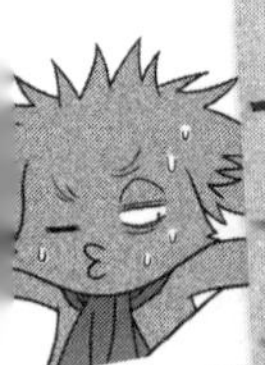

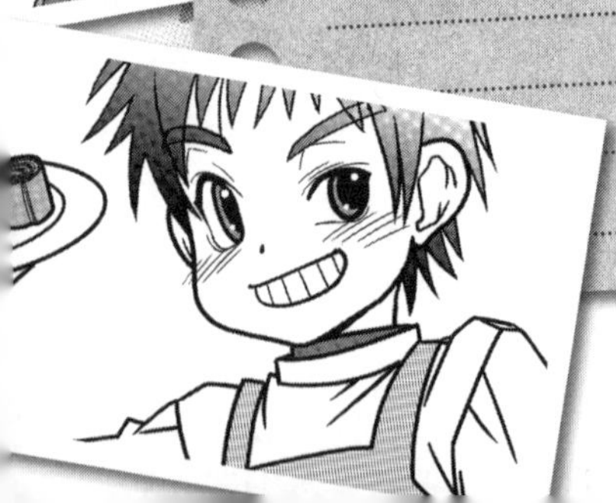

My Notes

My Notes

MANGA COOKBOOK

炊きたてご飯 Steamed Rice

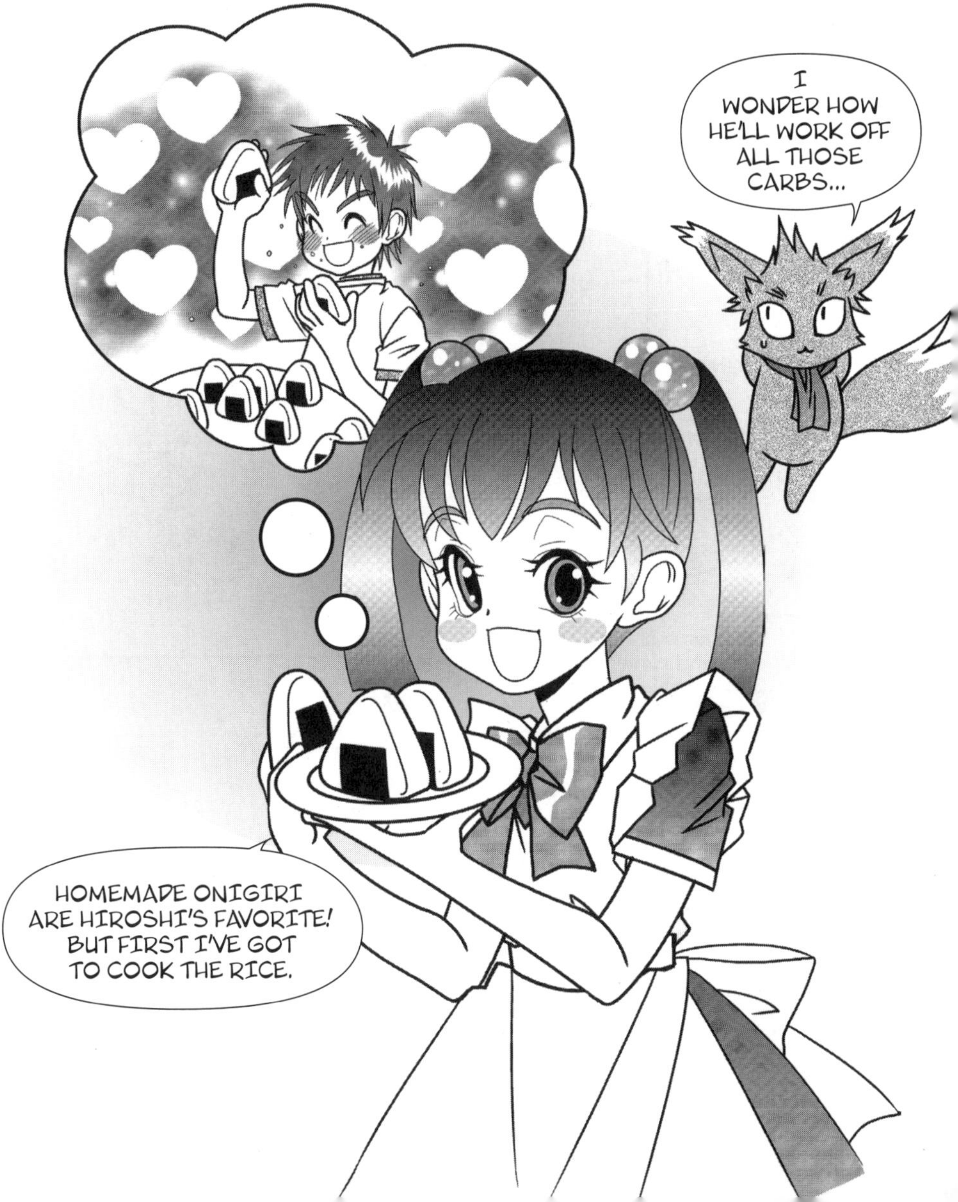
I WONDER HOW HE'LL WORK OFF ALL THOSE CARBS...
HOMEMADE ONIGIRI ARE HIROSHI'S FAVORITE! BUT FIRST I'VE GOT TO COOK THE RICE.

Steamed Rice for Two

171 calories
(per serving)

1½ cups uncooked white rice

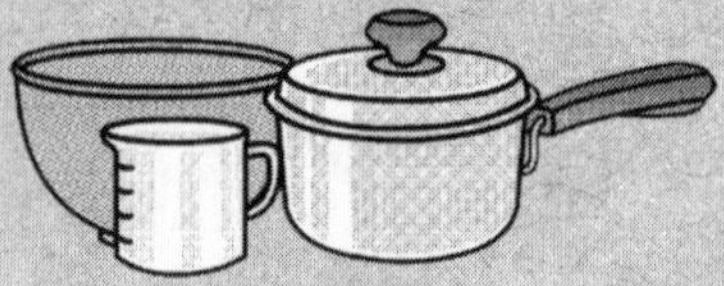

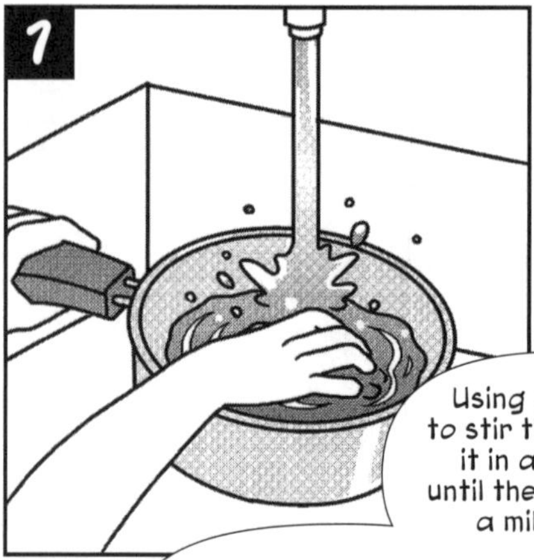
1
Using your hands to stir the rice, rinse it in a large pot until the water turns a milky white.

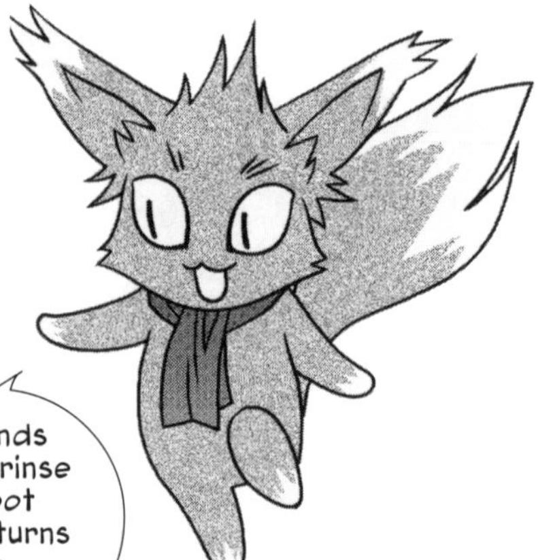

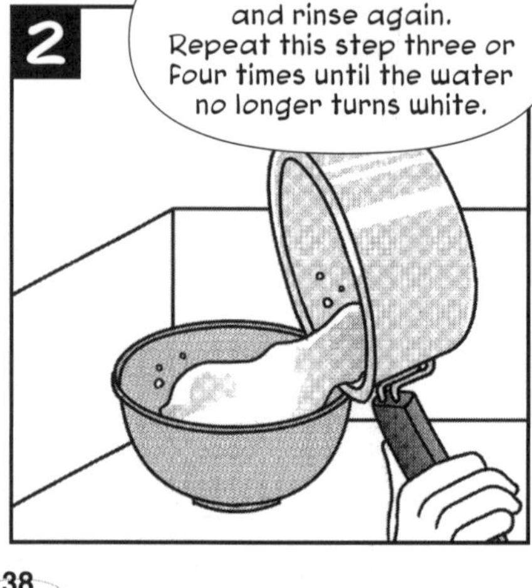
2
Pour out the water and rinse again. Repeat this step three or four times until the water no longer turns white.

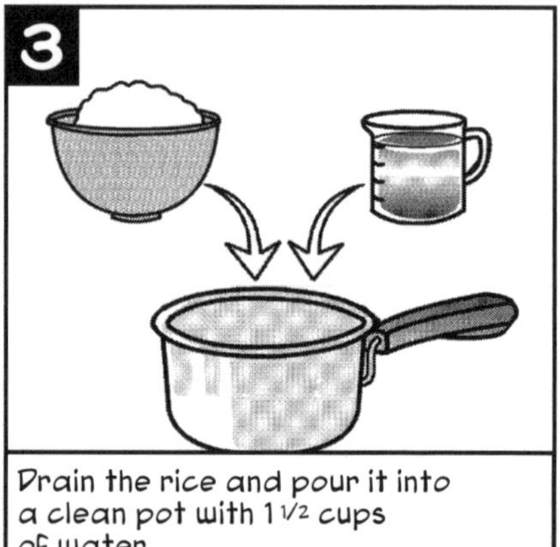
3

Drain the rice and pour it into a clean pot with 1 1/2 cups of water.

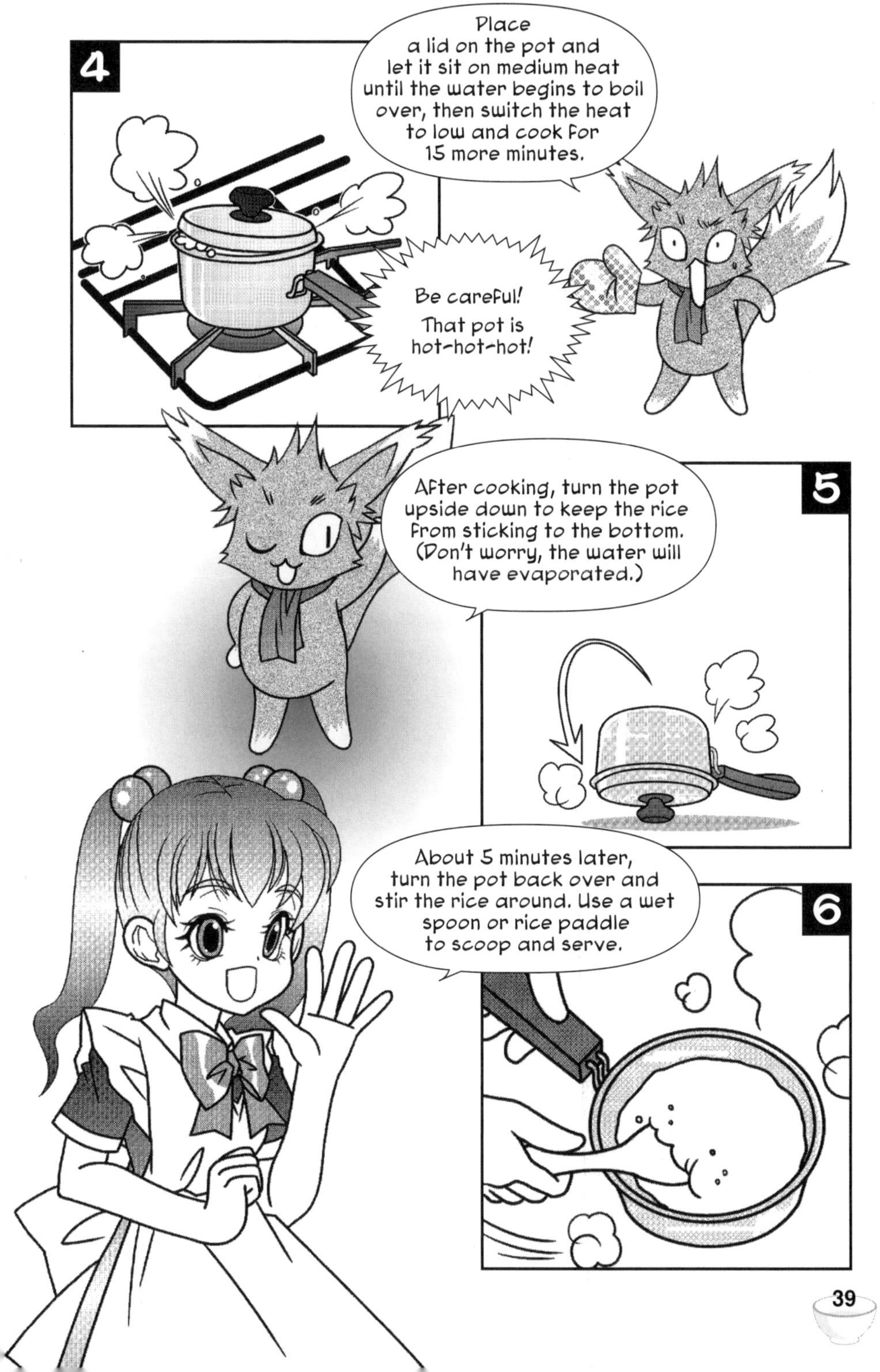

Place a lid on the pot and let it sit on medium heat until the water begins to boil over, then switch the heat to low and cook for 15 more minutes.
Be careful! That pot is hot-hot-hot!
After cooking, turn the pot upside down to keep the rice from sticking to the bottom. (Don't worry, the water will have evaporated.)
About 5 minutes later, turn the pot back over and stir the rice around. Use a wet spoon or rice paddle to scoop and serve.

Miyuki's Notes on Steamed Rice

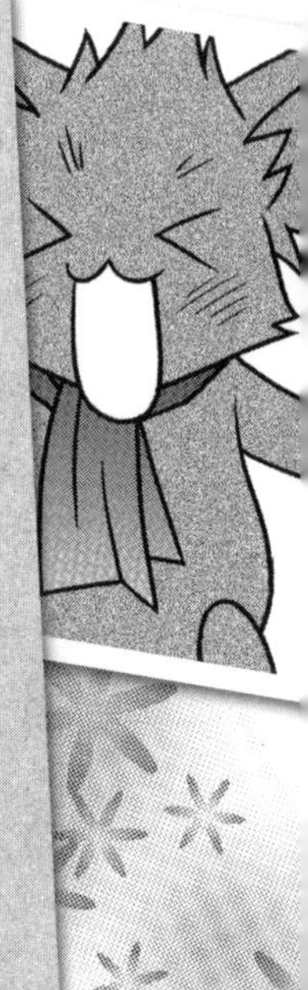

Rice is a staple of the Japanese diet. Each autumn the rice paddies are harvested, and the hard shells of the grain are peeled away. The result is raw white rice, which is then prepared in rice cookers until it is soft and sticky. (The shells are turned into a nutritious powder called rice bran, which can be mixed with salt and water for pickling vegetables.)

Japanese rice needs to be washed before cooking to remove any remaining bits and pieces of shell. Washing also stimulates the absorption of water in the rice.

Unlike bread, rice doesn't contain any oil or salt, making it easy to digest. Because rice can be turned into energy quickly, characters in sports-themed manga, such as "Prince of Tennis," are often shown eating it by the bowlful!

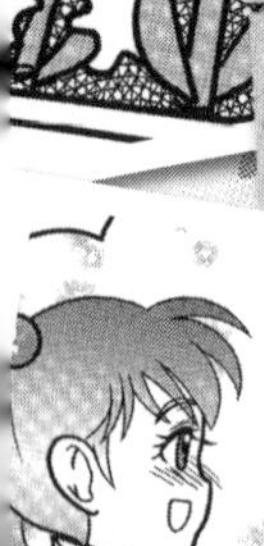

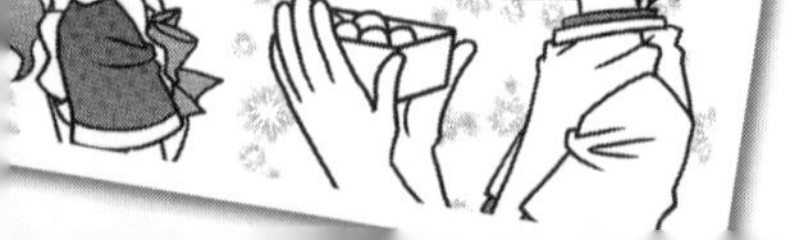

Onigiri
おにぎり

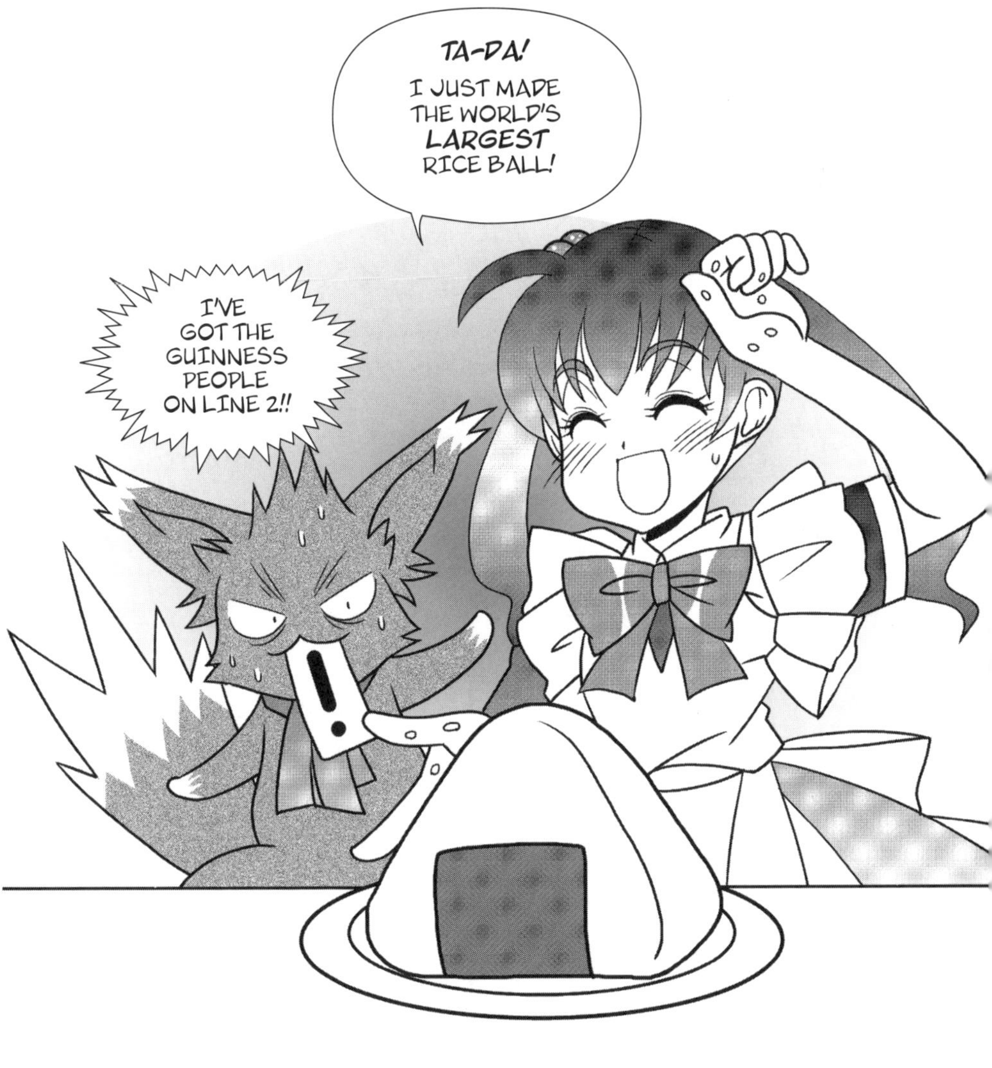
TA-DA! I JUST MADE THE WORLD'S **LARGEST** RICE BALL!
I'VE GOT THE GUINNESS PEOPLE ON LINE 2!!

Onigiri (rice balls)

160 calories
(per serving)

1½ cups steamed rice ....

A pinch of salt ....

1 sheet of nori (see page 19) ....

....

....

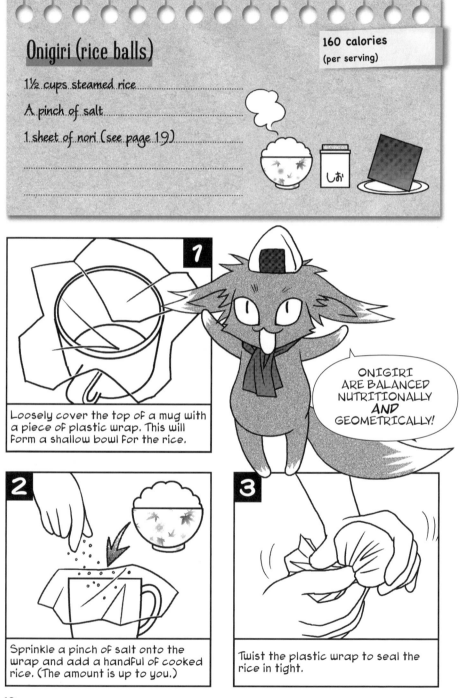

1

Loosely cover the top of a mug with a piece of plastic wrap. This will form a shallow bowl for the rice.

ONIGIRI ARE BALANCED NUTRITIONALLY **AND** GEOMETRICALLY!

2

Sprinkle a pinch of salt onto the wrap and add a handful of cooked rice. (The amount is up to you.)

3

Twist the plastic wrap to seal the rice in tight.

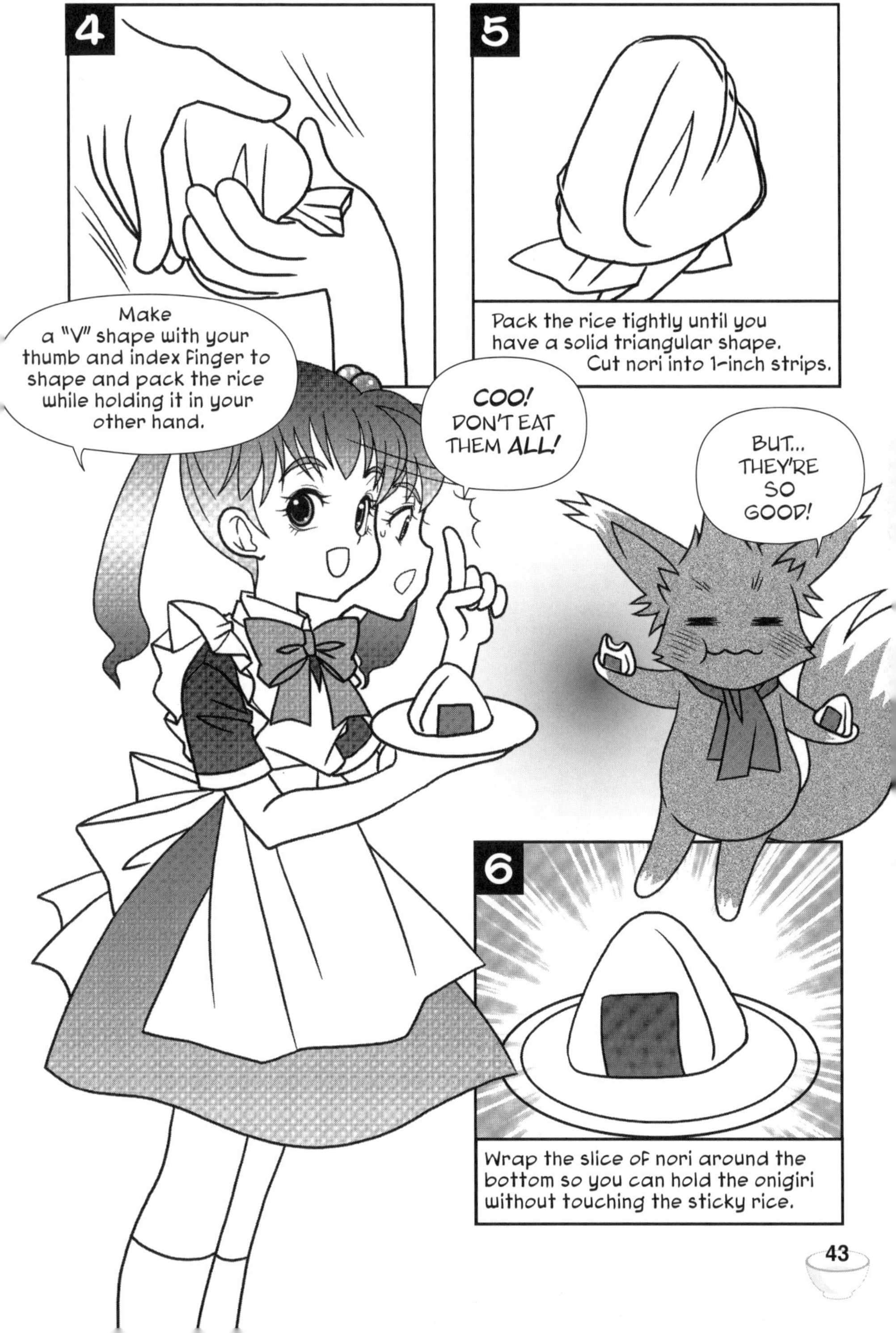
4
Make a "V" shape with your thumb and index finger to shape and pack the rice while holding it in your other hand.
5
Pack the rice tightly until you have a solid triangular shape. Cut nori into 1-inch strips.
COO! DON'T EAT THEM ALL!
BUT... THEY'RE SO GOOD!
6
Wrap the slice of nori around the bottom so you can hold the onigiri without touching the sticky rice.

Miyuki's Notes on Onigiri

In the West, students carry apples to school. In Japan, they bring onigiri. Unlike apples, though, onigiri do not grow on trees - something Tohru Honda knows all too well. The protagonist of Natsuki Takaya's "Fruits Basket" has painful memories of the childhood game upon which the manga series is named. Rather than being assigned a fruit nickname, as the rules require, Tohru is called "onigiri" by a mean-spirited classmate who wants to brand her an outsider.

In fact, onigiri are one of the most common of all Japanese foods. In ancient times, people would dry rice in the sun so the rice wouldn't spoil as they carried it on long trips. This practice is believed to be the origin of the rice ball. The Japanese word "omusubi" primarily refers to the standard, triangle-shaped rice ball, whereas the word onigiri can be used for any kind of hand-packed rice ball.

Tohru-chan eventually realizes that everyone in Japan loves onigiri. I think you will too!

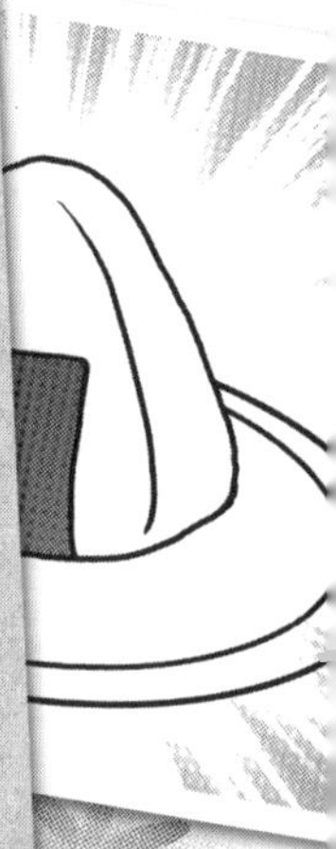

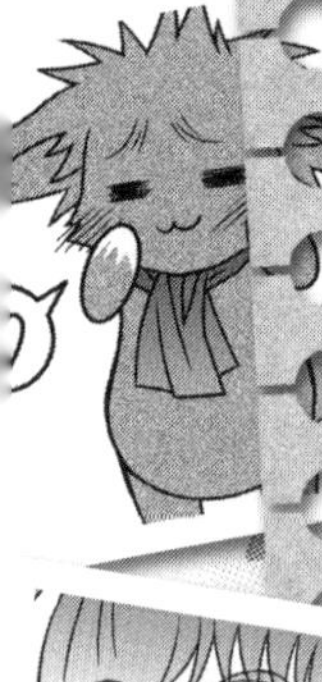

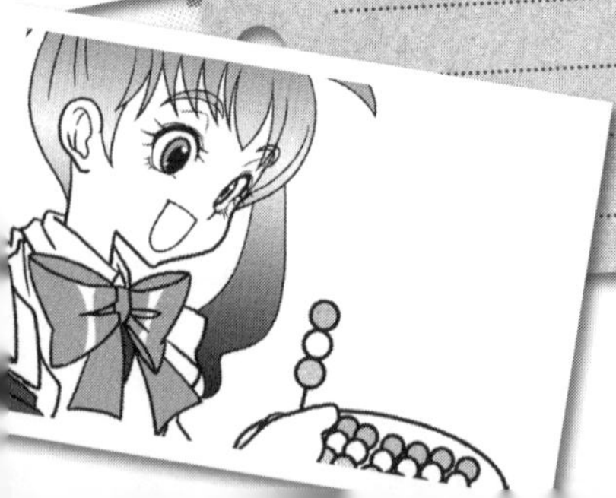

My Notes

My Notes

Bento Basics

Naruto Rolls
ナルト巻き

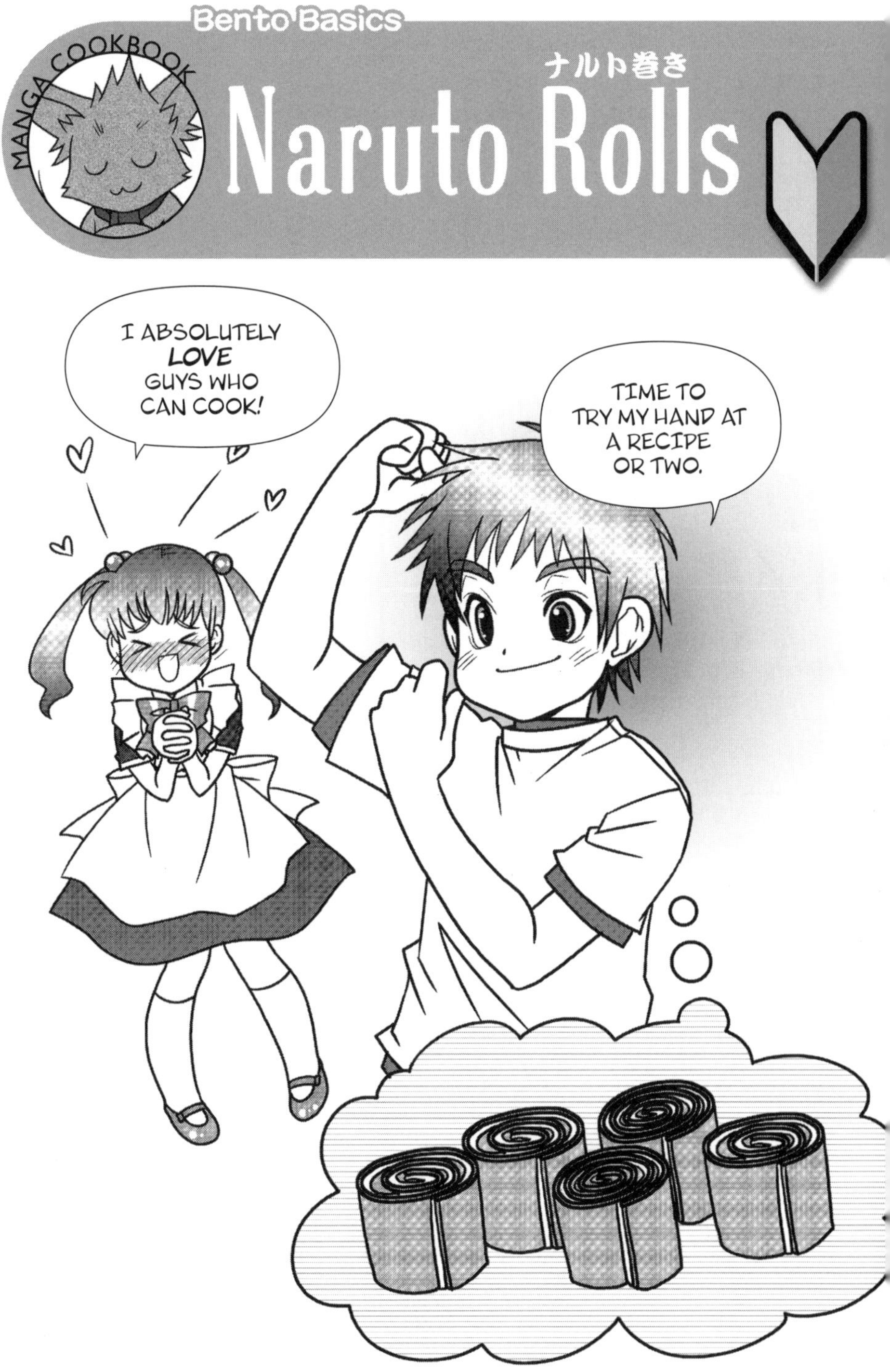
MANGA COOKBOOK
TIME TO TRY MY HAND AT A RECIPE OR TWO.
I ABSOLUTELY **LOVE** GUYS WHO CAN COOK!

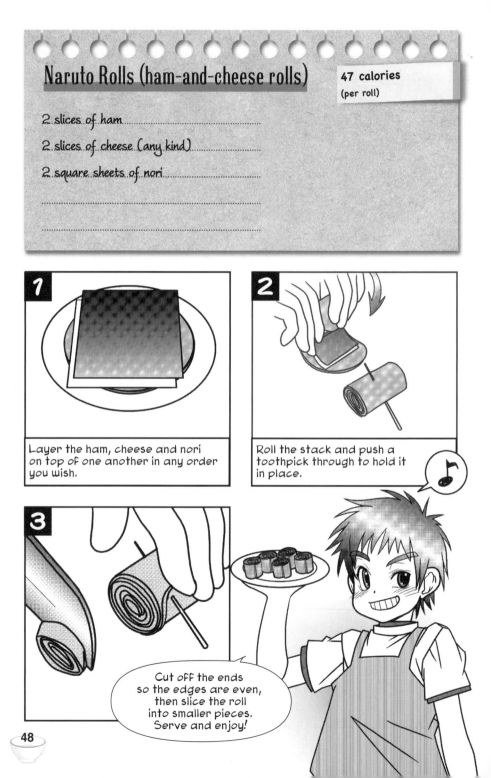

Naruto Rolls (ham-and-cheese rolls)

47 calories
(per roll)

2 slices of ham
2 slices of cheese (any kind)
2 square sheets of nori

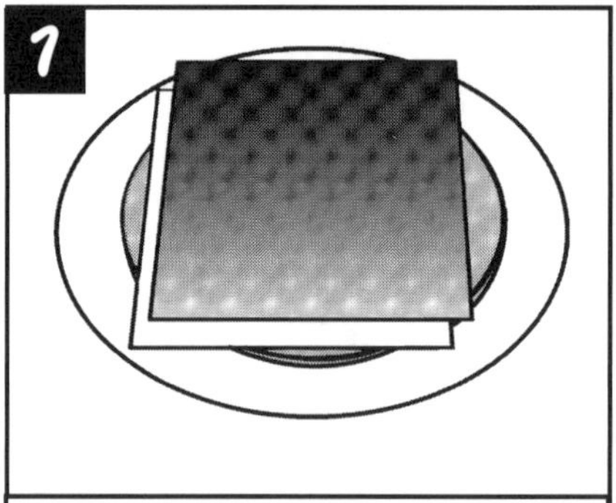
1

Layer the ham, cheese and nori on top of one another in any order you wish.

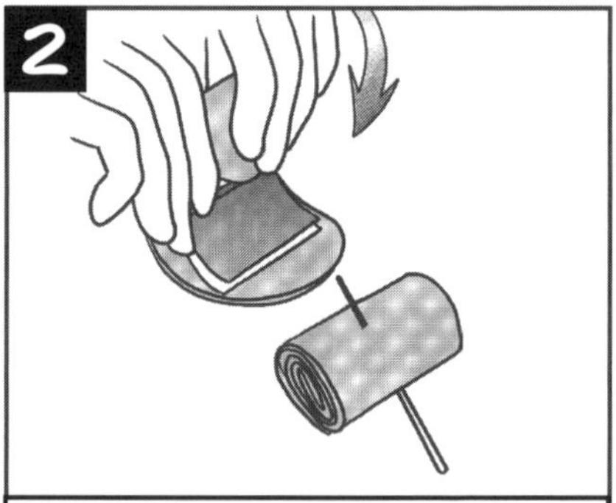
2

Roll the stack and push a toothpick through to hold it in place.

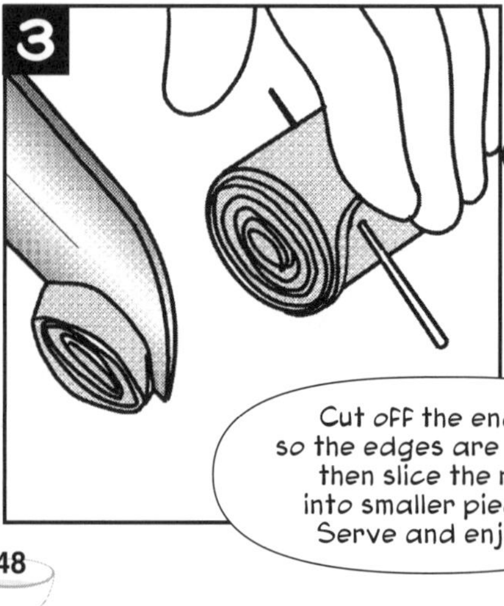
3

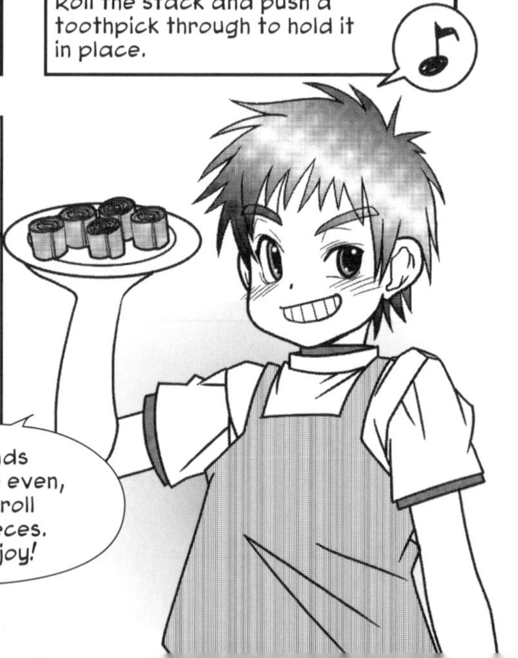
Cut off the ends so the edges are even, then slice the roll into smaller pieces. Serve and enjoy!

MANGA COOKBOOK

Nikumaki 肉巻き

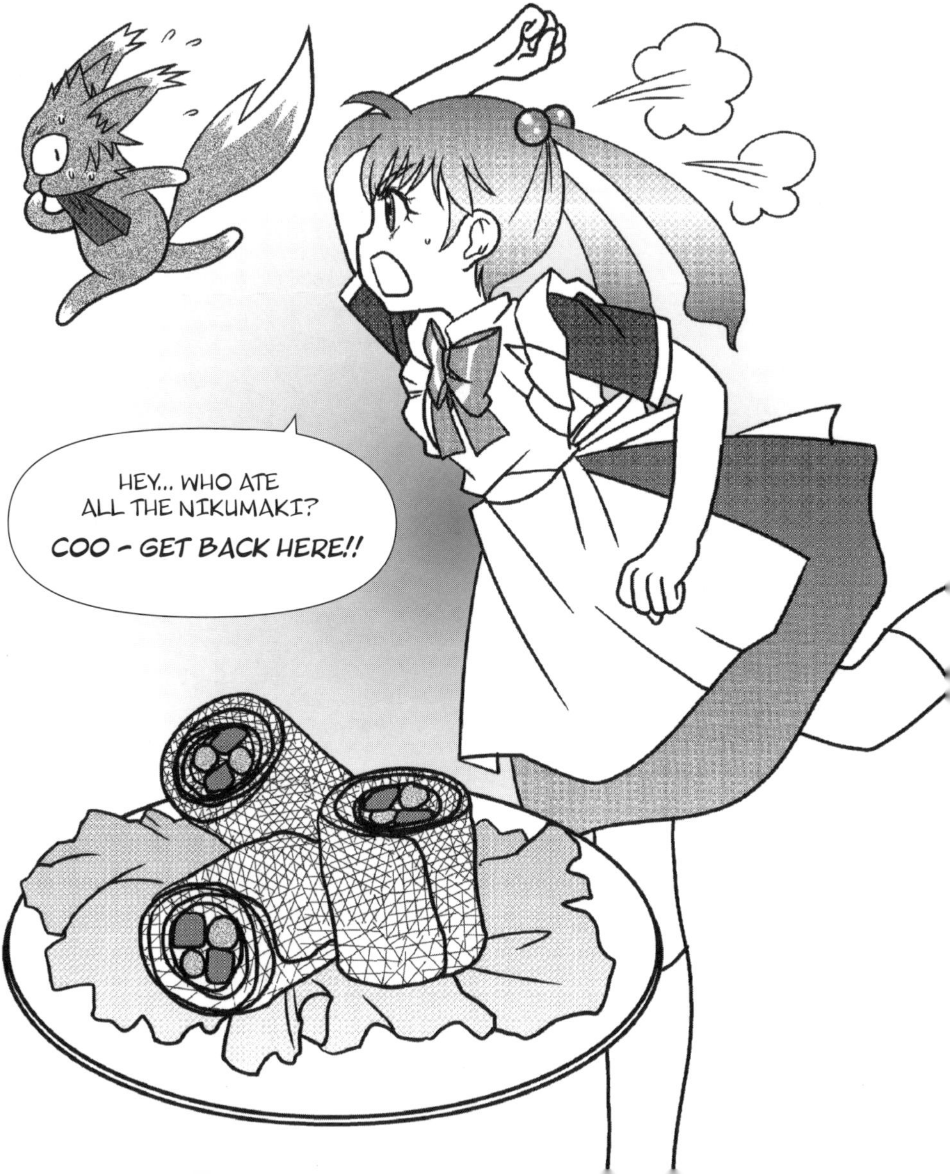
HEY... WHO ATE ALL THE NIKUMAKI?
COO - GET BACK HERE!!

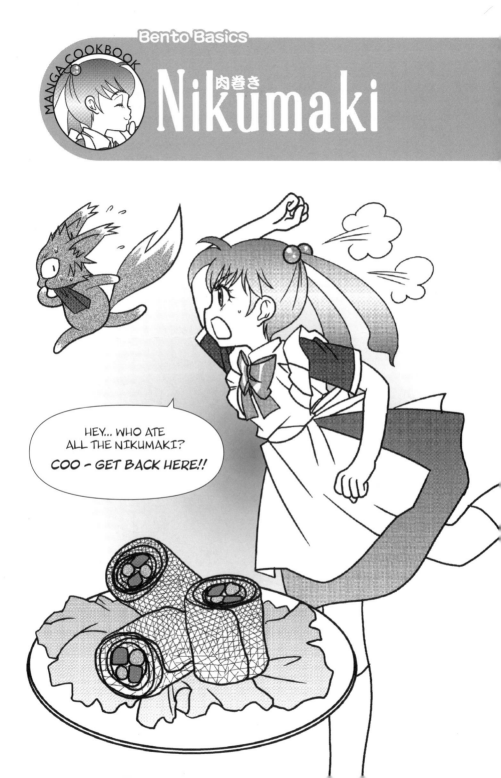

Nikumaki (meat rolls)

738 calories
(per serving)

- 1 pound thinly sliced pork (bacon or prosciutto work well)
- 3 carrot sticks cut to 4 inches
- 3 asparagus stalks cut to 4 inches
- 3 string beans cut to 4 inches
- 2 tablespoons sugar
- ½ cup teriyaki sauce (see page 109)

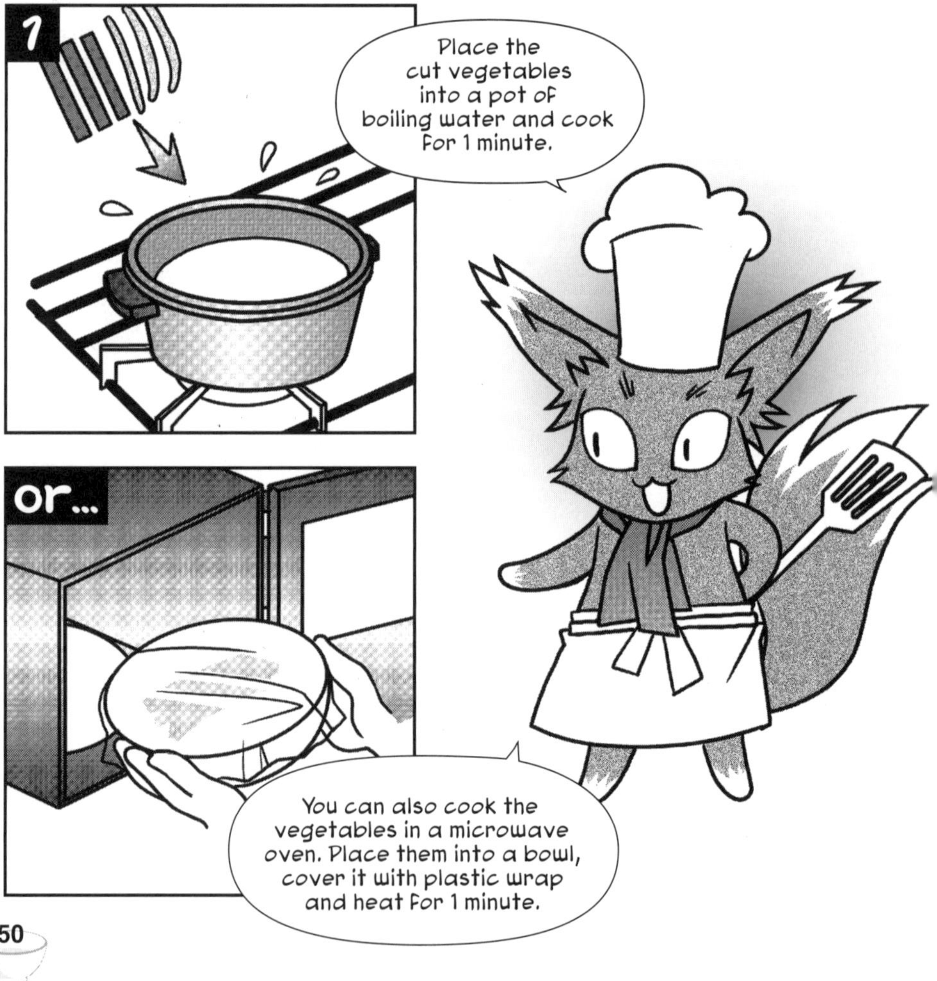
1
Place the cut vegetables into a pot of boiling water and cook for 1 minute.
or...
You can also cook the vegetables in a microwave oven. Place them into a bowl, cover it with plastic wrap and heat for 1 minute.

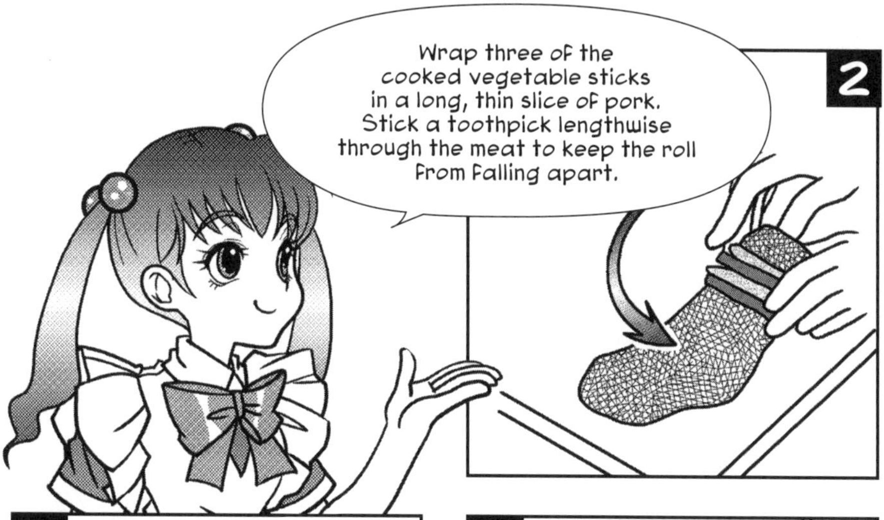
2
Wrap three of the cooked vegetable sticks in a long, thin slice of pork. Stick a toothpick lengthwise through the meat to keep the roll from falling apart.

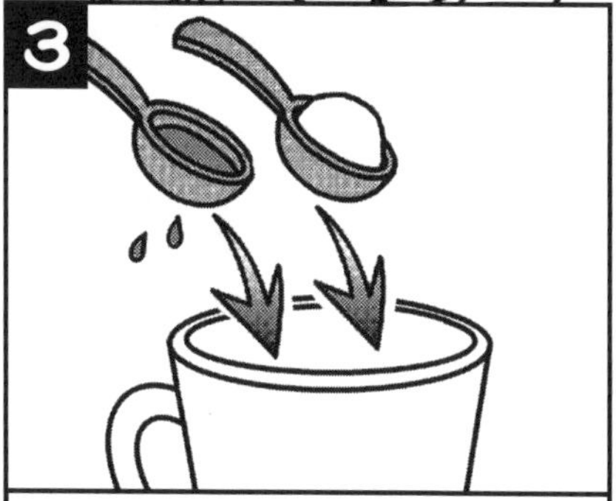
3

Mix the teriyaki sauce and sugar in a cup or bowl.

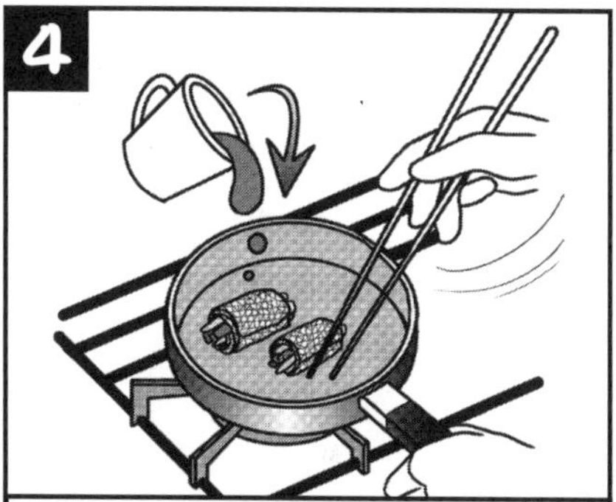
4

Fry the meat rolls on medium heat, then add the teriyaki sauce.

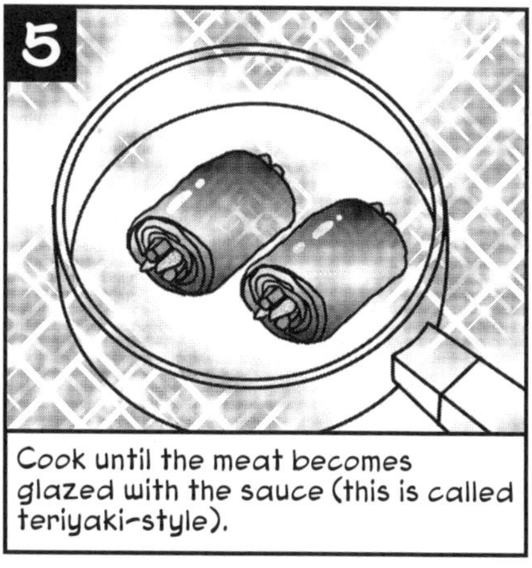
5

Cook until the meat becomes glazed with the sauce (this is called teriyaki-style).

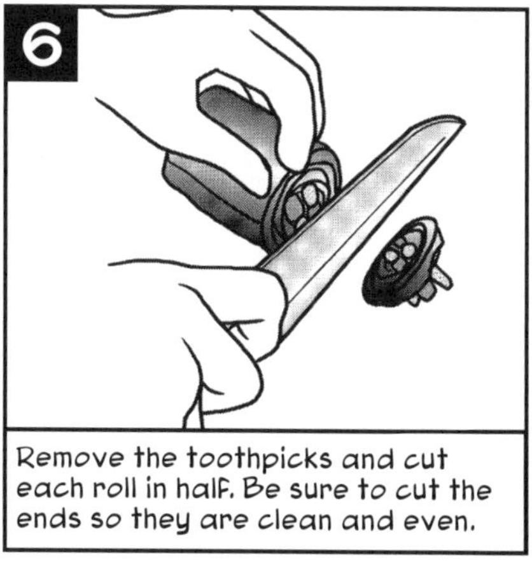
6

Remove the toothpicks and cut each roll in half. Be sure to cut the ends so they are clean and even.

Miyuki's Notes on "Omotenashi"

As noted earlier, Japanese food is both nutritious and delicious. However, the appearance of food is also very important. Savoring food not only with one's mouth but with one's eyes makes it all the more delicious and enjoyable. This is what is known as "omotenashi."

The Naturo Roll recipe may seem simple, but careful attention must be paid to how the food looks. The ends of the rolls should be very cleanly cut. You may recognize "Naruto" as the name of everyone's favorite manga ninja, but the word actually refers to a kind of kamaboko (see page 19) with a swirl pattern similar to the one on Naruto's jacket. Because the ingredients in the ham-and-cheese roll create the same pattern, I call this creation the Naruto Roll!

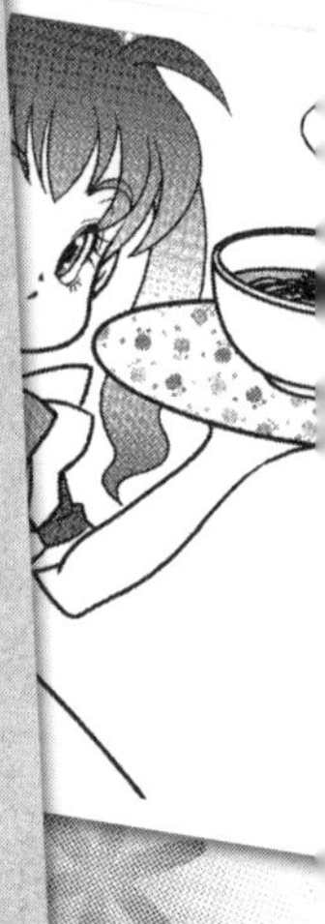

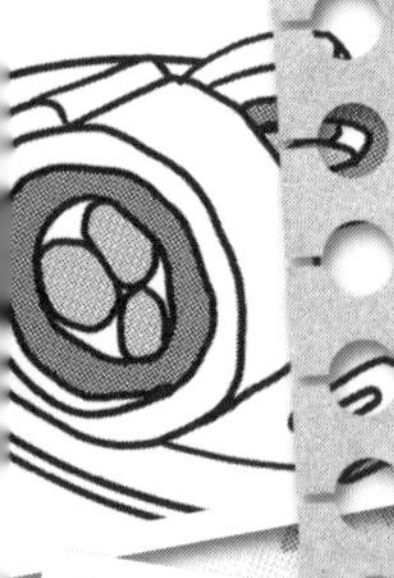

Toothpicks like the ones used in the roll recipe are almost always placed on a Japanese dinner table. They are useful when eating apples and other fruits, as well as fried chicken, potatoes, and other snacks. While it's not particularly good manners at the dinner table, toothpicks are still also used to remove food stuck between teeth.

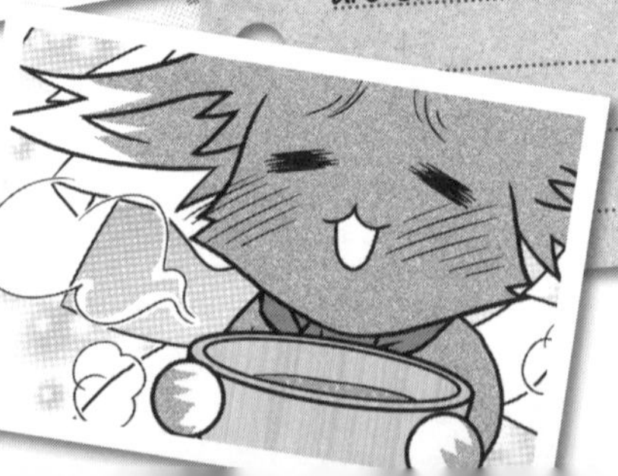

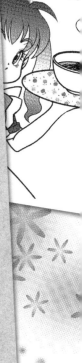

My Notes

My Notes

MANGA COOKBOOK

Bento Basics

Jagatama じゃが玉

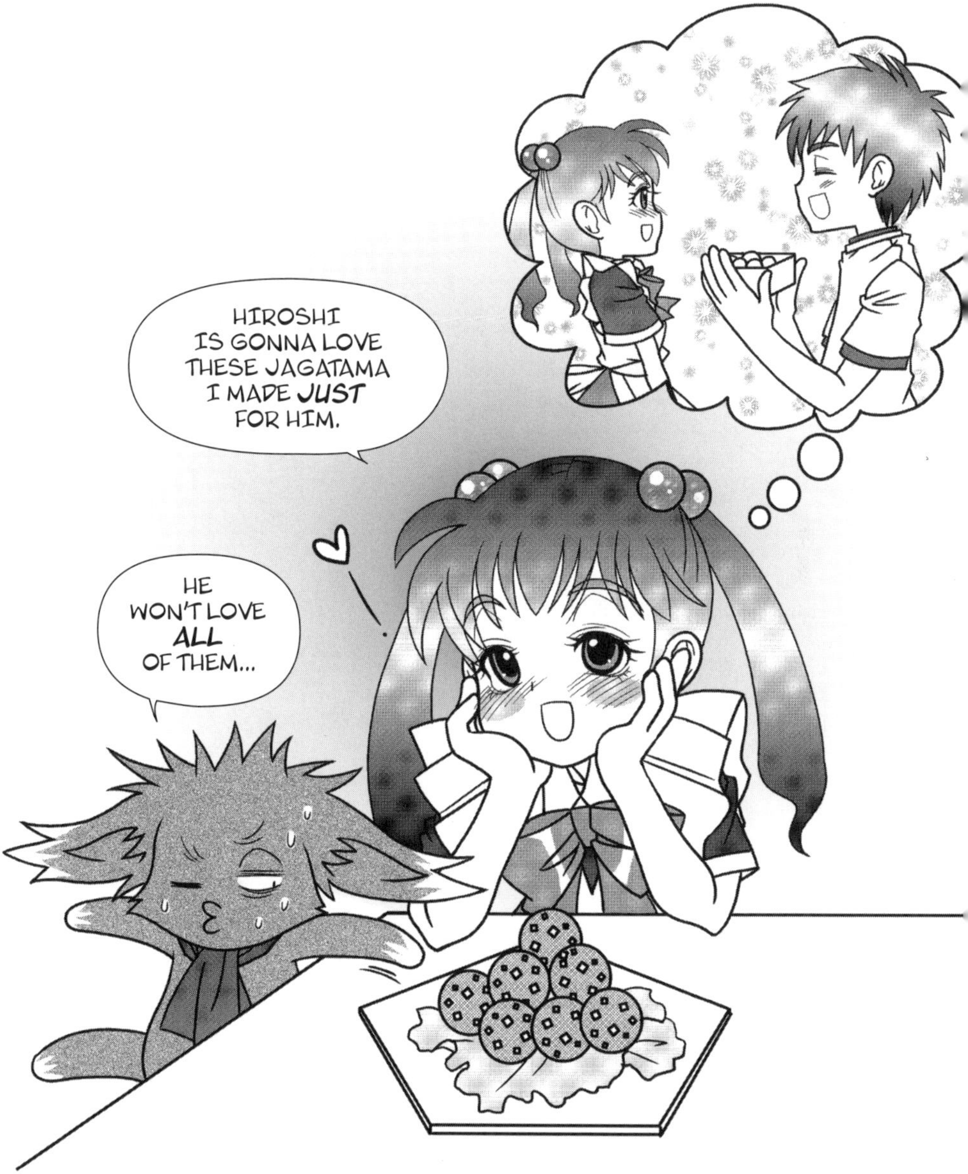
HIROSHI IS GONNA LOVE THESE JAGATAMA I MADE JUST FOR HIM.
HE WON'T LOVE ALL OF THEM...

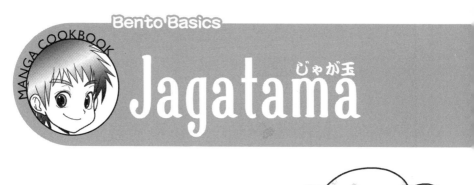

Jagatama (potato balls)

440 calories
(per serving)

- 2 potatoes, cut into cubes
- 4 tablespoons mixed frozen vegetables (cooked per package instructions)
- ⅓ cup mayonnaise
- 1 lemon
- Salt
- Sugar
- Curry powder

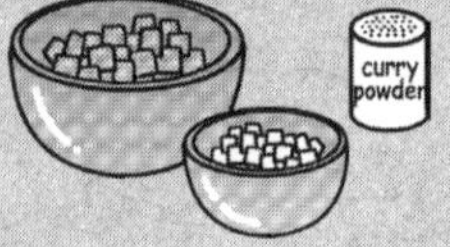
curry powder

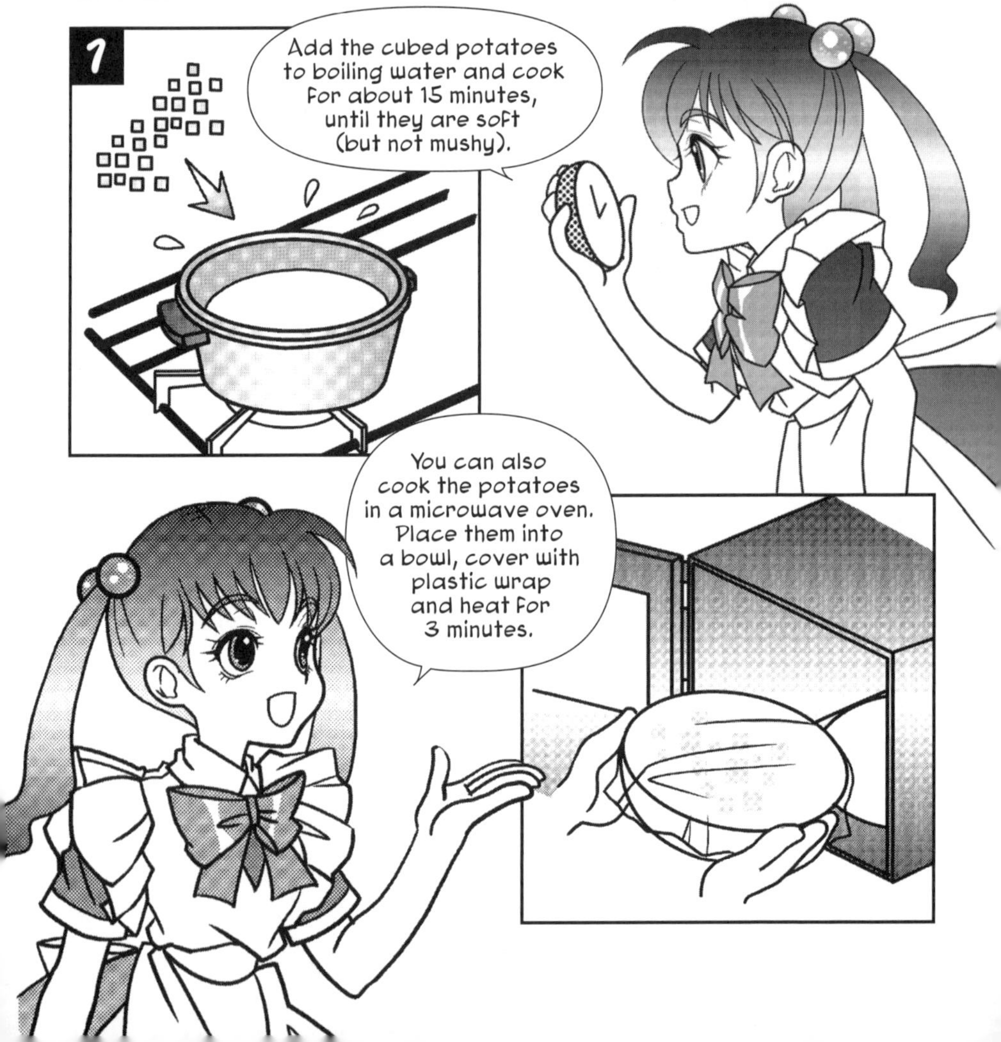
1
Add the cubed potatoes to boiling water and cook for about 15 minutes, until they are soft (but not mushy).
You can also cook the potatoes in a microwave oven. Place them into a bowl, cover with plastic wrap and heat for 3 minutes.

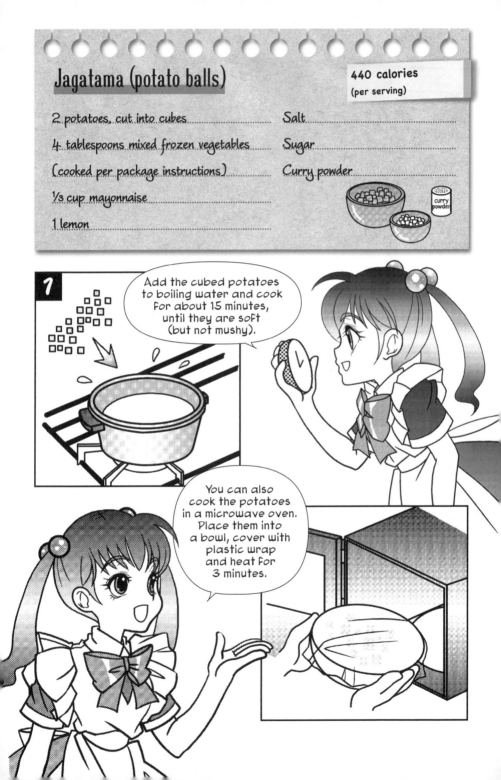

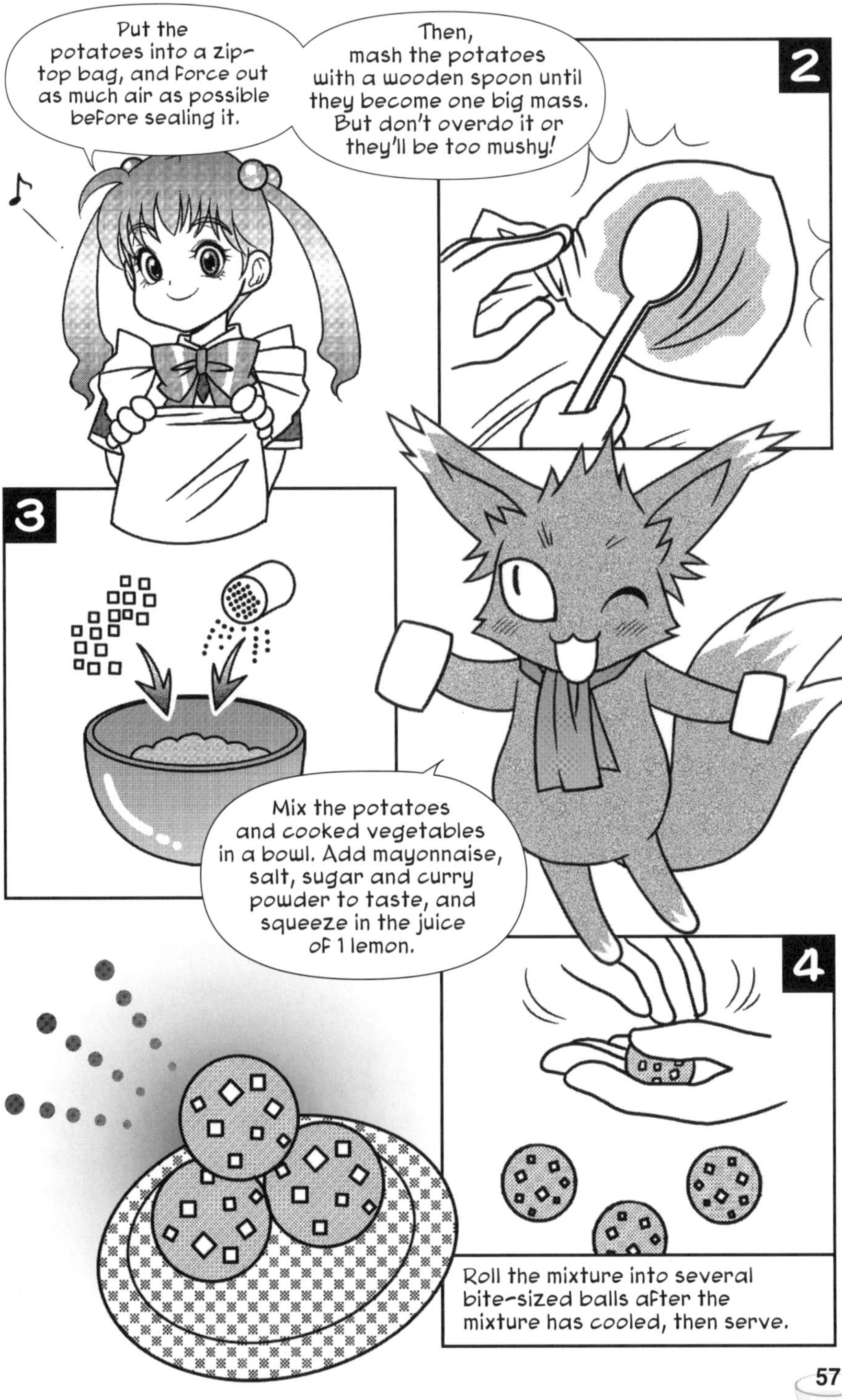
Put the potatoes into a zip-top bag, and force out as much air as possible before sealing it.
Then, mash the potatoes with a wooden spoon until they become one big mass. But don't overdo it or they'll be too mushy!
2
3
Mix the potatoes and cooked vegetables in a bowl. Add mayonnaise, salt, sugar and curry powder to taste, and squeeze in the juice of 1 lemon.
4
Roll the mixture into several bite-sized balls after the mixture has cooled, then serve.

Miyuki's Notes on Jagatama

The color scheme of a bento is very important. How you include both attractive and nutritionally balanced side dishes is key.

Like onigiri, you can roll a lot of ingredients into a ball without worrying as much about the appearance of the food. When you have a large number of vegetables you'd like to use, putting them into a ball form is both cute and economical.

Since potato salad balls are low in moisture, there is no risk of the flavors of other items in your bento being affected.

Though it will add calories, an extra helping of mayonnaise will yield a more moist potato salad. However, if you're more concerned about your diet, you can add more vinegar and lemon juice, and if you substitute olive oil for the extra mayonnaise, you can cut both the calories and cholesterol.

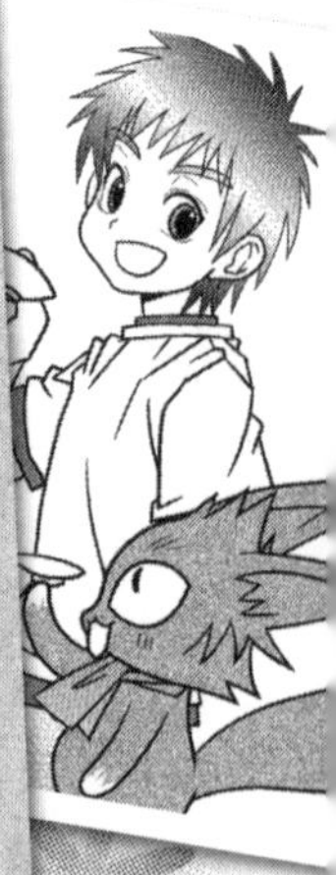

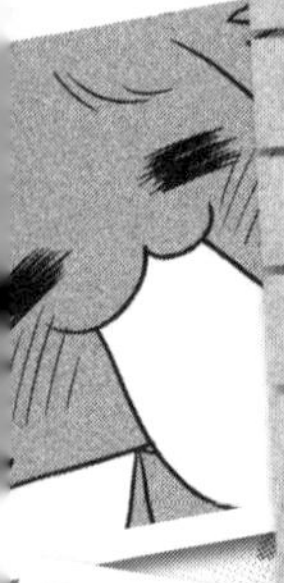

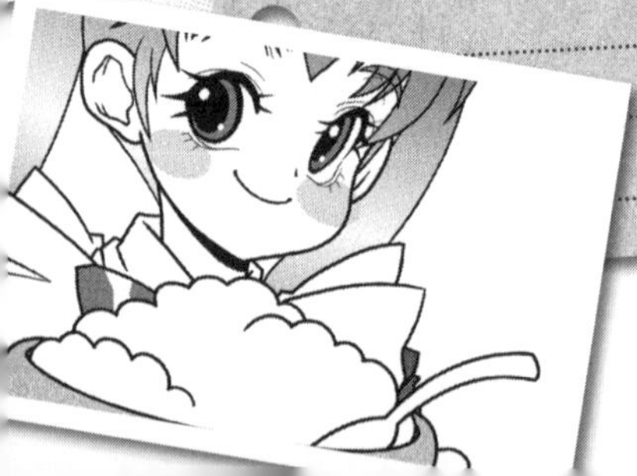

My Notes

My Notes

Bento Basics

MANGA COOKBOOK

Rice Burgers

ご飯バーガー

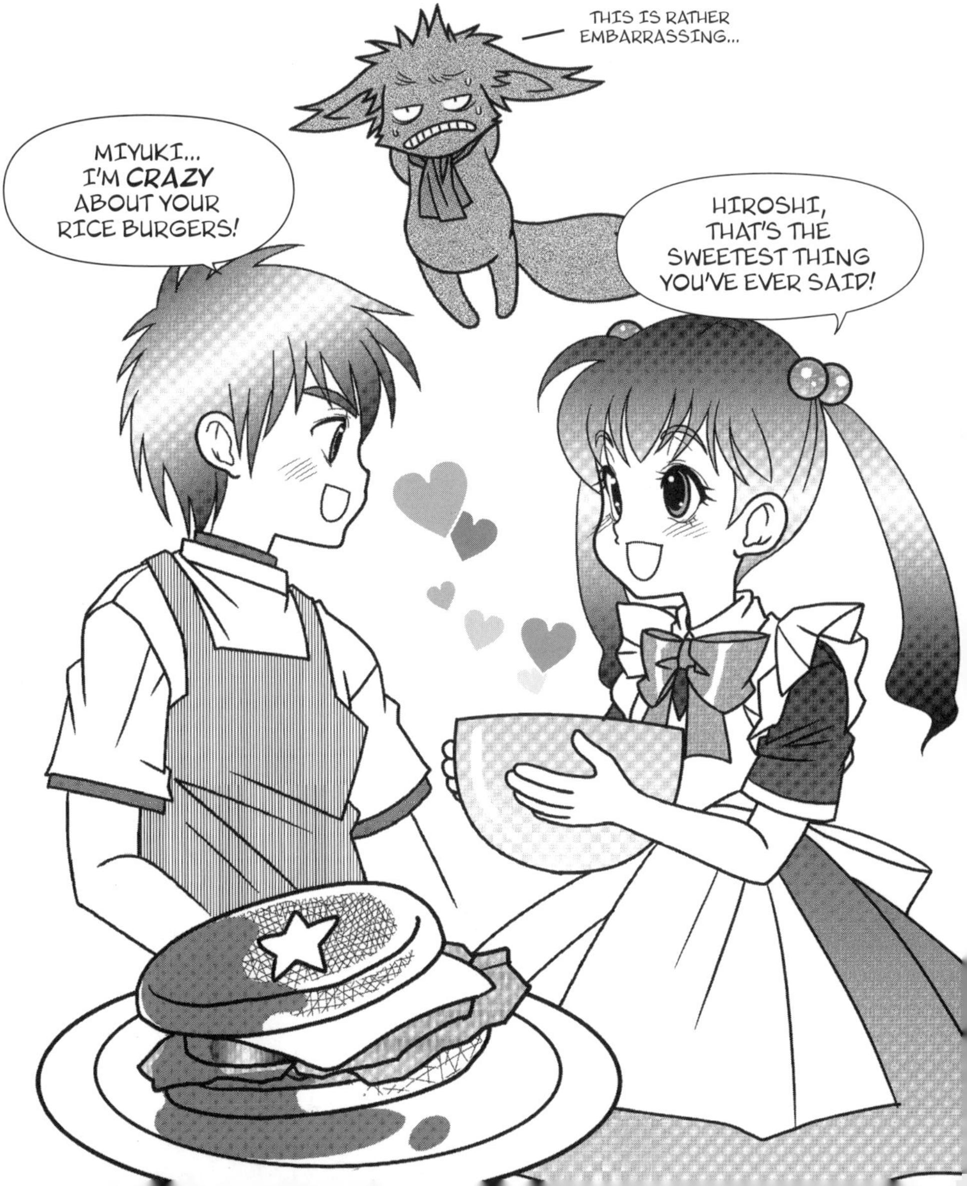

MIYUKI... I'M **CRAZY** ABOUT YOUR RICE BURGERS!
HIROSHI, THAT'S THE SWEETEST THING YOU'VE EVER SAID!
THIS IS RATHER EMBARRASSING...

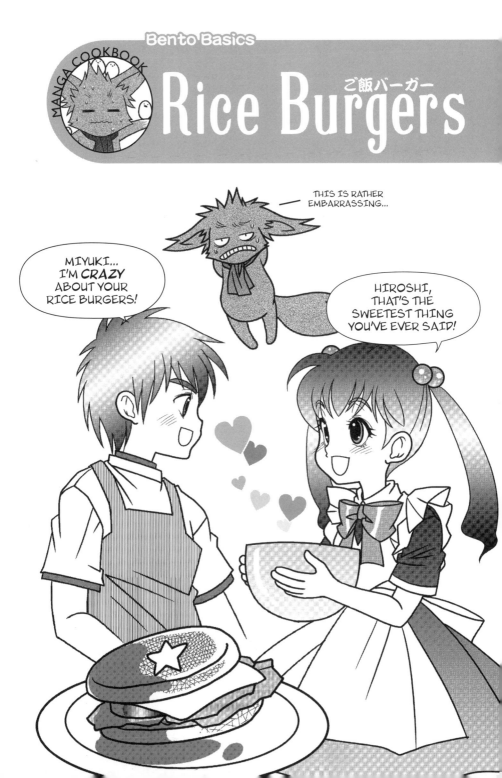

Rice Burgers

320 calories
(per burger)

2 cups steamed rice

1 tablespoon butter

The rest of the ingredients are up to you!

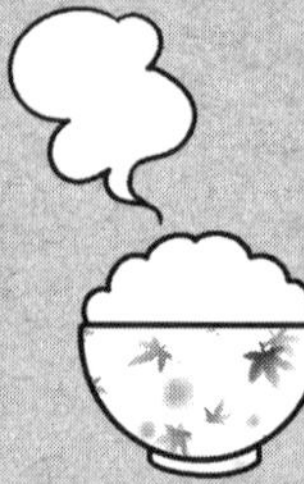

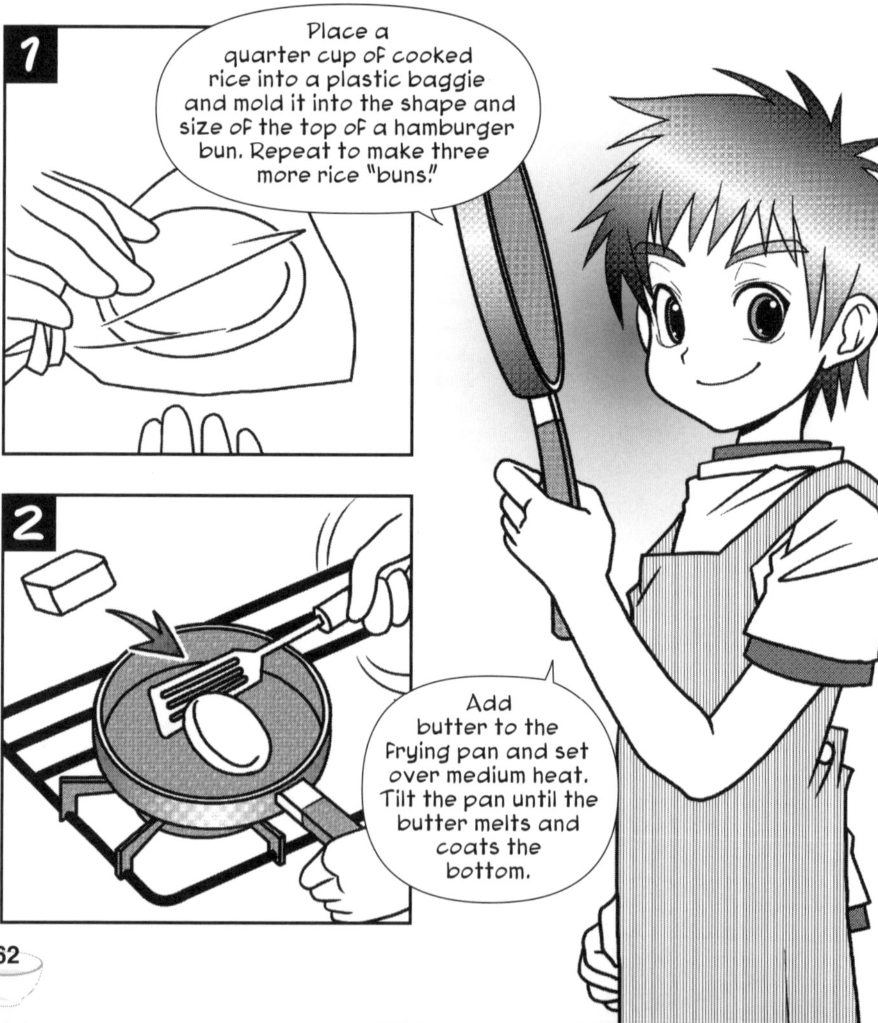
1
Place a quarter cup of cooked rice into a plastic baggie and mold it into the shape and size of the top of a hamburger bun. Repeat to make three more rice "buns."
2
Add butter to the frying pan and set over medium heat. Tilt the pan until the butter melts and coats the bottom.

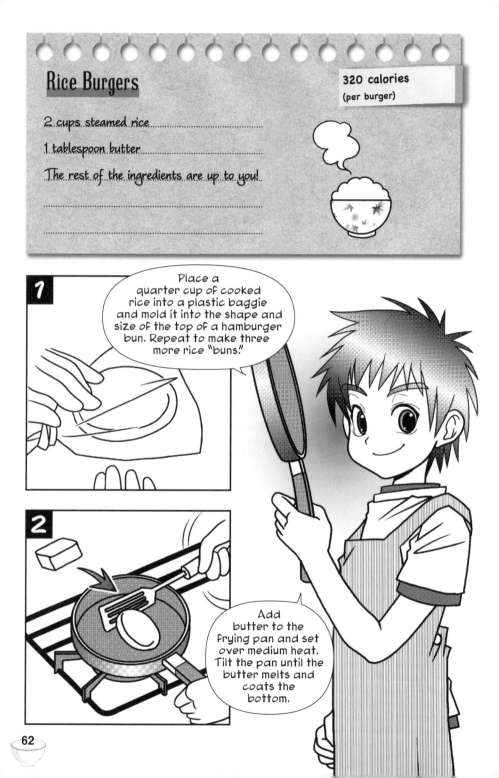

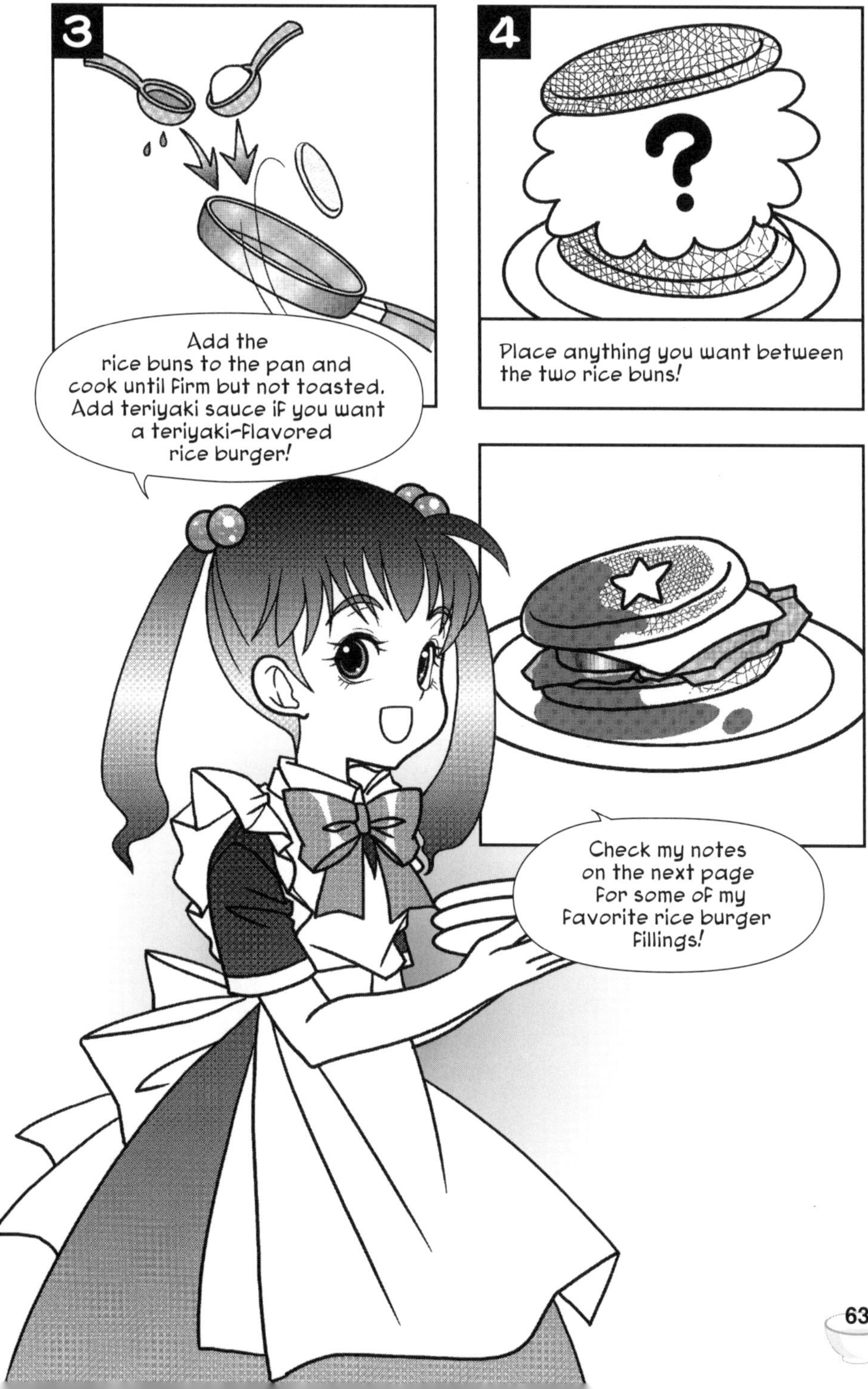
3
4
Add the rice buns to the pan and cook until firm but not toasted. Add teriyaki sauce if you want a teriyaki-flavored rice burger!
Place anything you want between the two rice buns!
?
Check my notes on the next page for some of my favorite rice burger fillings!

Miyuki's Notes on Rice Burgers

Rice burgers are popular at Japanese fast-food restaurants. Like the bread on a sandwich, rice patties can hold just about anything in between. For vegetarians, rice burgers are a godsend, since fast-food chains in Japan often serve them with only sautéed veggies in between.

Beef patties, cheese, sausage, fried chicken and fish are also some of my favorite fillings. Rice burgers can be topped with mayonnaise, ketchup or just about any condiment you like. Teriyaki sauce, soy sauce and sweet chili sauce are what I use – but feel free to experiment!

If you ever have leftover rice, don't throw it out — it'll make a perfectly delicious rice burger later! Just seal unused rice in plastic wrap and keep it in the freezer for as long as you like. When you're ready to use the rice, defrost it by heating it in a microwave oven for about 30 seconds before making your burger.

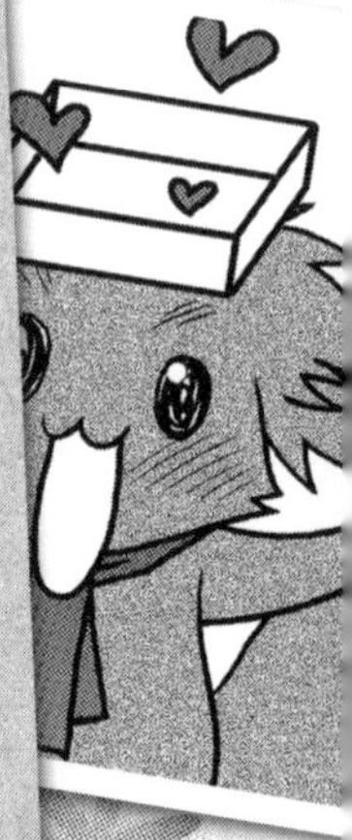

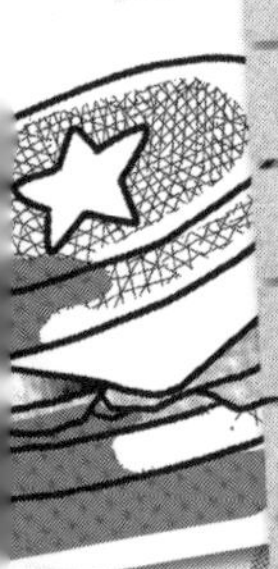

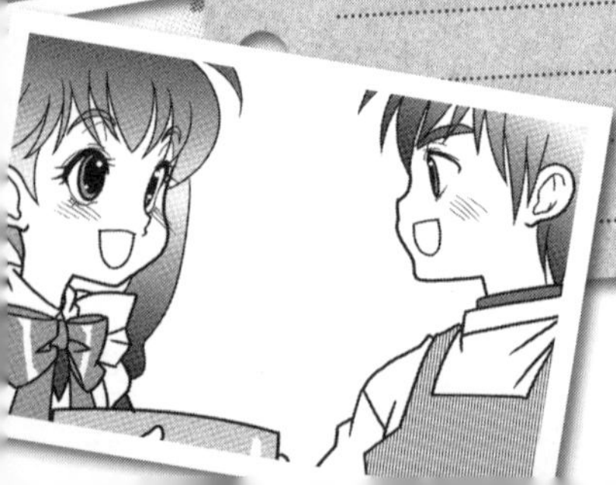

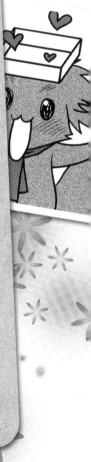

My Notes

My Notes

Bento Basics

MANGA COOKBOOK

Soboro Bento

そぼろ弁当

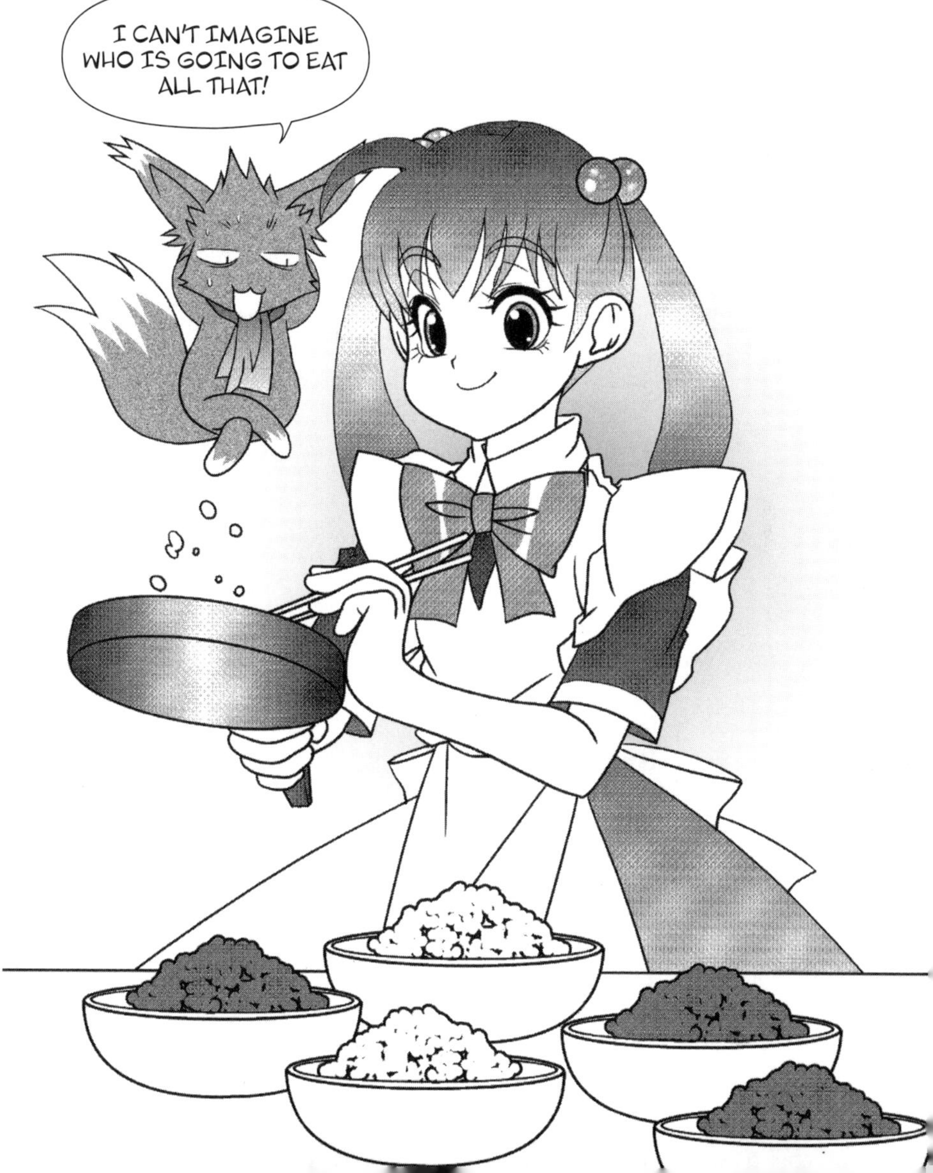
I CAN'T IMAGINE WHO IS GOING TO EAT ALL THAT!

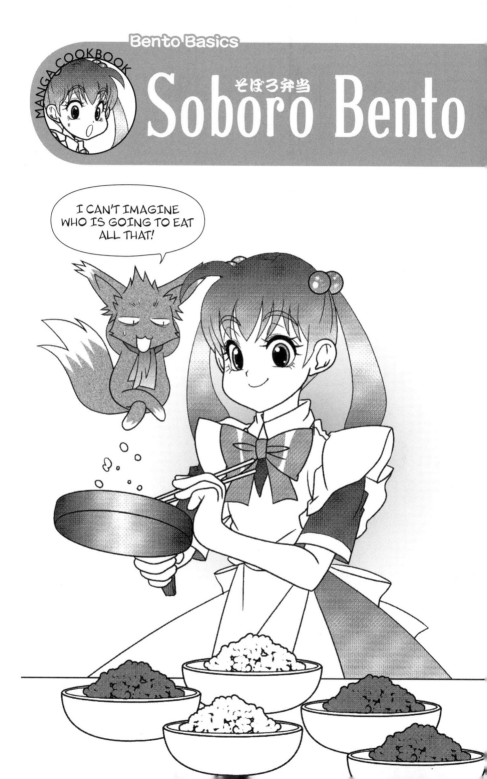

Soboro Bento (minced pork-and-egg)

657 calories
(per serving)

For the Meat:	For the Eggs:
1 pound ground pork	3 eggs
1 tablespoon olive oil	2 tablespoons sugar
3 tablespoons sugar	½ teaspoon salt
4 tablespoons teriyaki sauce (page 109)	2 tablespoons vegetable oil

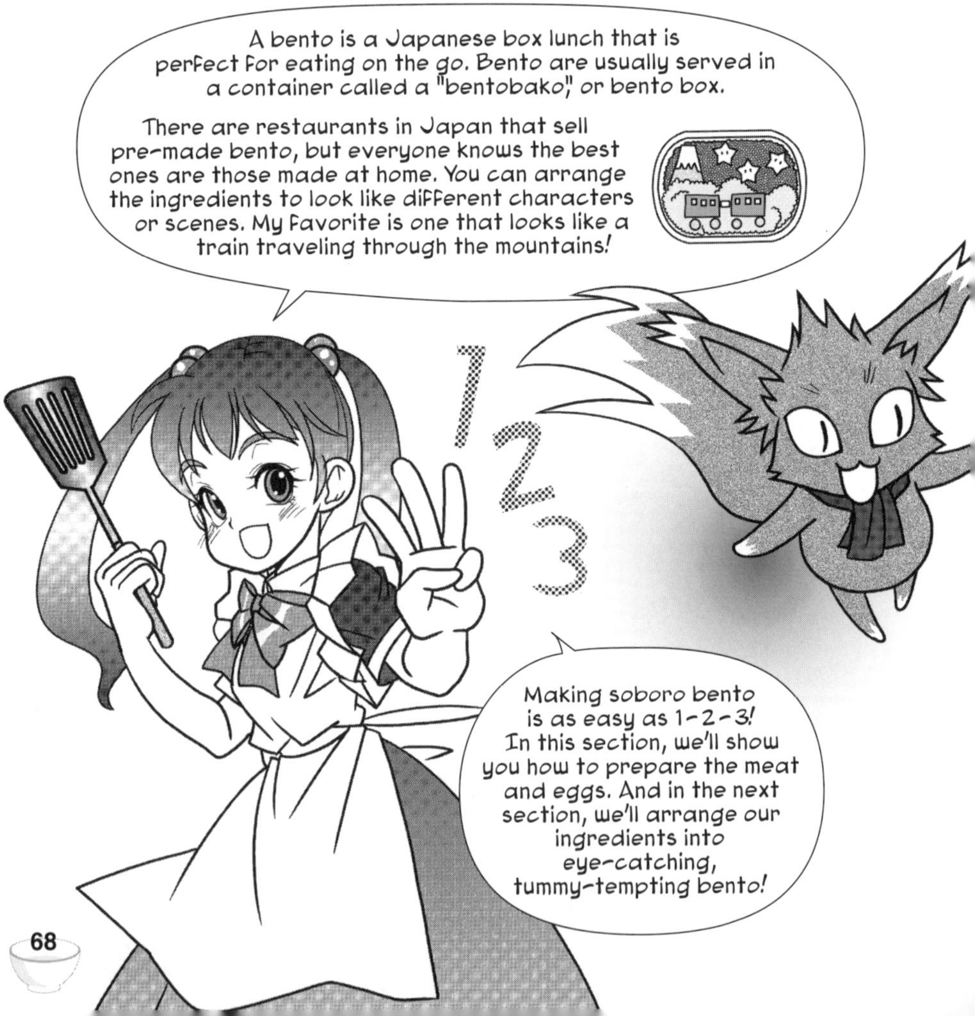
A bento is a Japanese box lunch that is perfect for eating on the go. Bento are usually served in a container called a "bentobako," or bento box.
There are restaurants in Japan that sell pre-made bento, but everyone knows the best ones are those made at home. You can arrange the ingredients to look like different characters or scenes. My favorite is one that looks like a train traveling through the mountains!
1
2
3
Making soboro bento is as easy as 1-2-3! In this section, we'll show you how to prepare the meat and eggs. And in the next section, we'll arrange our ingredients into eye-catching, tummy-tempting bento!

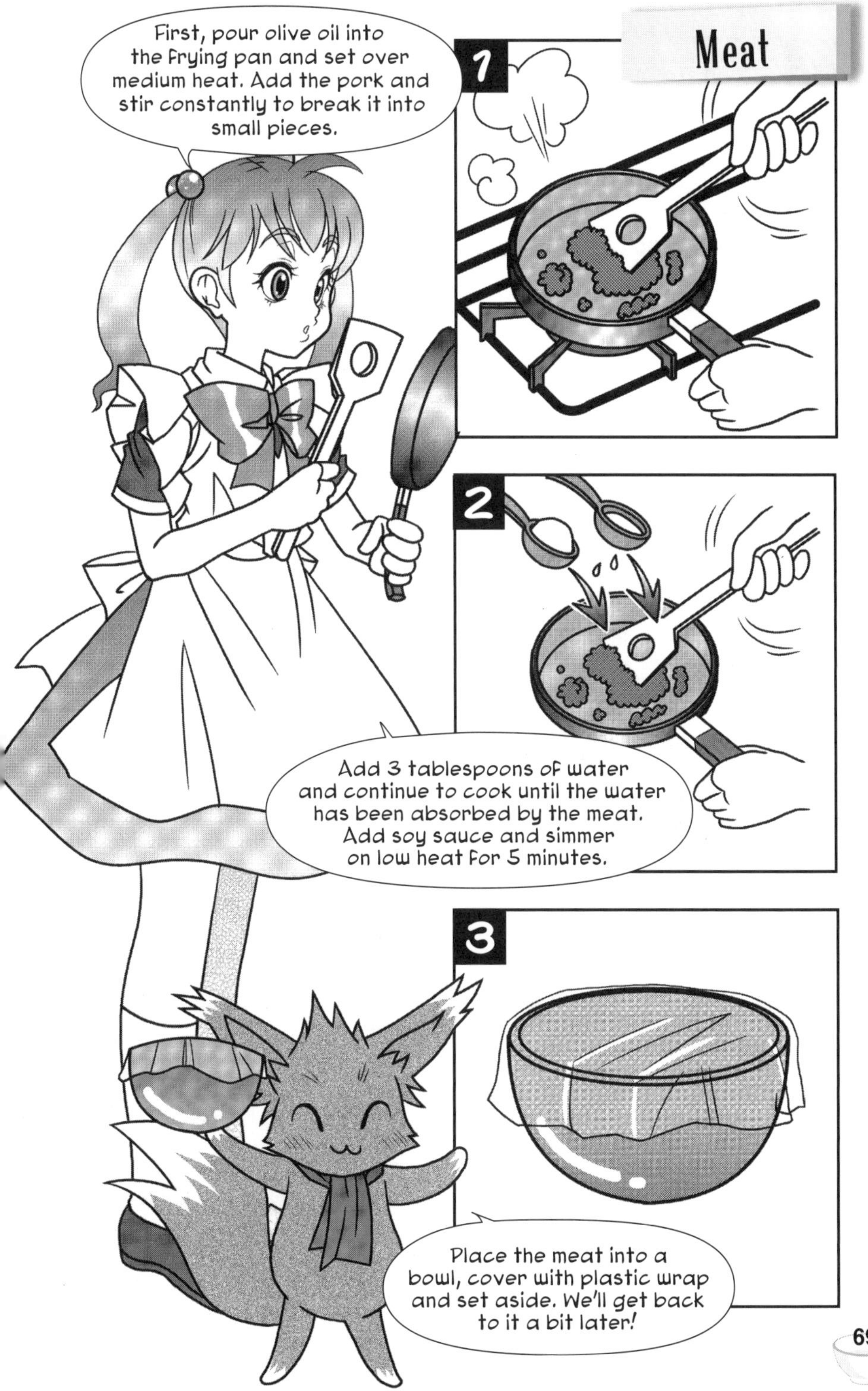
Meat
First, pour olive oil into the frying pan and set over medium heat. Add the pork and stir constantly to break it into small pieces.
1
2
Add 3 tablespoons of water and continue to cook until the water has been absorbed by the meat. Add soy sauce and simmer on low heat for 5 minutes.
3
Place the meat into a bowl, cover with plastic wrap and set aside. We'll get back to it a bit later!

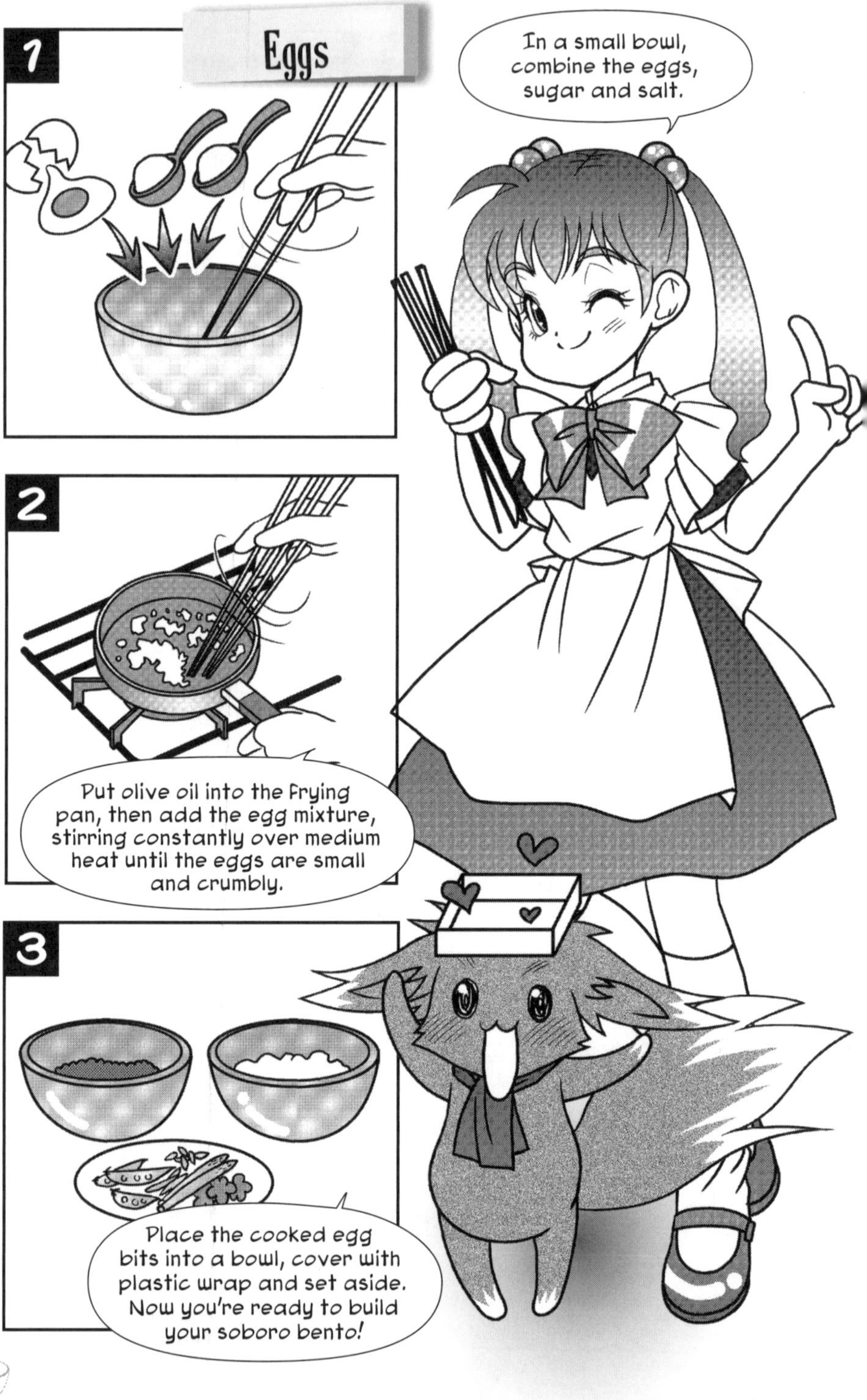
Eggs
1
In a small bowl, combine the eggs, sugar and salt.
2
Put olive oil into the frying pan, then add the egg mixture, stirring constantly over medium heat until the eggs are small and crumbly.
3
Place the cooked egg bits into a bowl, cover with plastic wrap and set aside. Now you're ready to build your soboro bento!

MANGA COOKBOOK

Build a Bento

お弁当を作ろう

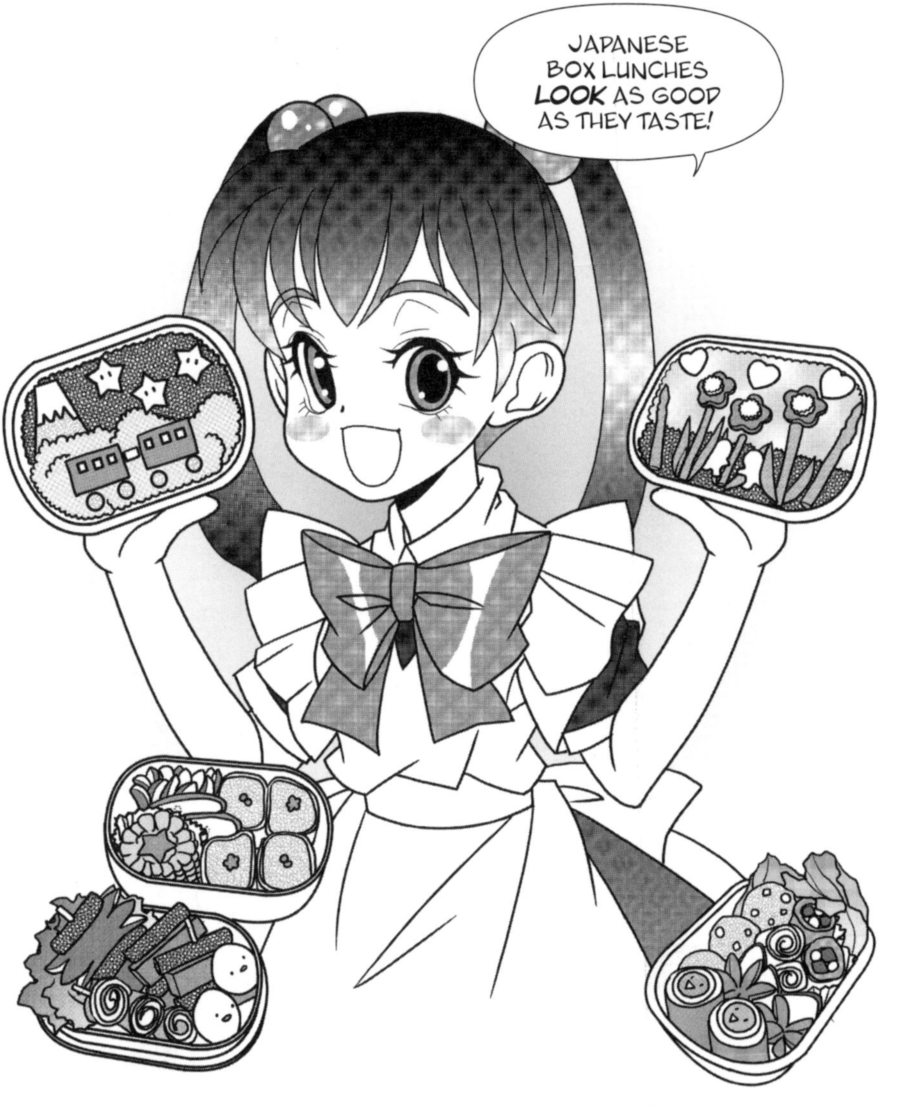
JAPANESE BOX LUNCHES LOOK AS GOOD AS THEY TASTE!

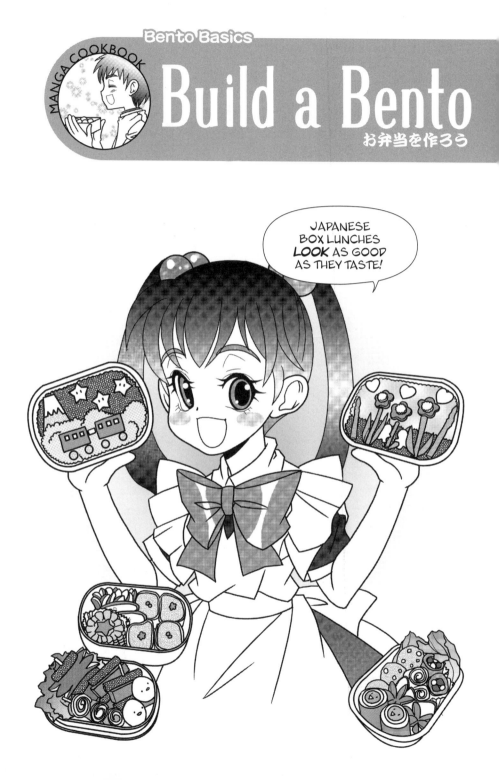

Train Bento

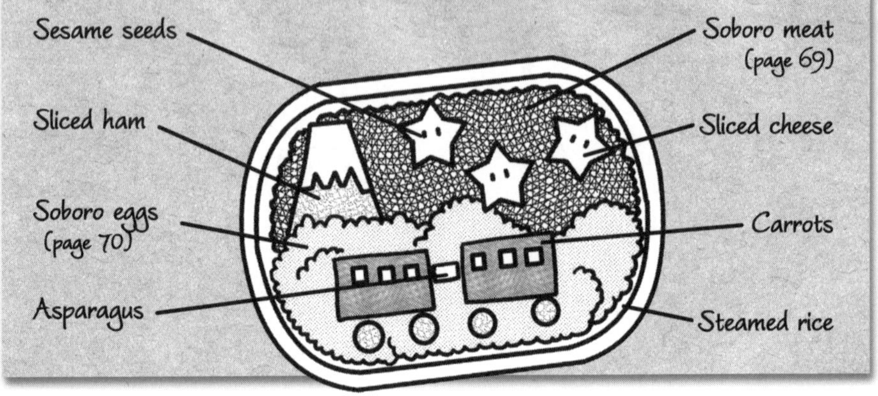
Sesame seeds
Soboro meat (page 69)
Sliced ham
Sliced cheese
Soboro eggs (page 70)
Carrots
Asparagus
Steamed rice

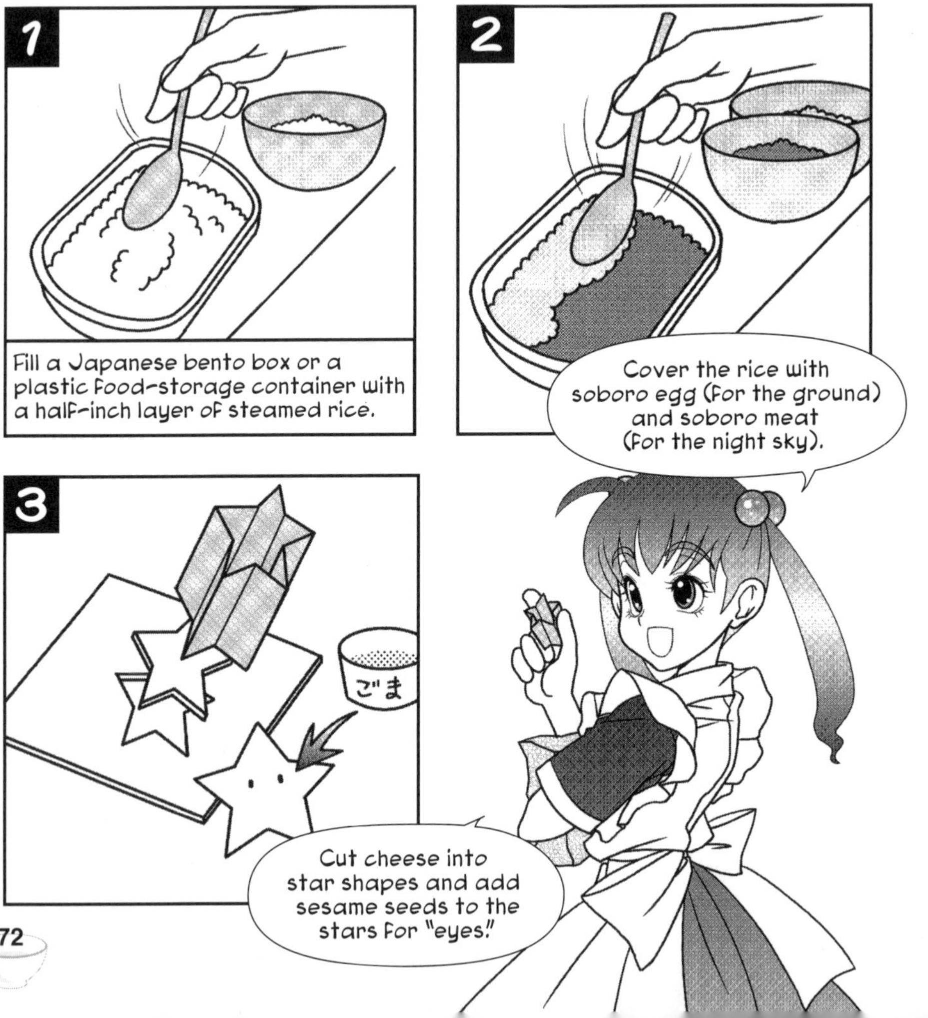
1
Fill a Japanese bento box or a plastic food-storage container with a half-inch layer of steamed rice.
2
Cover the rice with soboro egg (for the ground) and soboro meat (for the night sky).
3
ごま
Cut cheese into star shapes and add sesame seeds to the stars for "eyes."

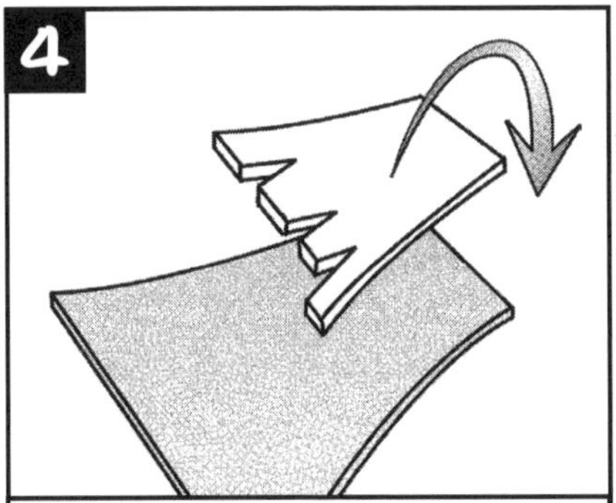

Cut a slice of ham into the shape of a mountain, and add a bit of cheese for the snowy top.

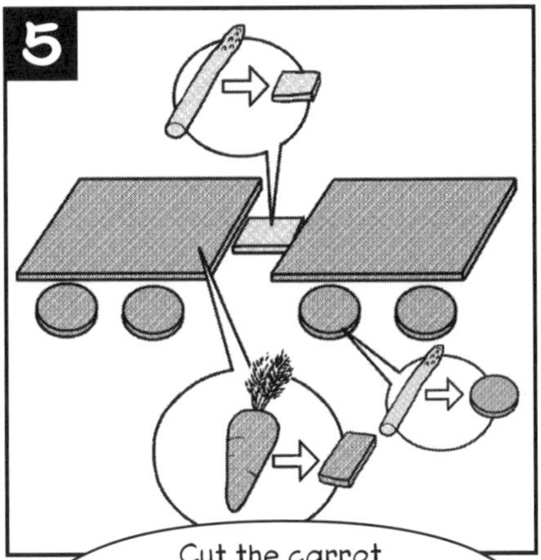

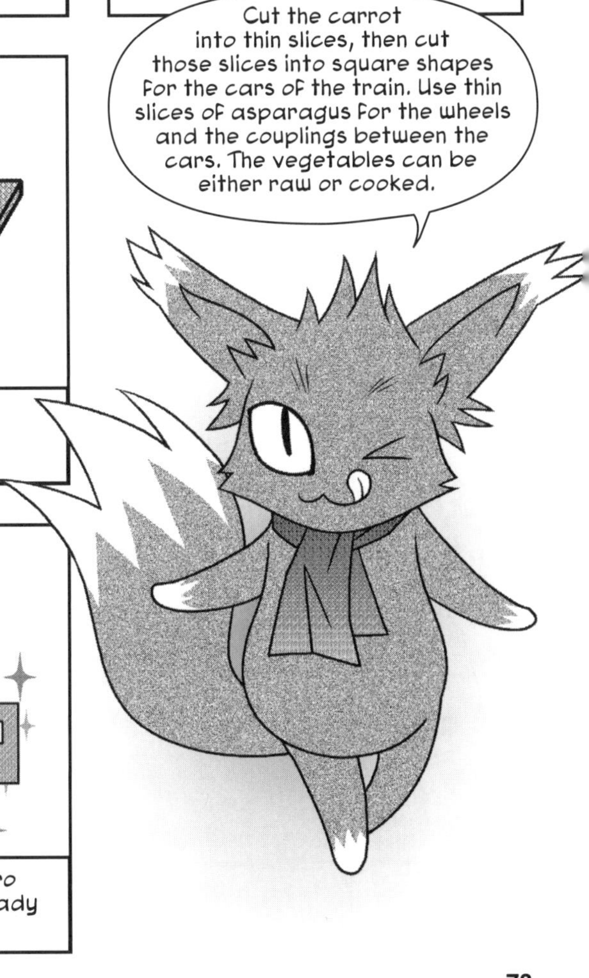
Cut the carrot into thin slices, then cut those slices into square shapes for the cars of the train. Use thin slices of asparagus for the wheels and the couplings between the cars. The vegetables can be either raw or cooked.

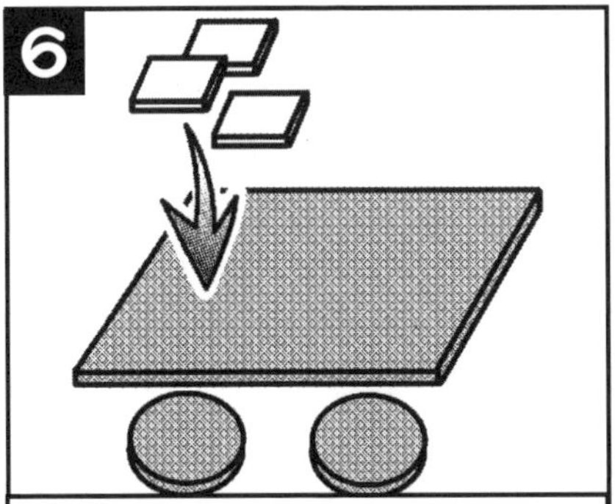

Small, square-shaped slices of cheese can be used for the windows of the train.

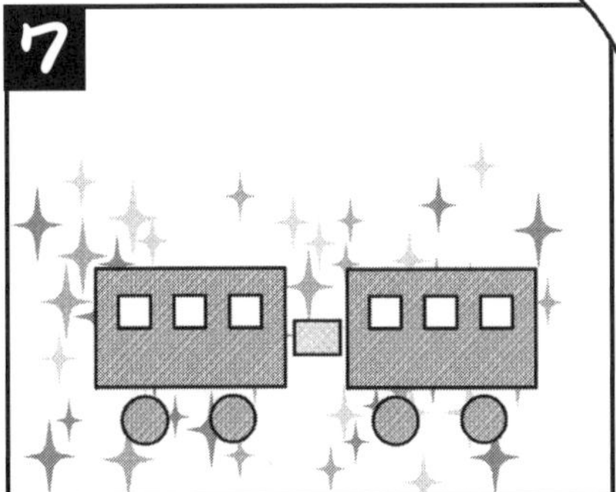

Place the train atop the soboro egg, and your bento is now ready for departure. "All aboard!"

Garden Bento

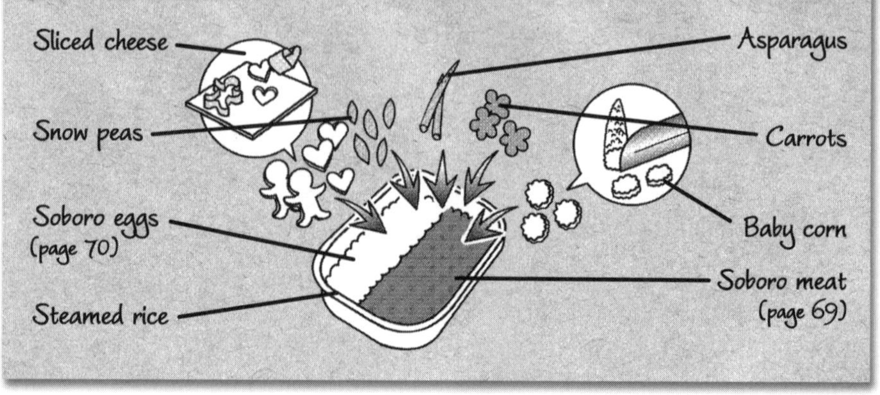

Sliced cheese
Snow peas
Soboro eggs (page 70)
Steamed rice
Asparagus
Carrots
Baby corn
Soboro meat (page 69)

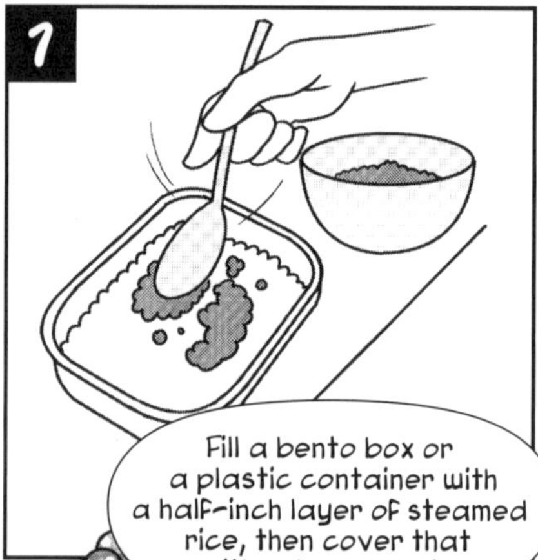

1

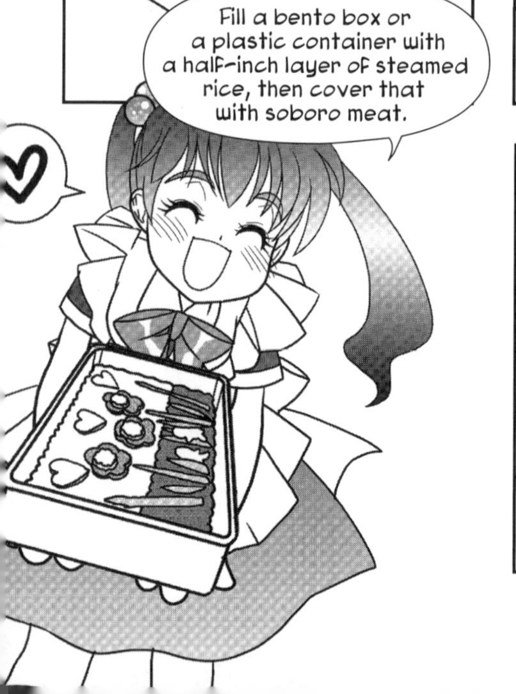

Fill a bento box or a plastic container with a half-inch layer of steamed rice, then cover that with soboro meat.

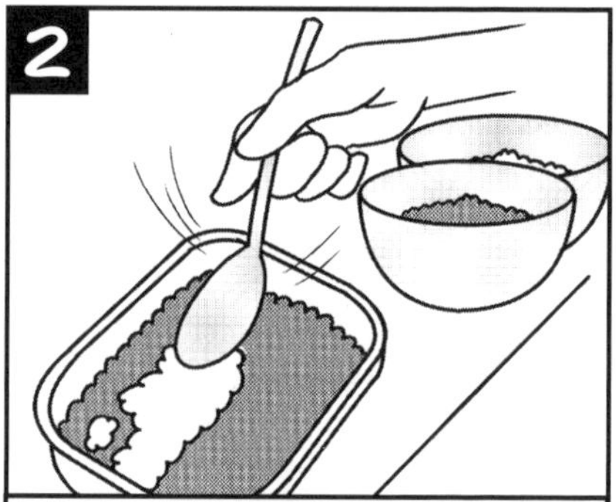

2

Add a layer of soboro eggs to the top two-thirds of the box to form the sky.

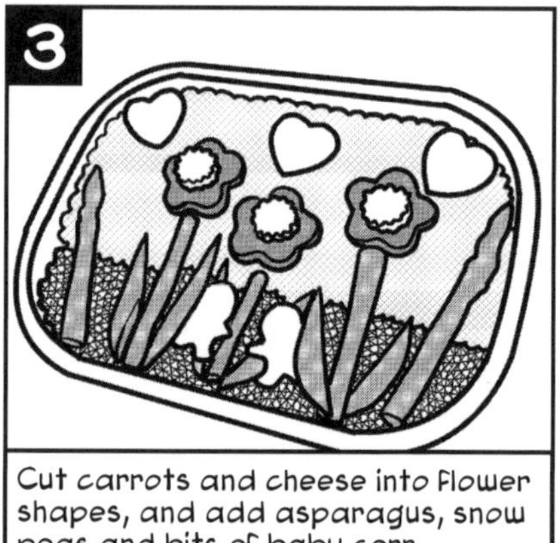

3

Cut carrots and cheese into flower shapes, and add asparagus, snow peas and bits of baby corn.

Bento Ideas

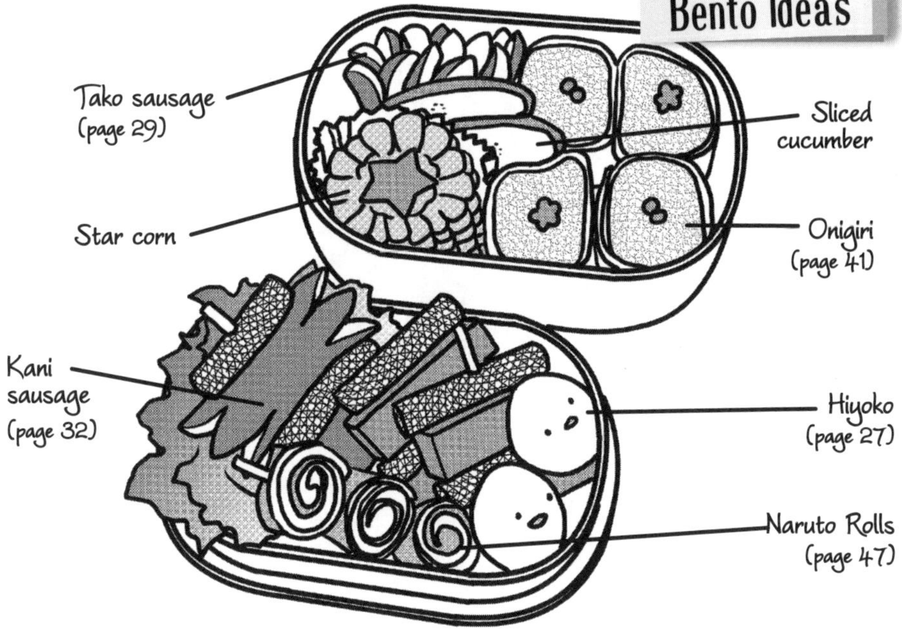
Tako sausage
(page 29)
Sliced cucumber
Star corn
Onigiri
(page 41)
Kani sausage
(page 32)
Hiyoko
(page 27)
Naruto Rolls
(page 47)

Star Corn

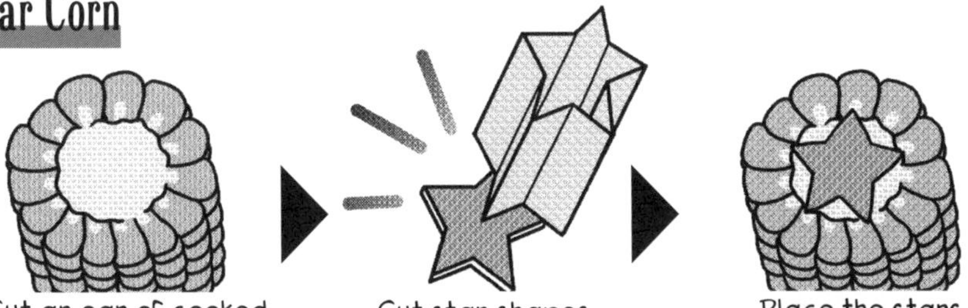

Cut an ear of cooked corn into slices about 1-inch thick.

Cut star shapes out of slices of cucumber.

Place the stars atop the slices of corn.

Crab Sticks

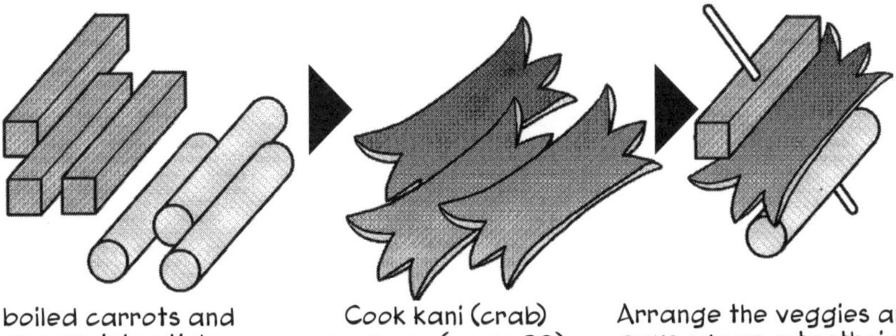

Cut boiled carrots and asparagus into sticks.

Cook kani (crab) sausage (page 32).

Arrange the veggies and sausage on a toothpick.

Bento Ideas

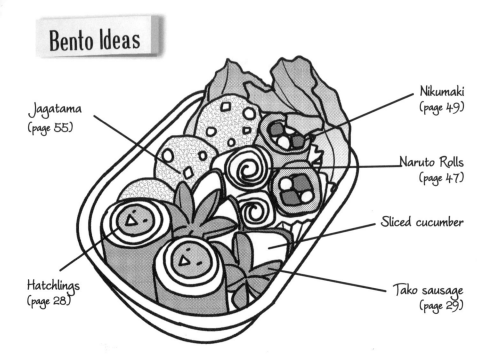

Jagatama
(page 55)

Nikumaki
(page 49)

Naruto Rolls
(page 47)

Sliced cucumber

Hatchlings
(page 28)

Tako sausage
(page 29)

Miyuki's Notes on Building a Bento

When assembling a bento, ask yourself: Is the bento nutritionally balanced? Does the color scheme work well?

Also, make sure there's no empty space in the box (that way when you carry it, the food won't get mixed up).

Fill your bento box while the food is cooling down (be sure it's not too hot).

To fill up empty space in your bento box, you can use paper cups (cupcake holders work, too), lettuce or other leafy vegetables, cherry tomatoes, small pieces of cheese, etc.

My Notes

My Notes

Oshinko お新香

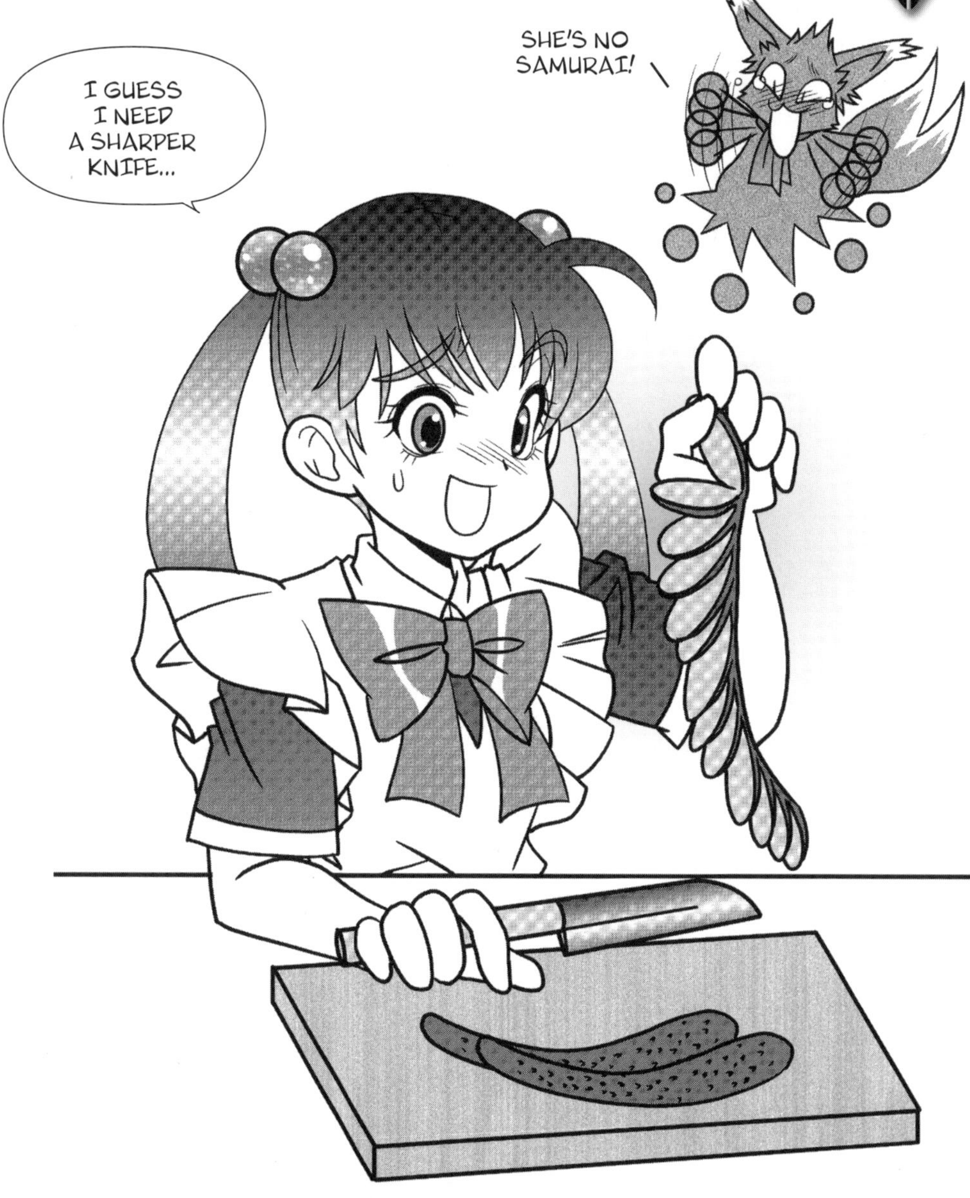
MANGA COOKBOOK
SHE'S NO SAMURAI!
I GUESS I NEED A SHARPER KNIFE...

Oshinko (pickled vegetables)

19 calories
(per serving)

- 2 large cabbage leaves
- ½ cucumber
- 1 teaspoon salt
- Juice of 1 lemon (optional)

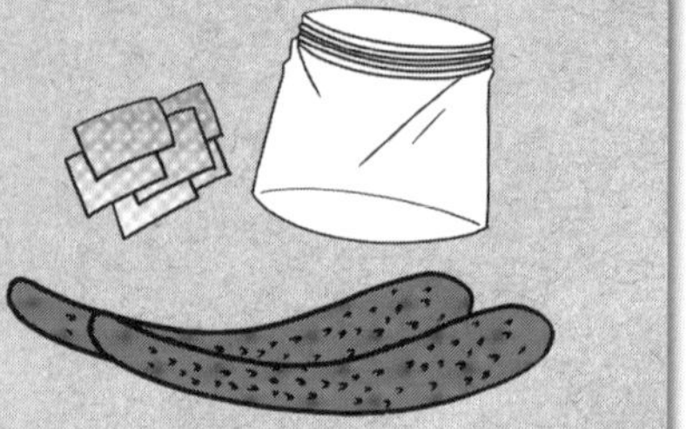

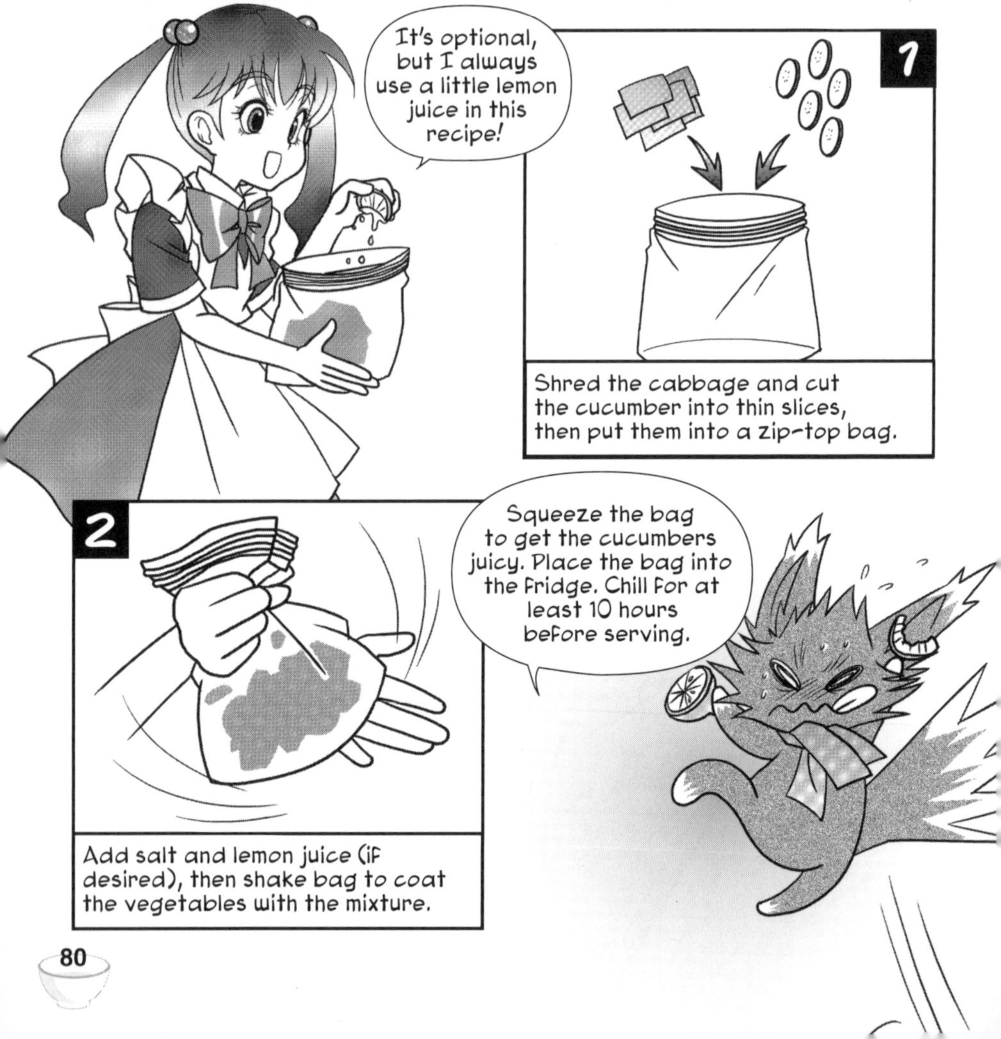

It's optional, but I always use a little lemon juice in this recipe!
1
Shred the cabbage and cut the cucumber into thin slices, then put them into a zip-top bag.
2
Add salt and lemon juice (if desired), then shake bag to coat the vegetables with the mixture.
Squeeze the bag to get the cucumbers juicy. Place the bag into the fridge. Chill for at least 10 hours before serving.

The Main Course

MANGA COOKBOOK

Miso Soup みそ汁

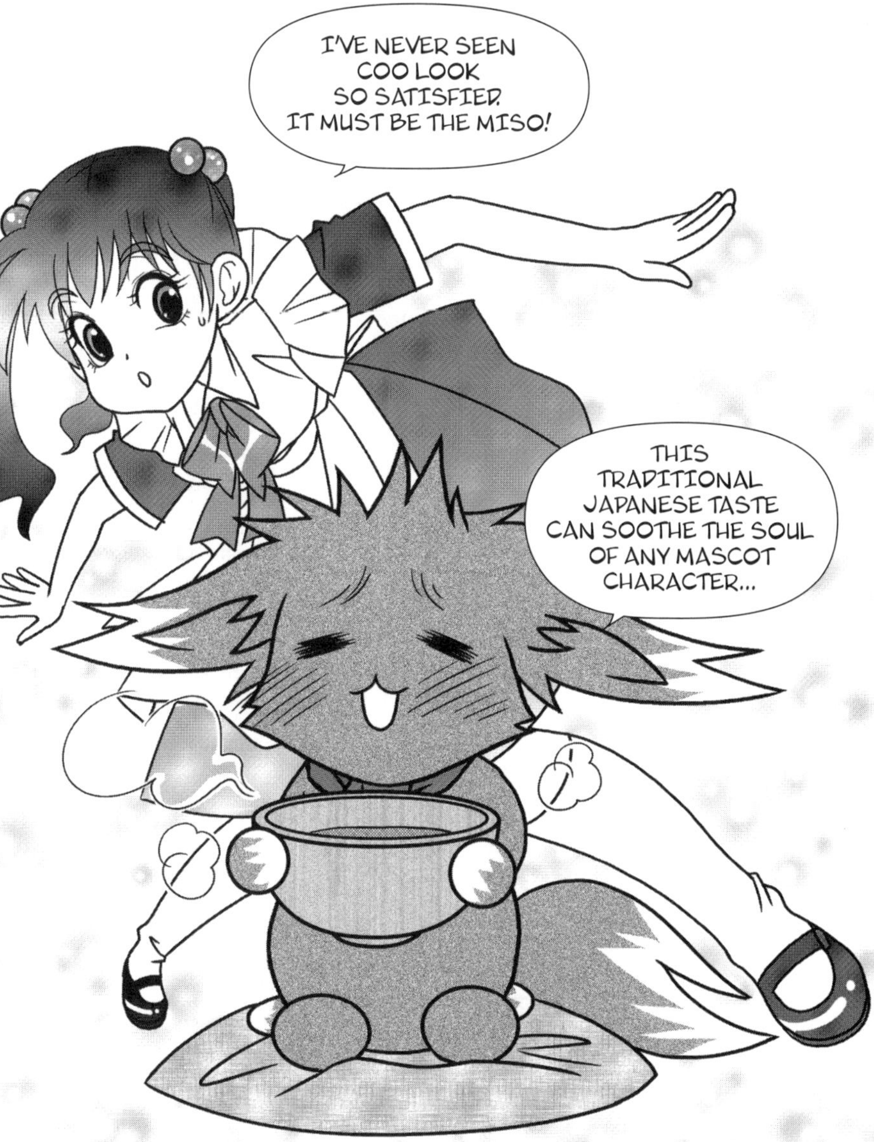
I'VE NEVER SEEN COO LOOK SO SATISFIED. IT MUST BE THE MISO!
THIS TRADITIONAL JAPANESE TASTE CAN SOOTHE THE SOUL OF ANY MASCOT CHARACTER...

Miso Soup (soybean soup)

52 calories
(per serving)

2 tablespoons miso paste (see page 19)

1¼ tablespoons dashi stock (see page 20)

⅓ block of tofu (see page 19)

1 green onion

だし　みそ

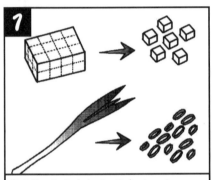

1

Cut the tofu into half-inch cubes, then cut the green onion into thin slices. (Don't eat the leafy part.)

2

Bring the dashi stock and 2 cups of water to a boil in a pot, then stir in the miso paste.

3

Add tofu to the soup just before serving. Add green onions to taste.

Cooking tofu requires a gentle touch. Don't stir too hard or it will break apart. Practice makes perfect!

The Main Course

MANGA COOKBOOK

Tamagoyaki 卵焼き

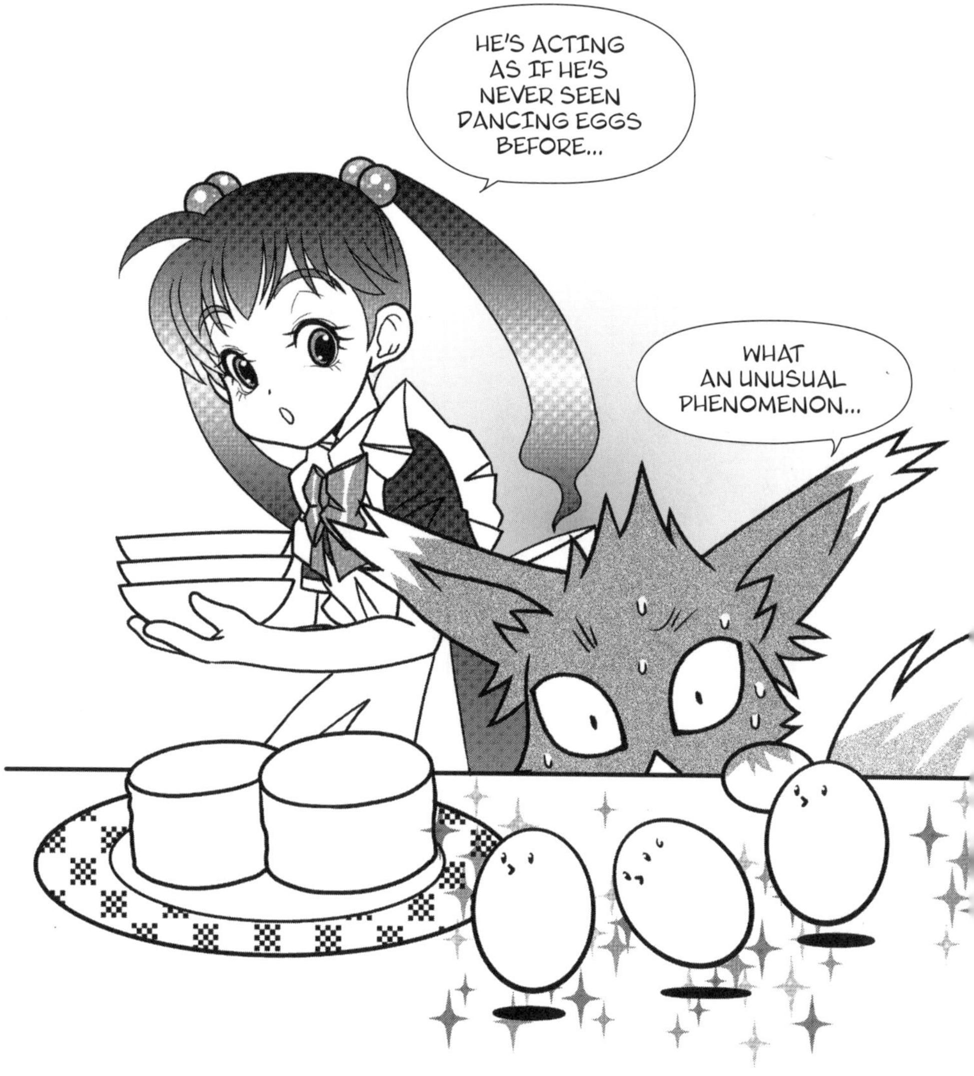
WHAT AN UNUSUAL PHENOMENON...
HE'S ACTING AS IF HE'S NEVER SEEN DANCING EGGS BEFORE...

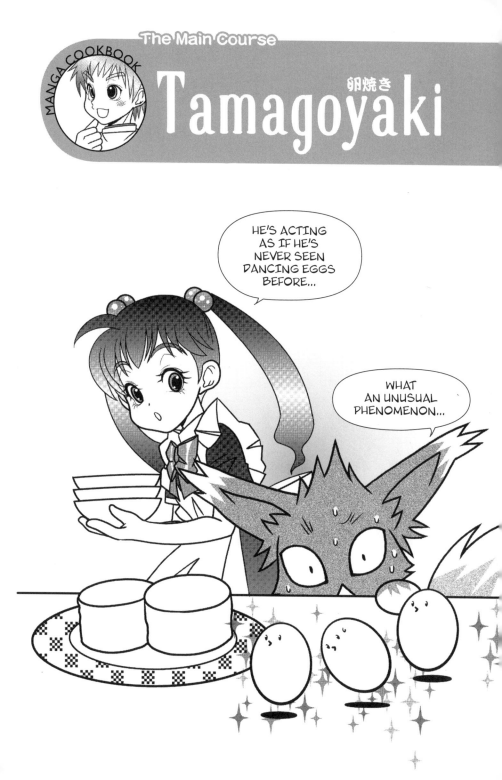

Tamagoyaki (Japanese-style omlette)

152 calories
(per serving)

3 eggs
2 teaspoons sugar
¼ teaspoon salt
2 teaspoons milk (optional)
1 tablespoon vegetable oil

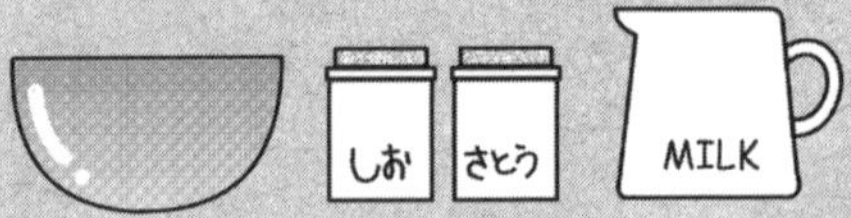
しお
さとう
MILK

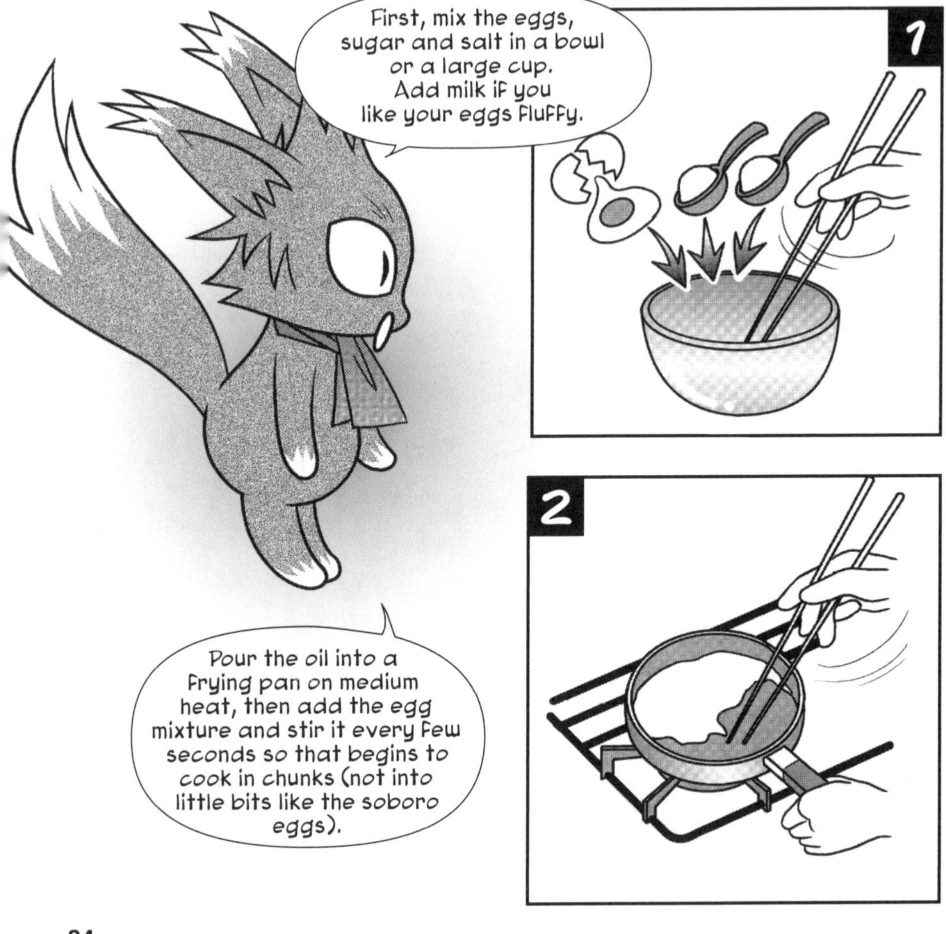
First, mix the eggs, sugar and salt in a bowl or a large cup. Add milk if you like your eggs fluffy.
1
2
Pour the oil into a frying pan on medium heat, then add the egg mixture and stir it every few seconds so that begins to cook in chunks (not into little bits like the soboro eggs).

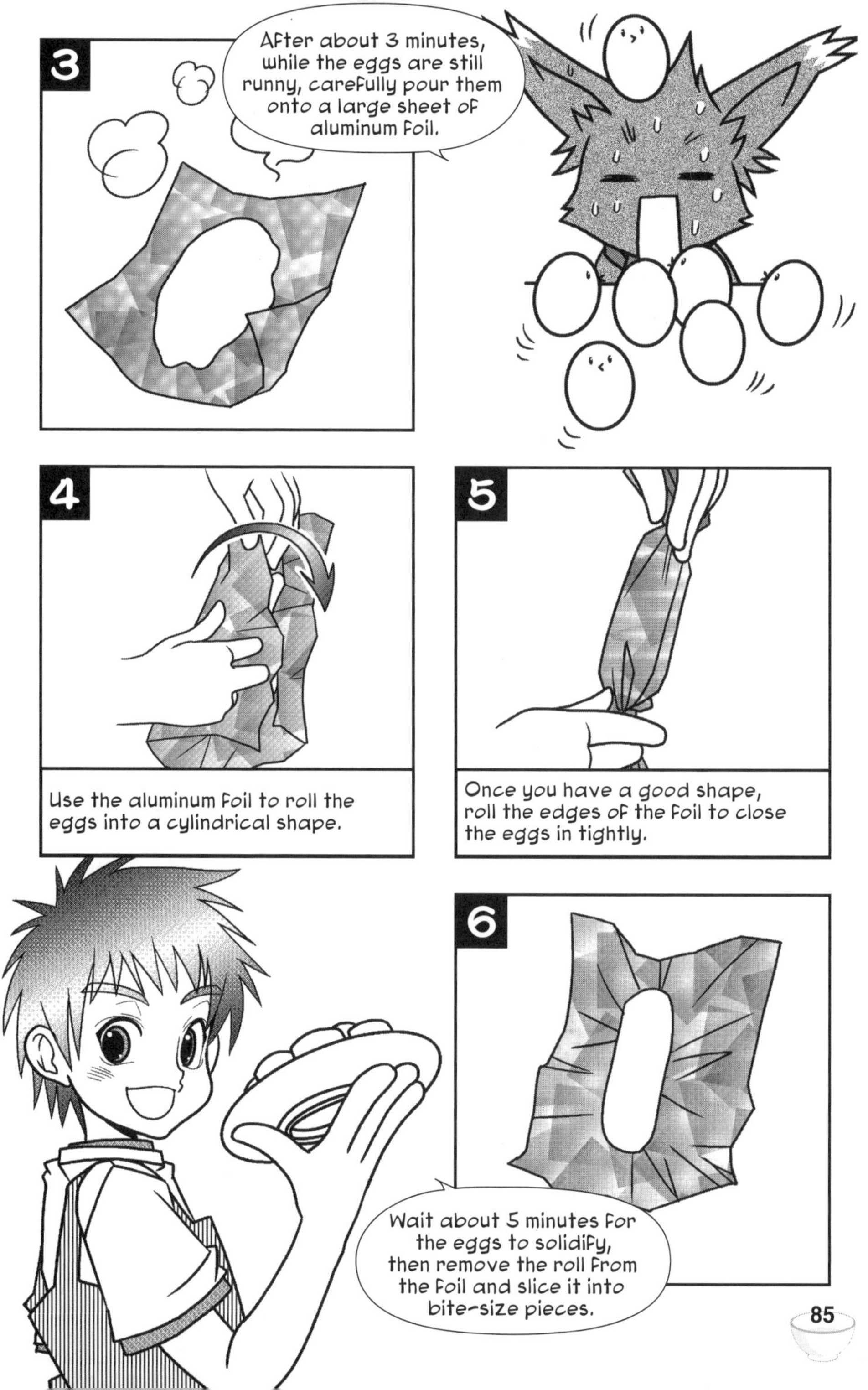
3
After about 3 minutes, while the eggs are still runny, carefully pour them onto a large sheet of aluminum foil.
4
Use the aluminum foil to roll the eggs into a cylindrical shape.
5
Once you have a good shape, roll the edges of the foil to close the eggs in tightly.
6
Wait about 5 minutes for the eggs to solidify, then remove the roll from the foil and slice it into bite-size pieces.

Miyuki's Notes on Eggs

The egg is a magical ingredient. Eggs are of course delicious by themselves — they can be served sunny side up or as omelets — and they are also a key ingredient in cakes, custards, flan, pancakes, cream puffs and tempura batter. You can use eggs in so many things that they're always on the table in one form or another.

When you eat a piece of tamagoyaki, it should be sweet and fluffy. We Japanese love tamagoyaki so much, we even have special frying pans just for making it!

At Japanese "oshogatsu" (New Year's celebrations), there is a special cuisine called "osechiryori." Eggs are mixed with fish to create an omelet called "datemaki," and the whites and yolk of the eggs are separated to make a cake called "kinshitamago." The yellows and whites of the eggs create a pretty color scheme that is regularly on display on the holiday dinner table.

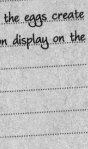

My Notes

My Notes

The Main Course

Sushi Rice すめし

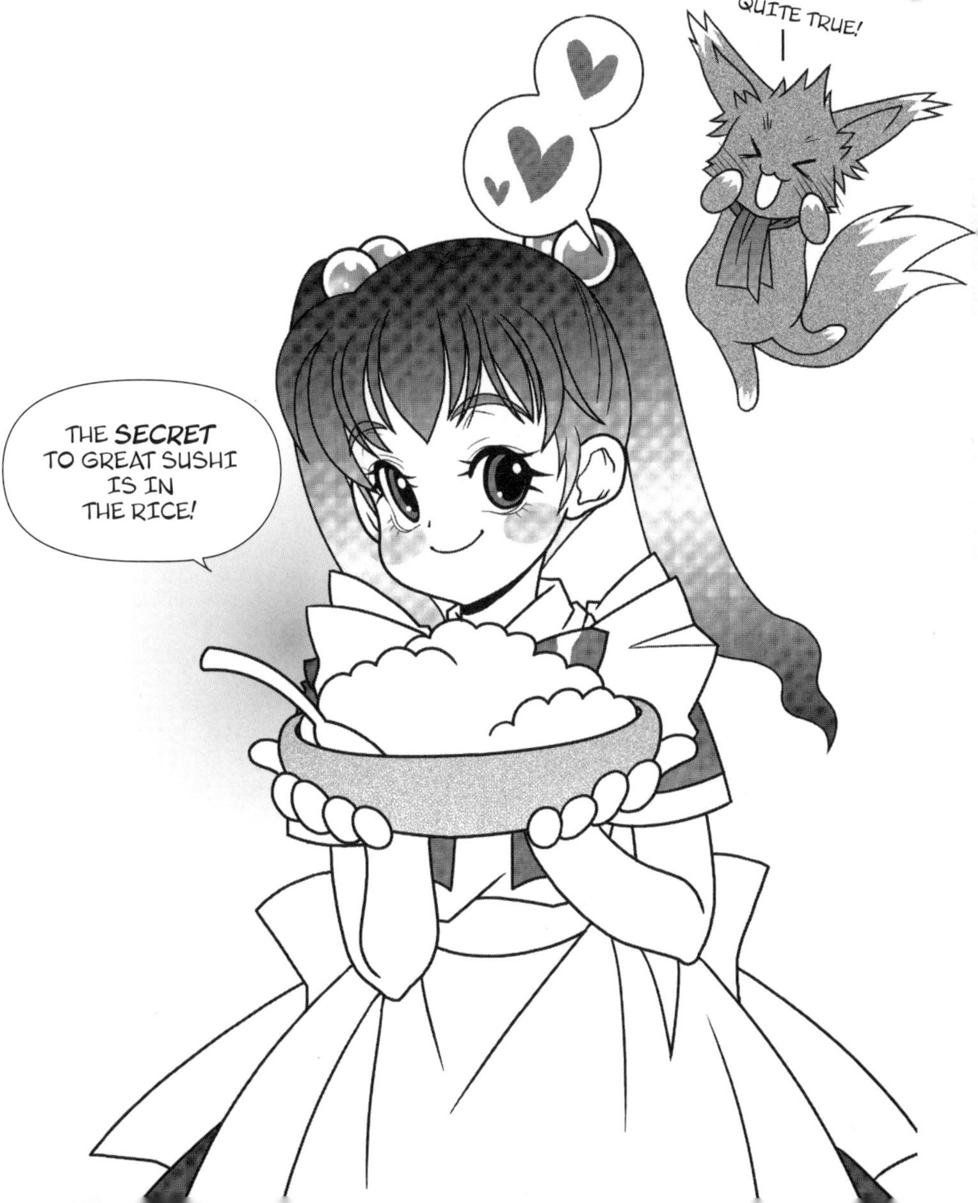

THE SECRET TO GREAT SUSHI IS IN THE RICE!
QUITE TRUE!

Sushi Rice

240 calories
(per serving)

4 cups cooked steamed rice
1 tablespoon vinegar
1 tablespoon sugar
1 teaspoon salt

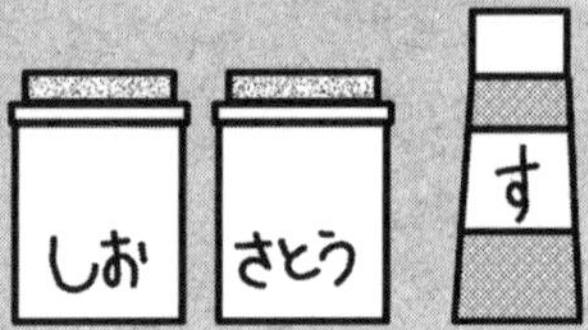

しお
さとう
す

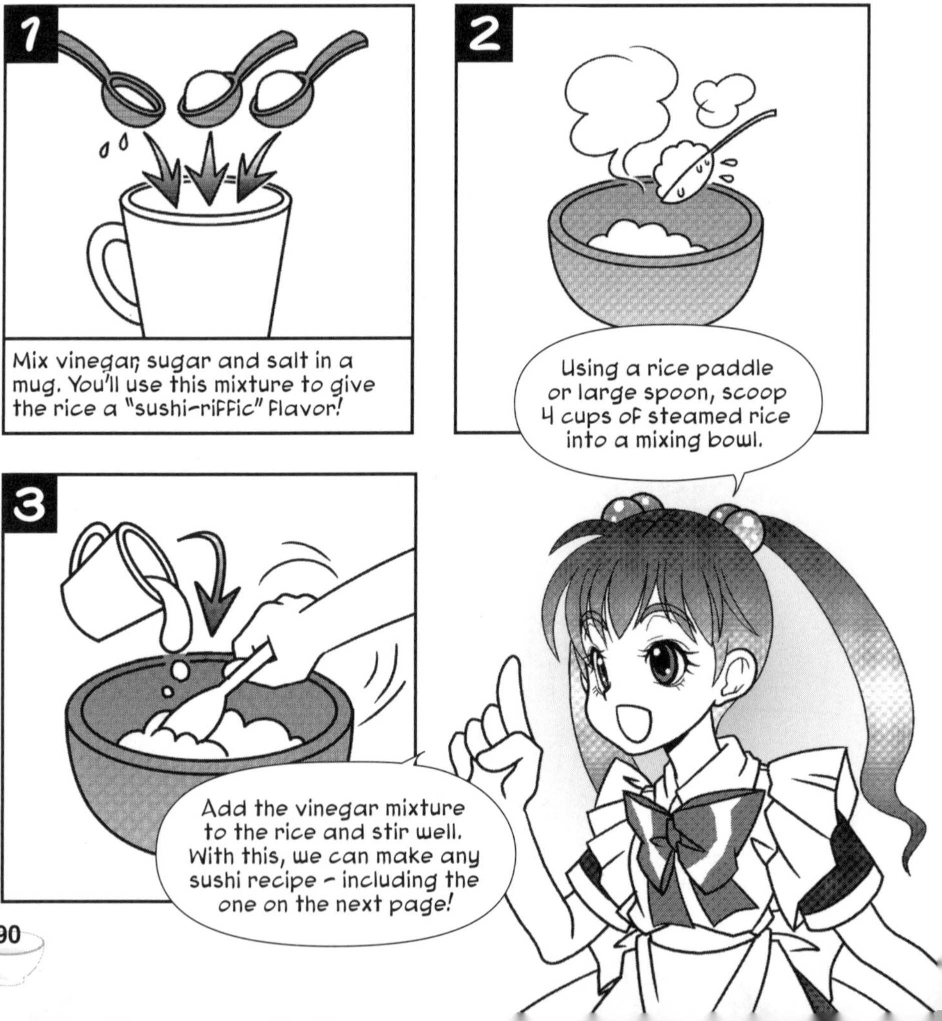

1
Mix vinegar, sugar and salt in a mug. You'll use this mixture to give the rice a "sushi-riffic" flavor!
2
Using a rice paddle or large spoon, scoop 4 cups of steamed rice into a mixing bowl.
3
Add the vinegar mixture to the rice and stir well. With this, we can make any sushi recipe – including the one on the next page!

MANGA COOKBOOK

The Main Course

California Roll

カリフォルニア・ロール

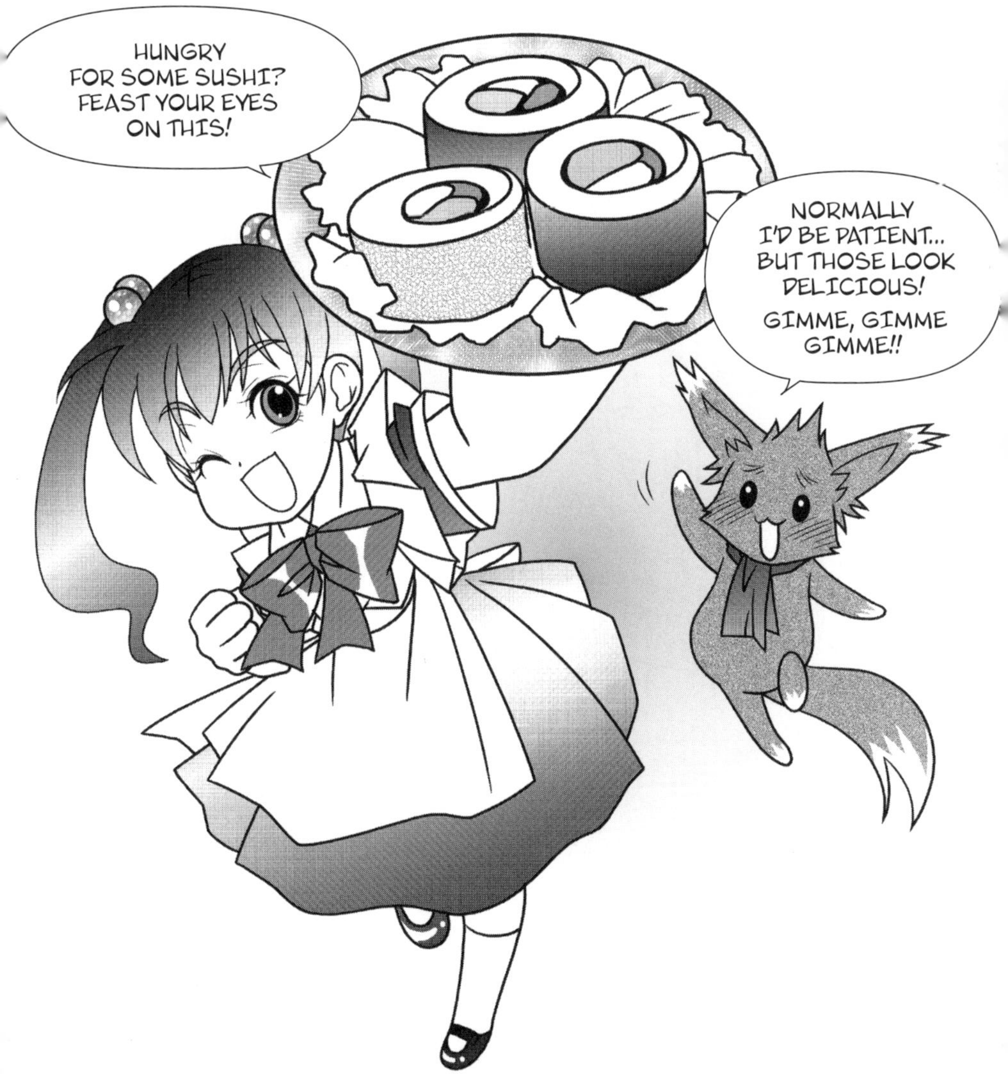
HUNGRY FOR SOME SUSHI? FEAST YOUR EYES ON THIS!
NORMALLY I'D BE PATIENT... BUT THOSE LOOK DELICIOUS! GIMME, GIMME GIMME!!

California Roll

57 calories
(per roll)

2 sheets of nori (see page 19)
1 avocado
2 strips of kamaboko (see page 20)
1 cup sushi rice
1 cucumber

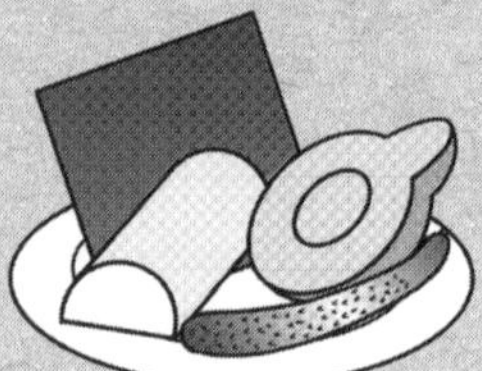

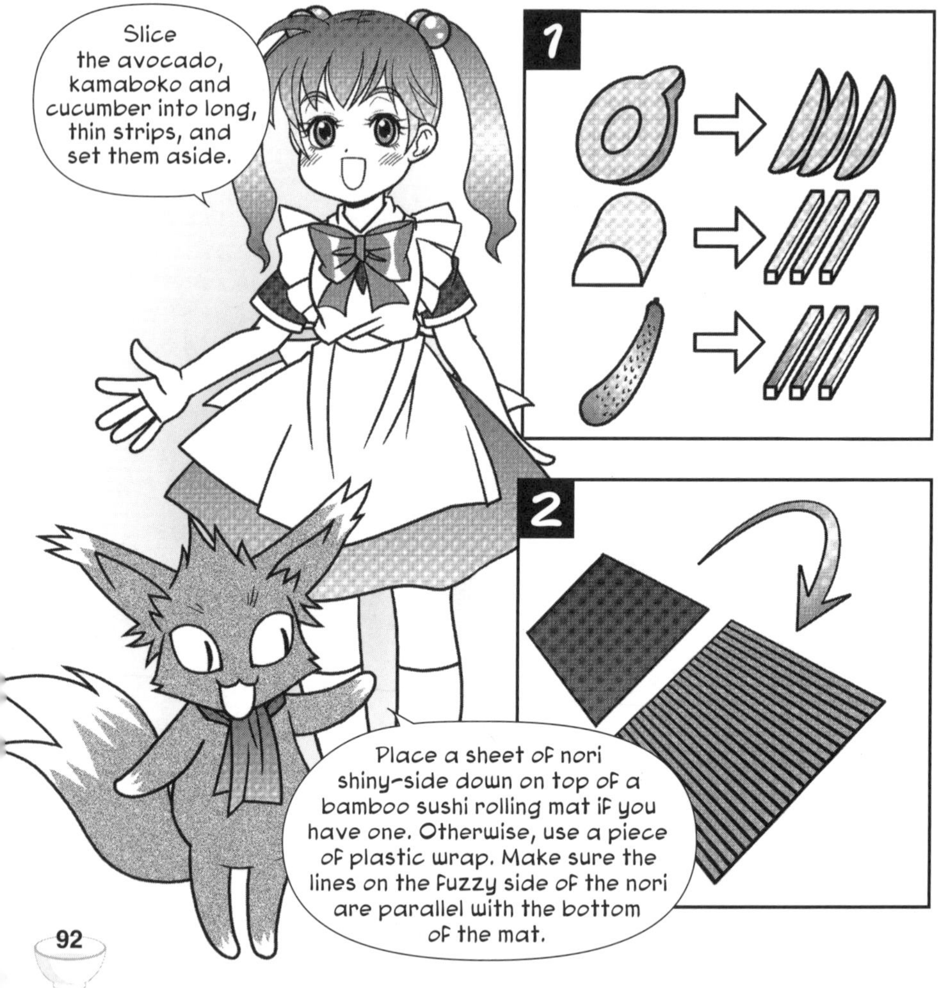

Slice the avocado, kamaboko and cucumber into long, thin strips, and set them aside.
1
2
Place a sheet of nori shiny-side down on top of a bamboo sushi rolling mat if you have one. Otherwise, use a piece of plastic wrap. Make sure the lines on the fuzzy side of the nori are parallel with the bottom of the mat.

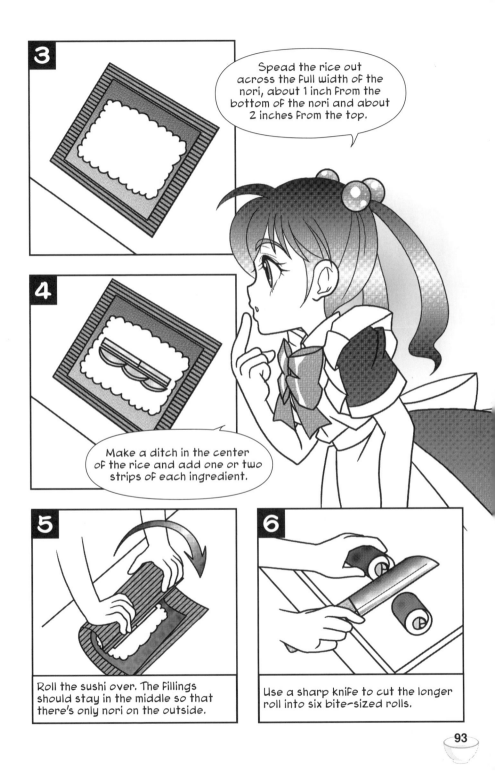

3

Spead the rice out across the Full width of the nori, about 1 inch From the bottom of the nori and about 2 inches From the top.

4

Make a ditch in the center of the rice and add one or two strips of each ingredient.

5

Roll the sushi over. The fillings should stay in the middle so that there's only nori on the outside.

6

Use a sharp knife to cut the longer roll into six bite-sized rolls.

Miyuki's Notes on Sushi

Once considered exotic, sushi today is enjoyed around the world. The sushi we eat in Japan was originally created to preserve raw fish for long stretches of time, as the vinegar contains preservatives that keep food from going bad.

Because oil is not used in sushi, it is low in calories, but since it is mainly flavored with salt, you should be careful not to eat too much so your body does not take in too much sodium.

"Norimaki" (seaweed-roll sushi) is often served at celebrations or when congratulations are in order. It is also said that sushi should be eaten when everything is going well or when something good has just happened.

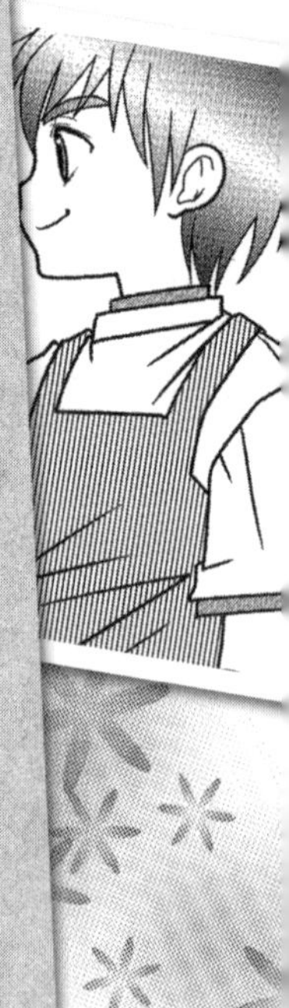

Nowadays in Japan, you can buy sushi just about any time, anywhere.

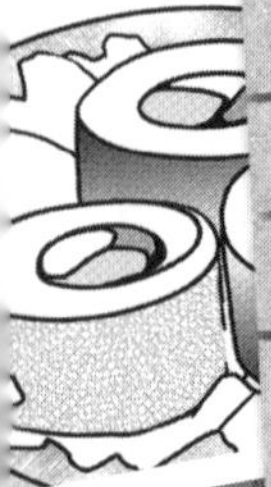

If you want to make an inside-out roll (rice on the outside) sprinkle some sesame seeds on the rice you just layed out, flip the whole thing over, place the filling on the shiny side of the nori, and then roll it.

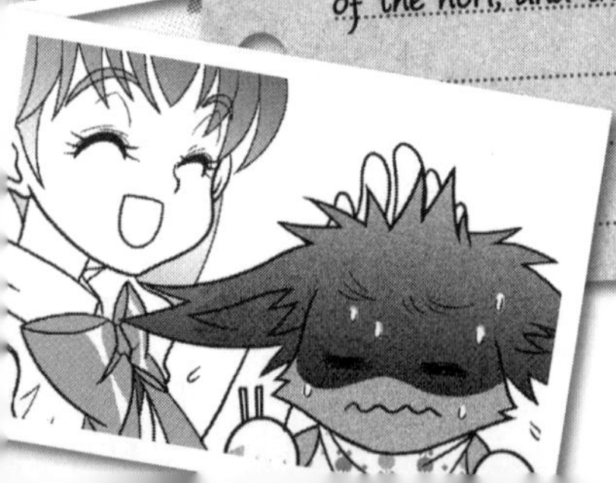

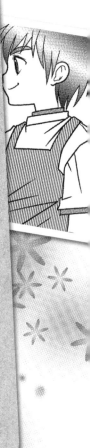

My Notes

My Notes

The Main Course

MANGA COOKBOOK

Tonkatsu トンカツ

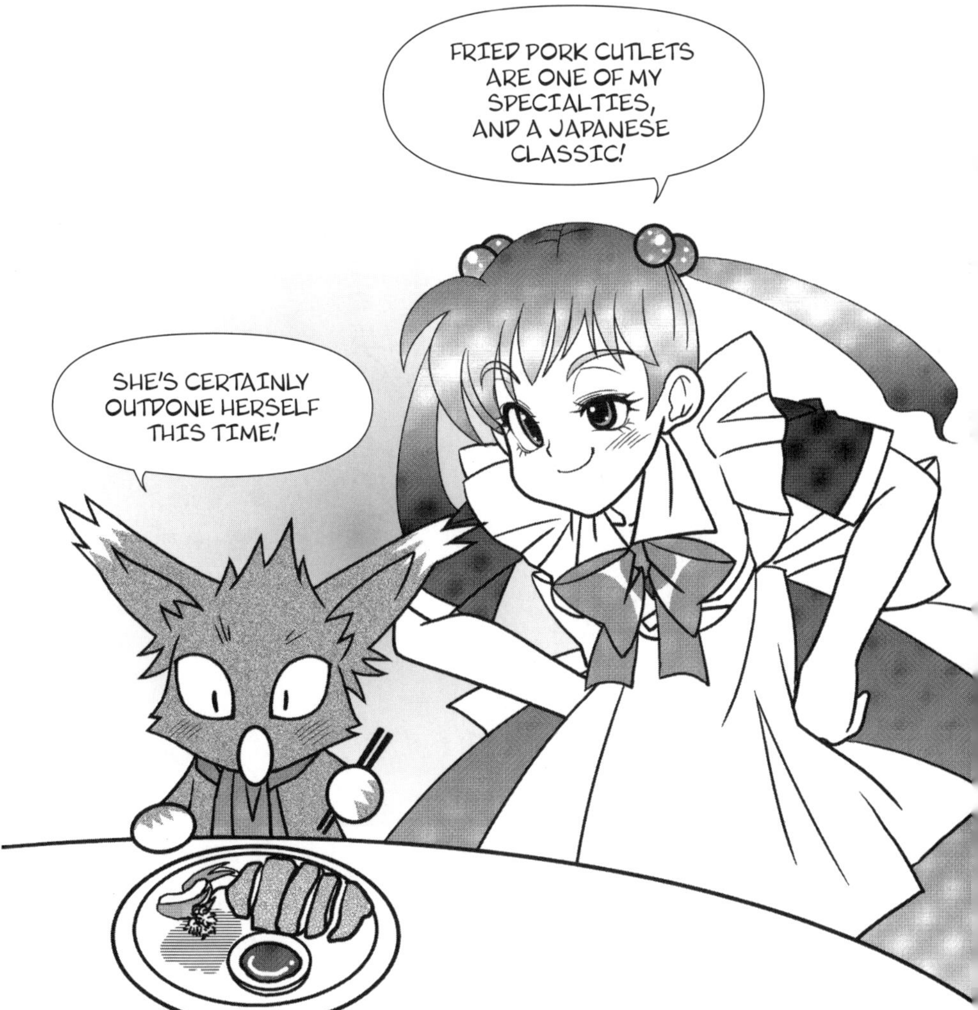
FRIED PORK CUTLETS ARE ONE OF MY SPECIALTIES, AND A JAPANESE CLASSIC!
SHE'S CERTAINLY OUTDONE HERSELF THIS TIME!

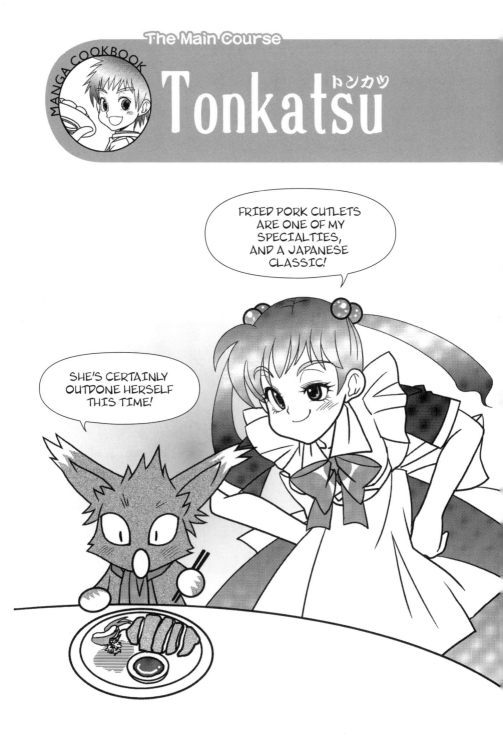

Tonkatsu (fried pork cutlet)

858 calories
(per serving)

2 pork tenderloin slices (8–10 ounces each)

1 egg mixed with 2 tablespoons water

Enough wheat flour to coat the pork

Enough panko (see page 20) to coat the pork

½ cup vegetable oil

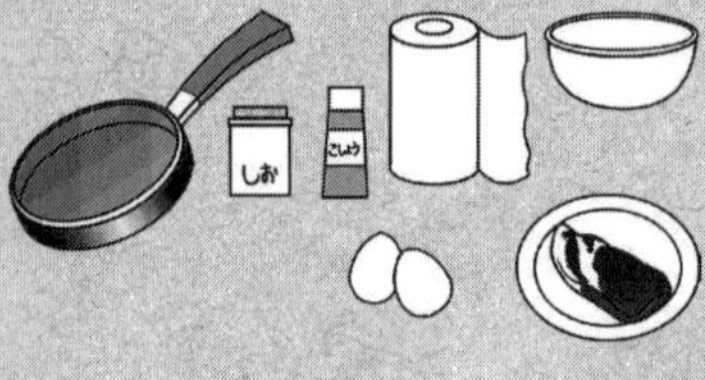

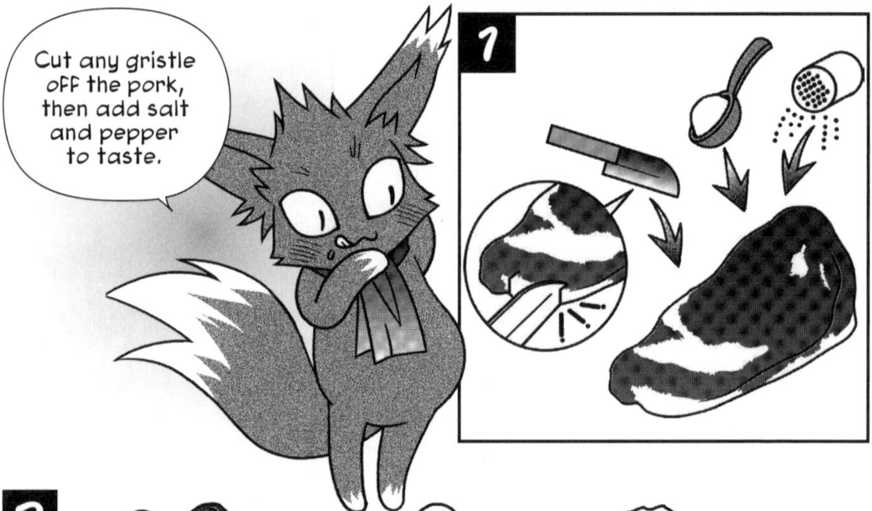

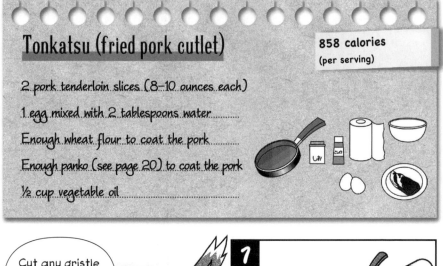

Cut any gristle off the pork, then add salt and pepper to taste.
1

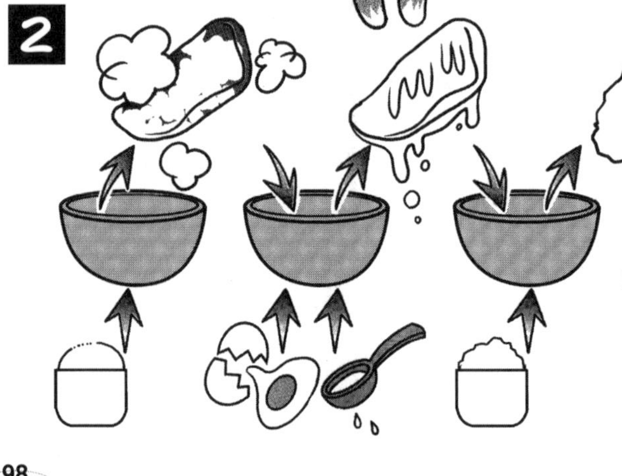

2

Put the wheat flour into one bowl, the egg and water into a second bowl, and the breadcrumbs into a third bowl. One by one, move each piece of pork from bowl to bowl, coating them first with the flour, then with the egg, and finally the breadcrumbs.

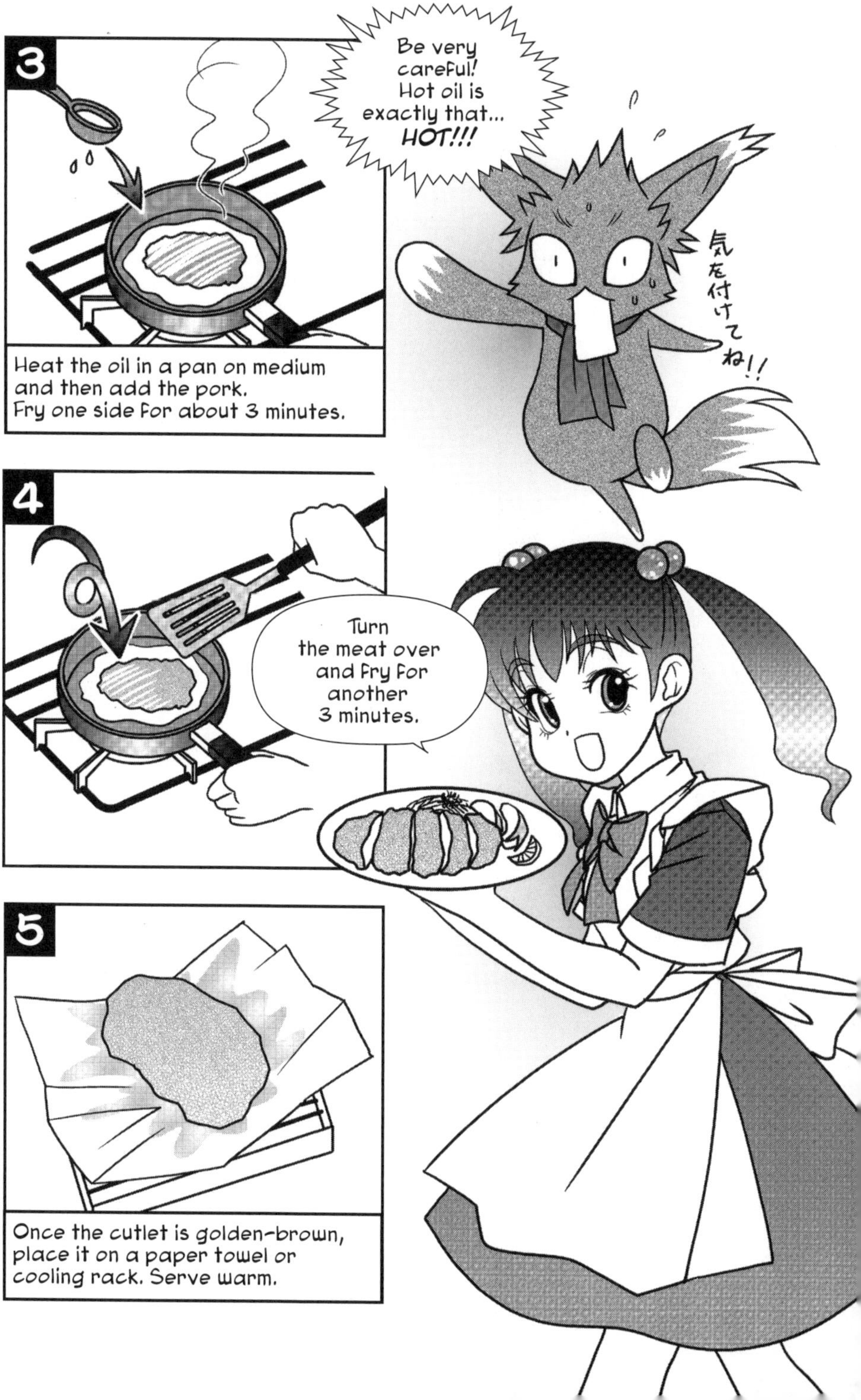
3
Heat the oil in a pan on medium and then add the pork. Fry one side for about 3 minutes.
Be very careful! Hot oil is exactly that... HOT!!!
気を付けてね!!
4
Turn the meat over and fry for another 3 minutes.
5
Once the cutlet is golden-brown, place it on a paper towel or cooling rack. Serve warm.

Miyuki's Notes on Tonkatsu

Up until about 150 years ago, Japan was completely cut off from the rest of the world by law. But that changed with the Meiji Restoration, and Japan began to integrate foreign cultures as it embarked on an ambitious period of modernization.

From that time on, there were also changes in the Japanese diet. For example, meat was not commonly eaten in Japan until then, when they began to import it from Australia and Europe. The emperor even encouraged his subjects to eat meat – in the hopes of developing Western physiques.

Tonkatsu was invented at that time by pan-frying beef, pork or chicken covered in panko, or Japanese breadcrumbs.

Today in Japan, tonkatsu is often on the dinner table, and is always available in stores as either a full dish or part of a bento.

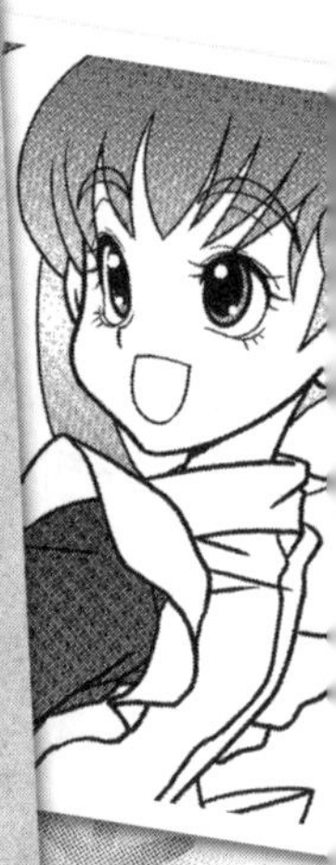

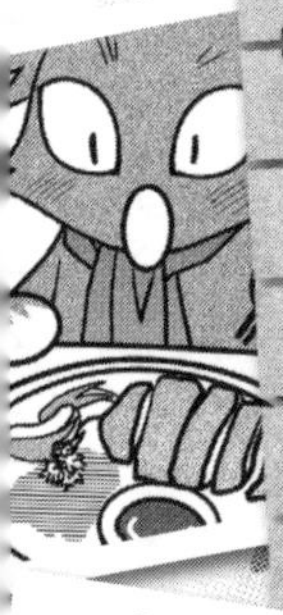

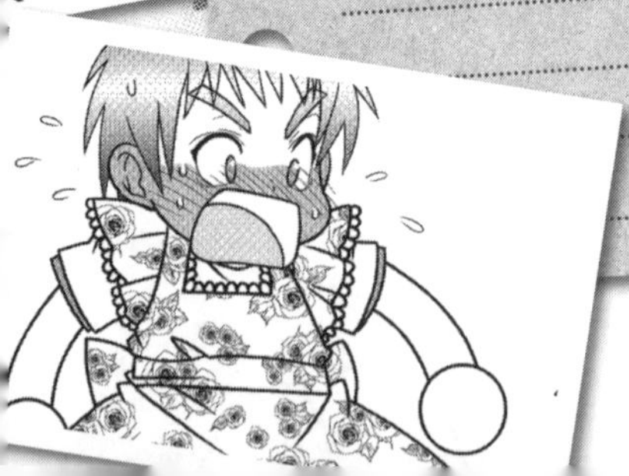

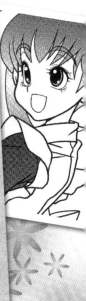

My Notes

My Notes

The Main Course

Karaage 唐揚げ

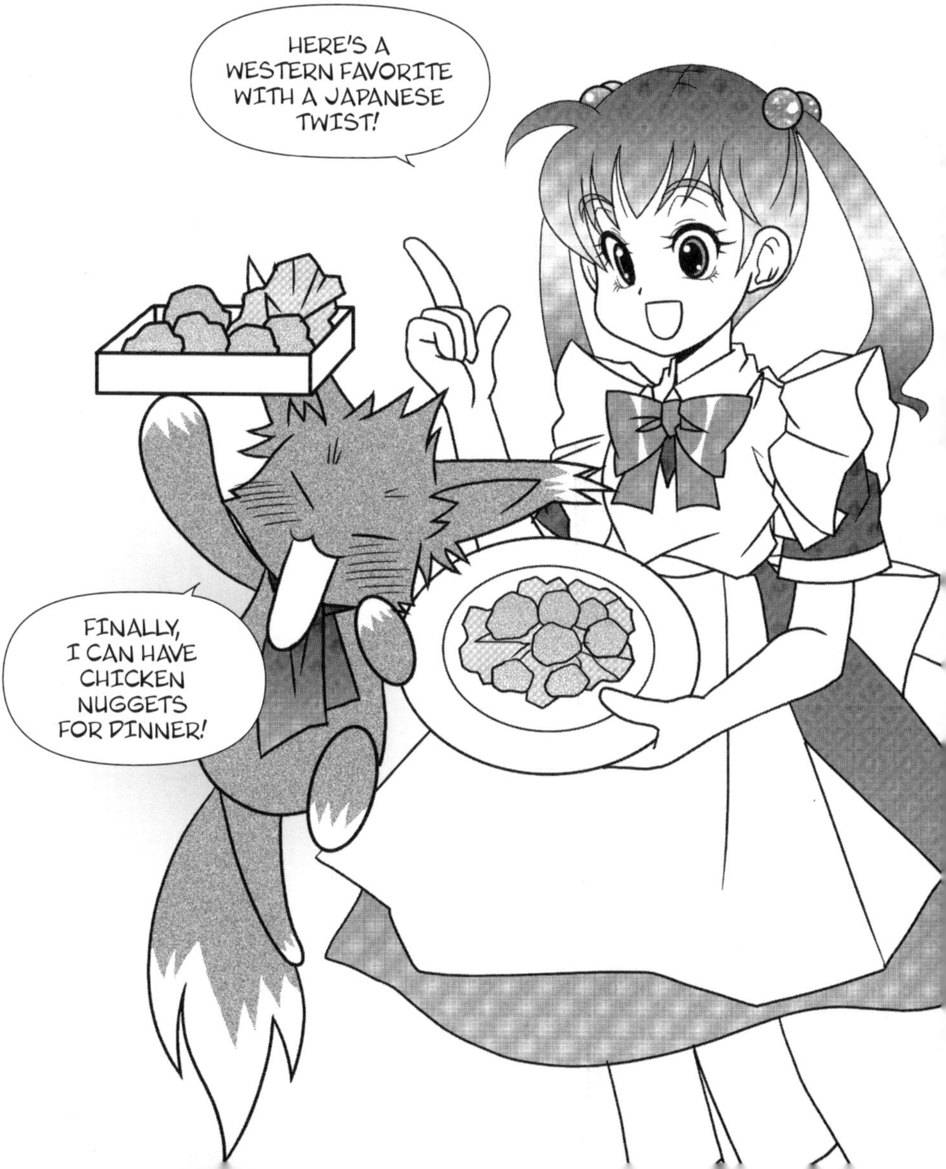
HERE'S A WESTERN FAVORITE WITH A JAPANESE TWIST!
FINALLY, I CAN HAVE CHICKEN NUGGETS FOR DINNER!

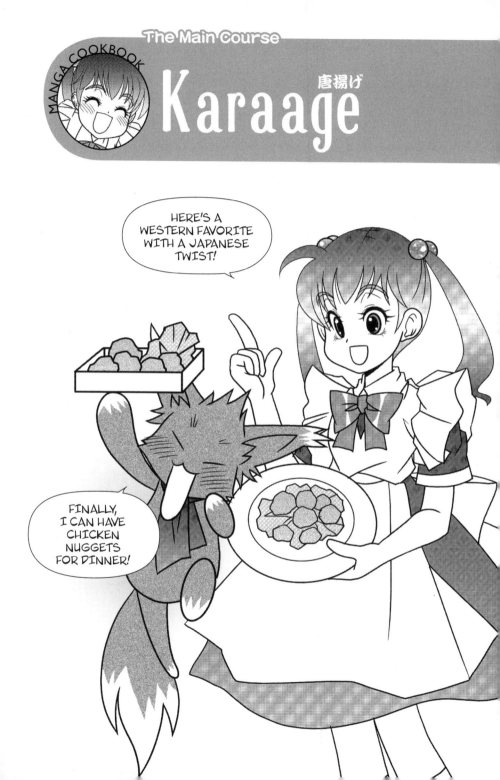

Karaage (Japanese-style chicken nuggets)

582 calories
(per serving)

1 pound chicken thighs (boneless)

Enough cornstarch to coat the chicken

1 lemon

Enough vegetable oil to cover the chicken

For the Marinade:

½ cup soy sauce

1 teaspoon grated ginger

2 cloves chopped garlic

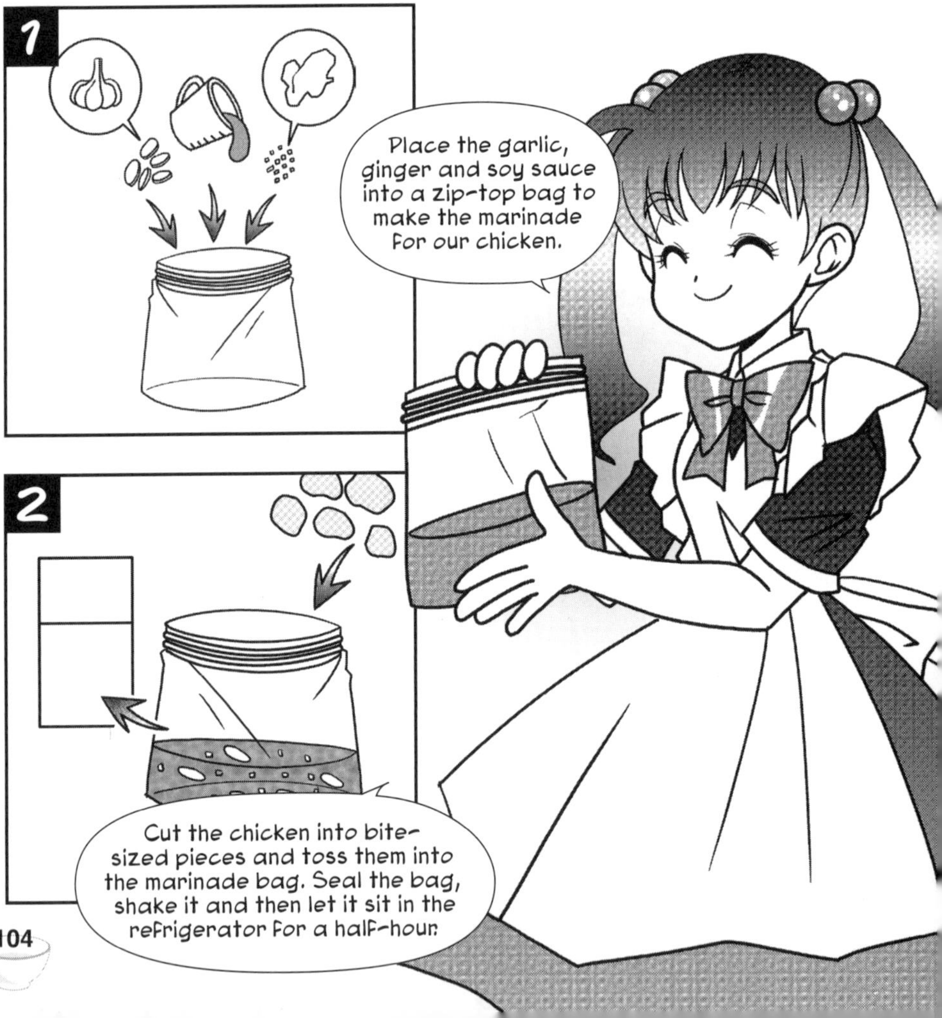
1
Place the garlic, ginger and soy sauce into a zip-top bag to make the marinade for our chicken.
2
Cut the chicken into bite-sized pieces and toss them into the marinade bag. Seal the bag, shake it and then let it sit in the refrigerator for a half-hour.

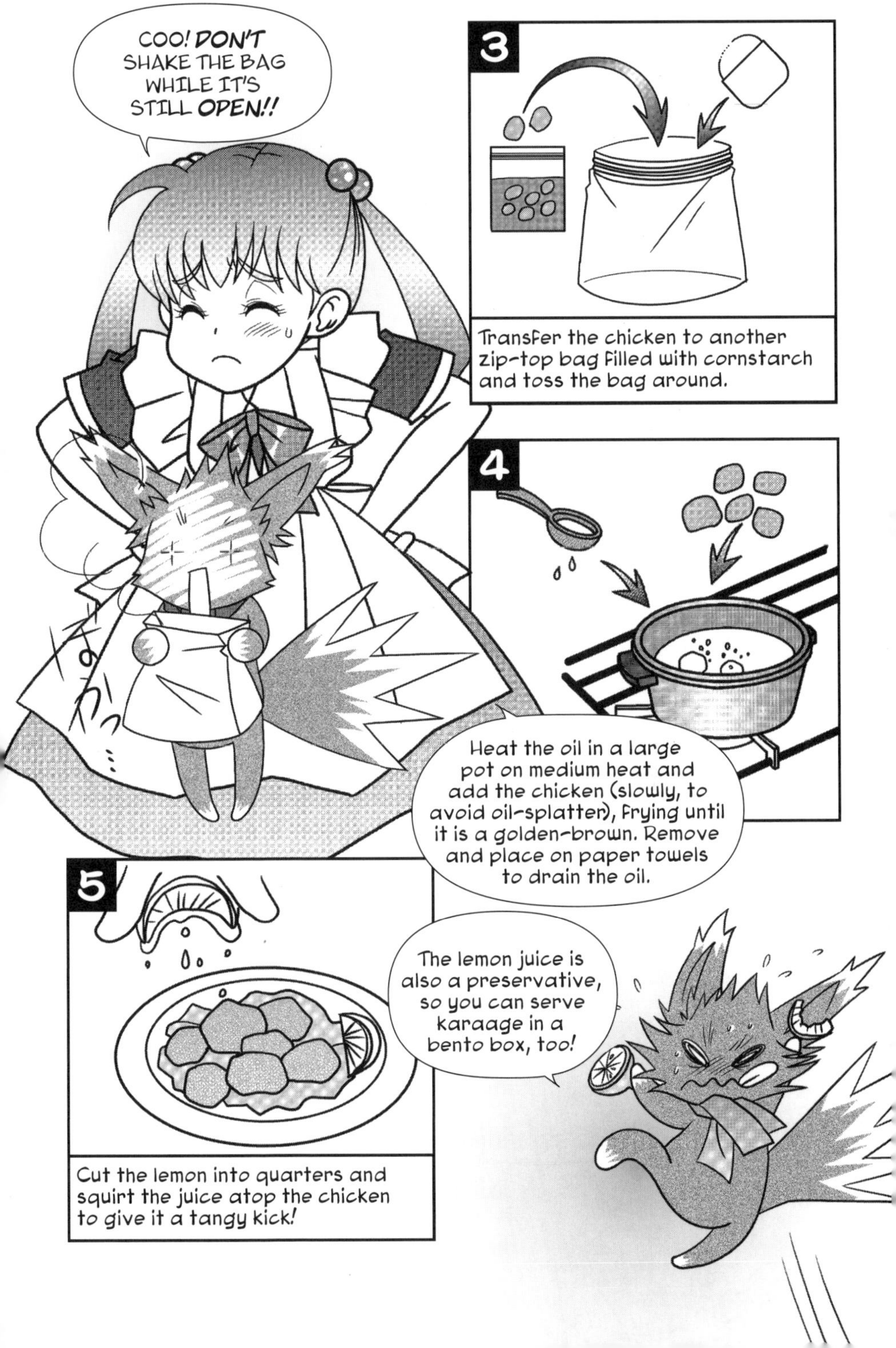
3
Transfer the chicken to another zip-top bag filled with cornstarch and toss the bag around.
COO! DON'T SHAKE THE BAG WHILE IT'S STILL OPEN!!
4
Heat the oil in a large pot on medium heat and add the chicken (slowly, to avoid oil-splatter), frying until it is a golden-brown. Remove and place on paper towels to drain the oil.
5
Cut the lemon into quarters and squirt the juice atop the chicken to give it a tangy kick!
The lemon juice is also a preservative, so you can serve karaage in a bento box, too!

Miyuki's Notes on Karaage

Karaage is believed to have its origins in Chinese cuisine. Soy sauce is used as flavoring, while garlic and ginger are added as aromatics.

Because karaage is crispy on the outside, the chicken remains juicy even when it cools down. So, just as you might pack cold fried chicken for a picnic lunch, we Japanese often fill our bento boxes with karaage.

Just about everyone in Japan loves the taste and texture of this east-west fusion food. No outdoor event is complete without it! When I was a young child, my mom always brought karaage to my "undokai," or school sports festivals, to share with the whole family. Nowadays, whenever Hiroshi and I go on a picnic, he always calls the night before to say, "Don't forget the karaage!"

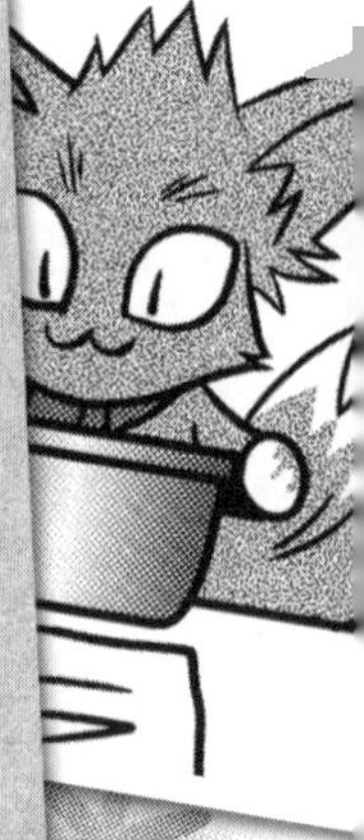

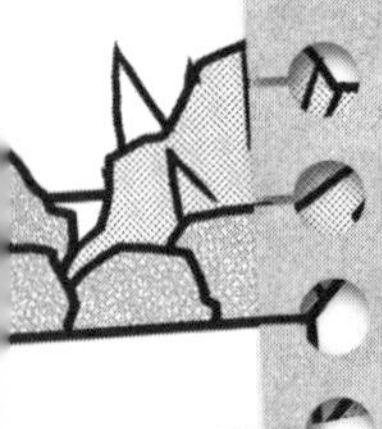

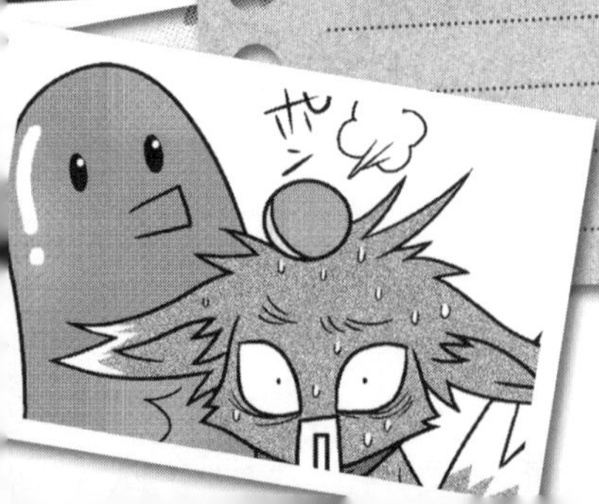

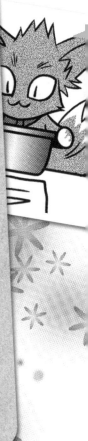

My Notes

My Notes

MANGA COOKBOOK

Teriyaki Sauce 照焼きソース

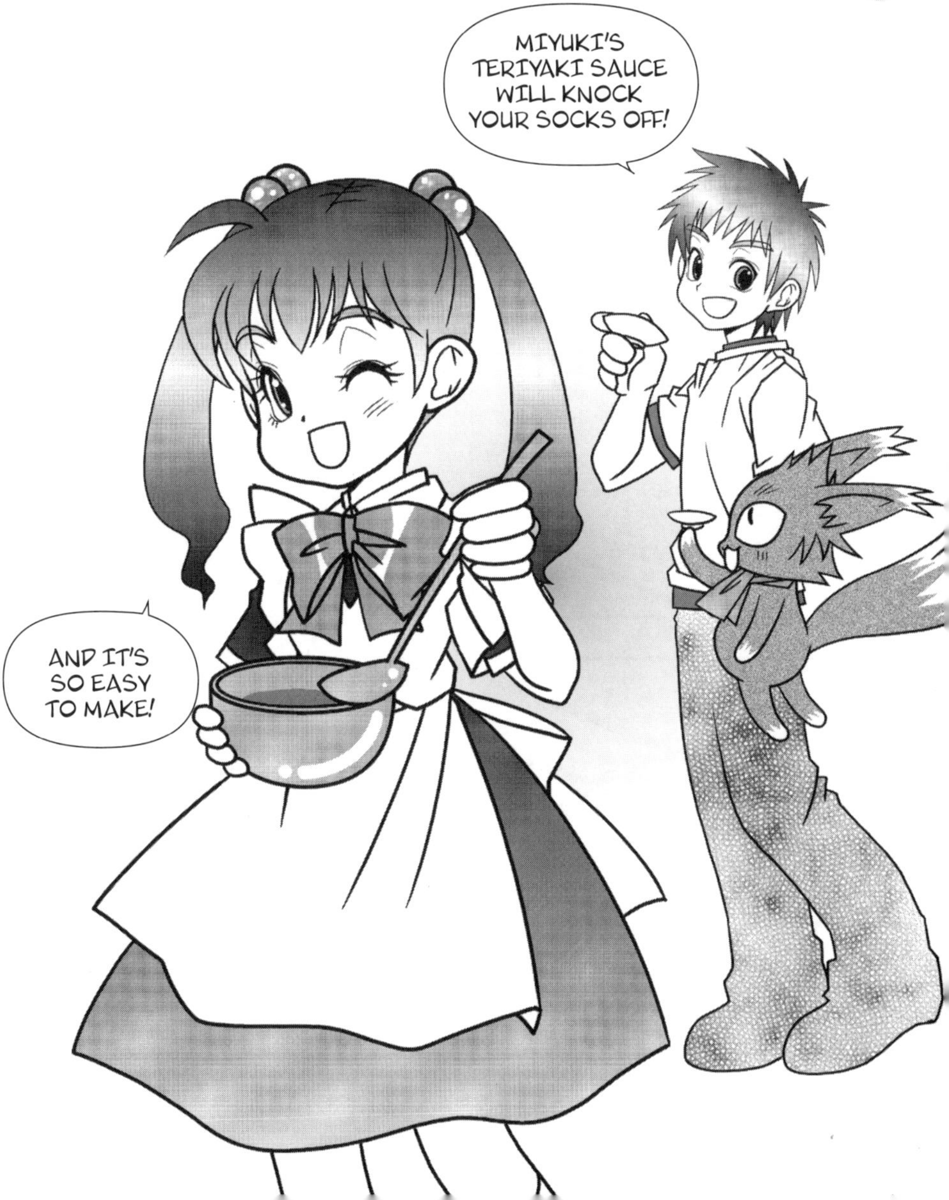
MIYUKI'S TERIYAKI SAUCE WILL KNOCK YOUR SOCKS OFF!
AND IT'S SO EASY TO MAKE!

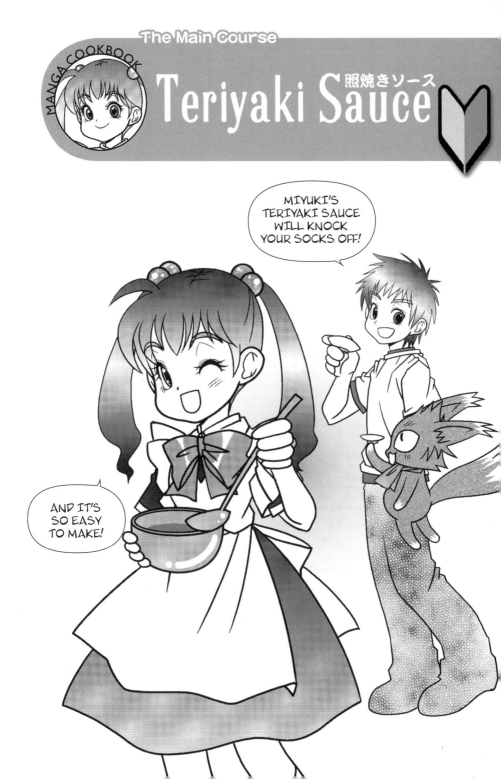

Teriyaki Sauce

21 calories
(per serving)

1 cup soy sauce

1 cup cooking sake

1 cup mirin (see page 19)

1 cup sugar

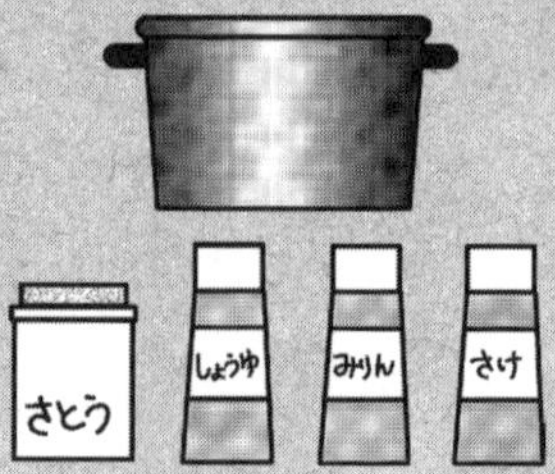
さとう
しょうゆ
みりん
さけ

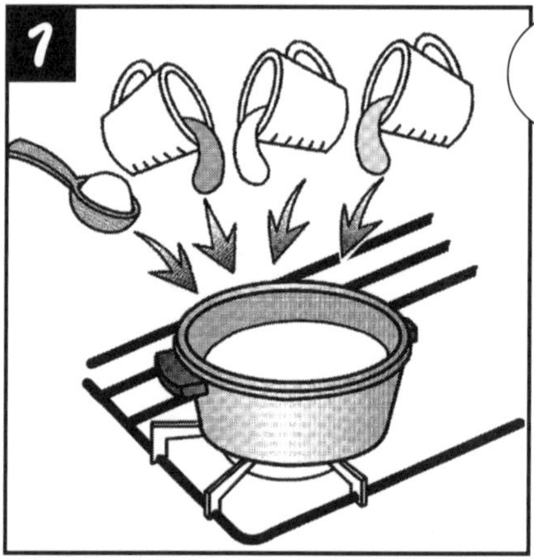
1

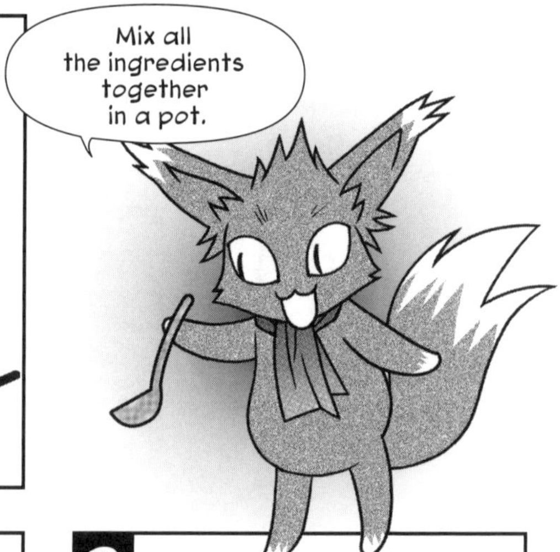
Mix all the ingredients together in a pot.

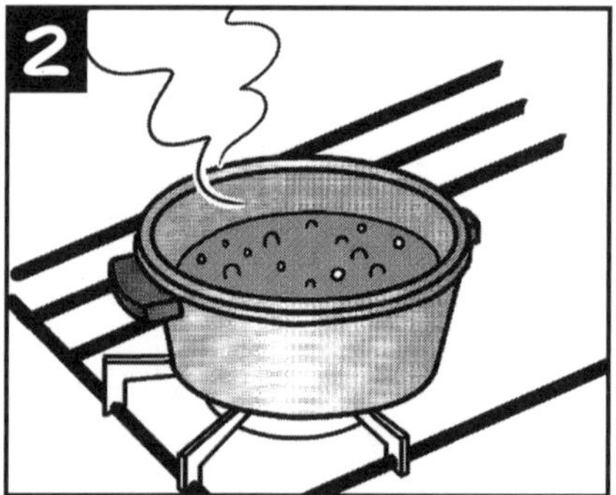
2

Bring the sauce to a slow boil on medium heat, allowing the sugar to dissolve.

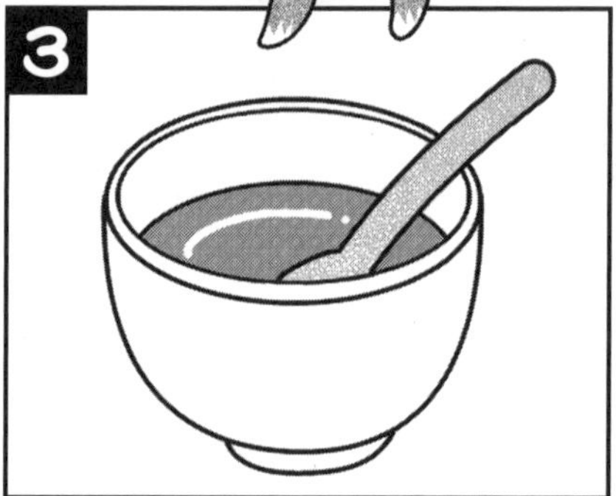
3

Remove from heat about 7 minutes later, when the sauce begins to thicken. Try it with the next recipe!

The Main Course

MANGA COOKBOOK

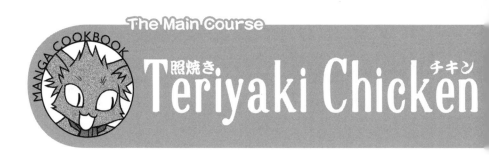

照焼き Teriyaki Chicken チキン

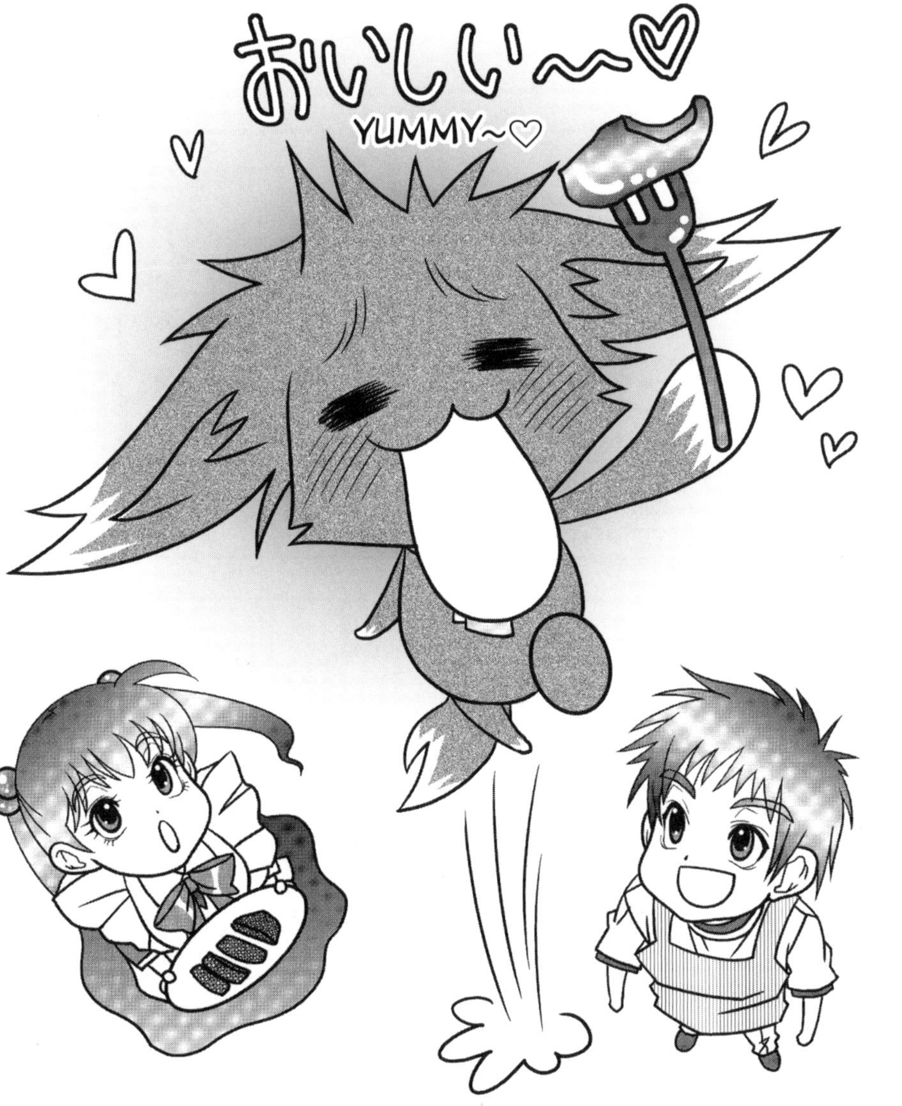
おいしい～♡
YUMMY～♡

Teriyaki Chicken

329 calories
(per serving)

1 pound chicken thighs (boneless)...................

½ cup teriyaki sauce (see page 109)..........

1 tablespoon sugar...................

1 teaspoon vegetable oil...................

Add oil to a frying pan over medium heat. Place chicken skin-side down and cook for about 3 minutes.

Turn the chicken over, cover the pan with a lid and cook for 2 more minutes.

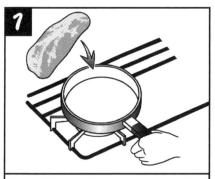
Remove the lid and add the teriyaki sauce and sugar.

When the sauce starts to bubble, reduce the heat to low and cook 3 more minutes. Slice and serve!

The Main Course

MANGA COOKBOOK

Yakitori 焼き鳥

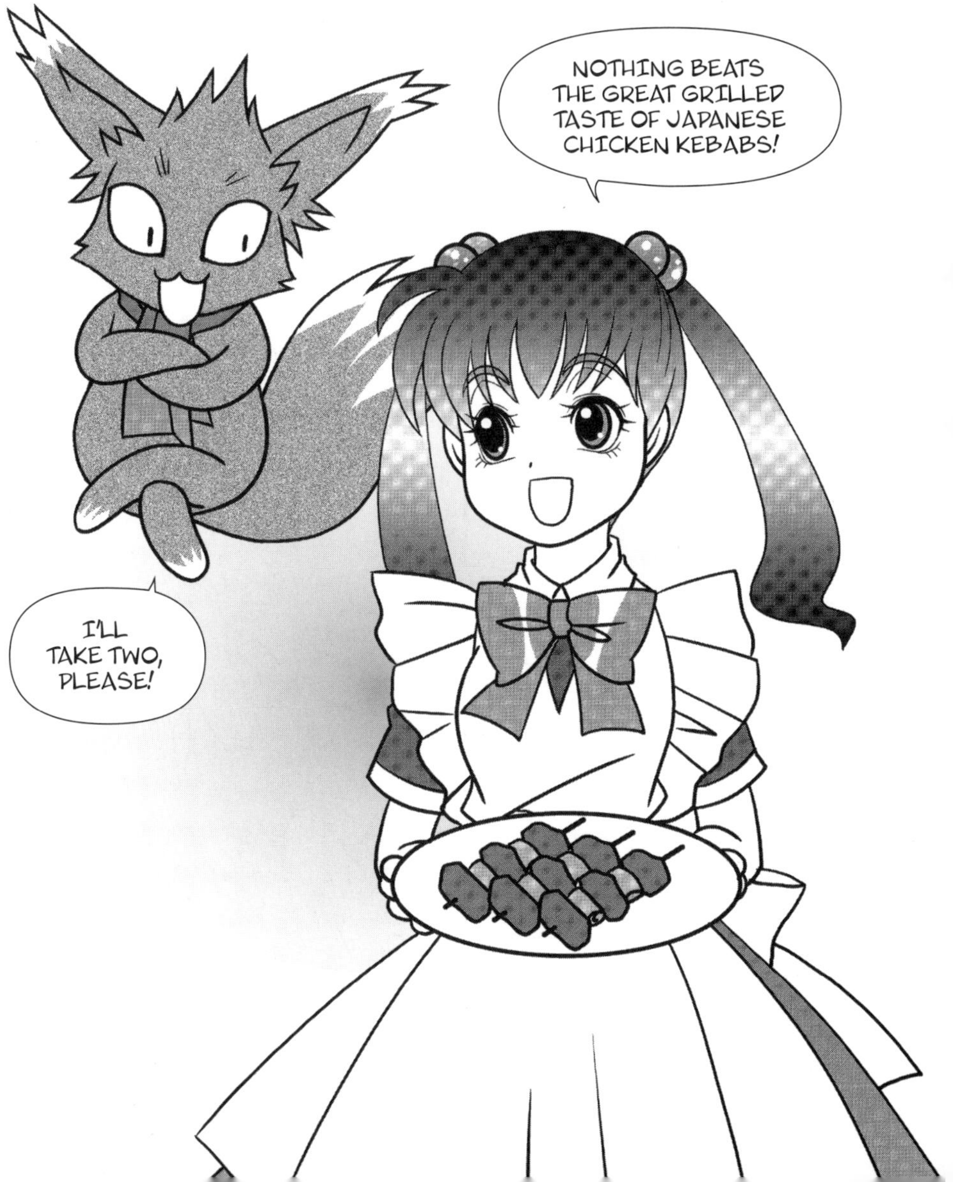
NOTHING BEATS THE GREAT GRILLED TASTE OF JAPANESE CHICKEN KEBABS!
I'LL TAKE TWO, PLEASE!

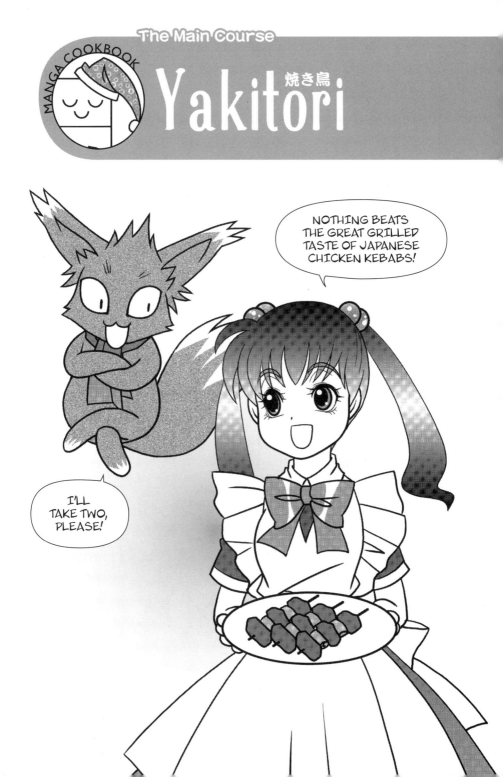

Yakitori (chicken kebabs)

329 calories
(per serving)

- 1½ pounds chicken thighs (boneless)
- 2 leeks
- 1⅓ pounds ground chicken
- ⅓ cup sesame seeds
- ⅓ cup cornstarch
- 2 tablespoons miso
- 2 eggs

For the Sauce:

- 1½ tablespoons sugar
- 3 tablespoons teriyaki sauce (page 109)

Negima

1

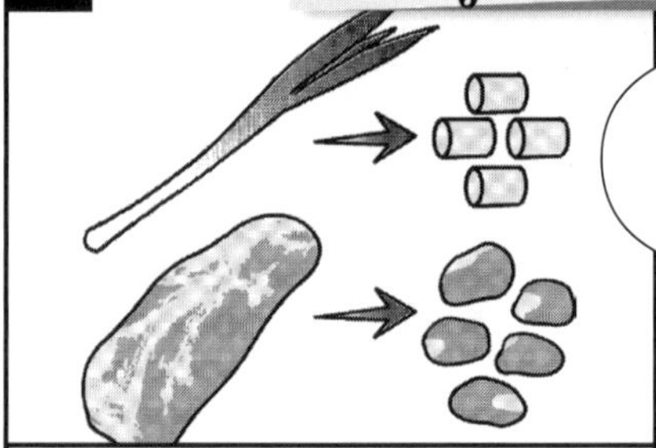

Cut the chicken breast into bite-sized chunks and 1 leek into 1-inch lengths.

2

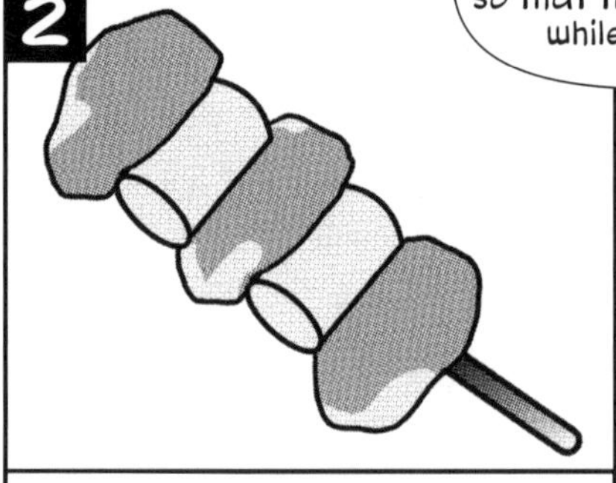

Arrange the chicken and leeks on the skewers as shown.

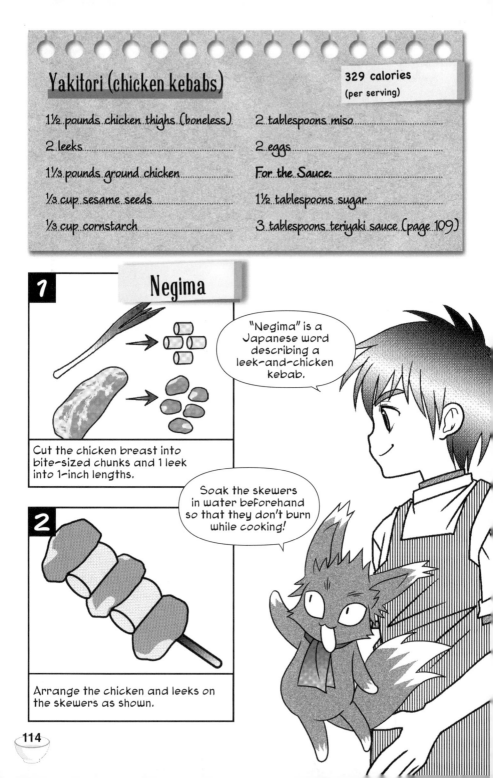

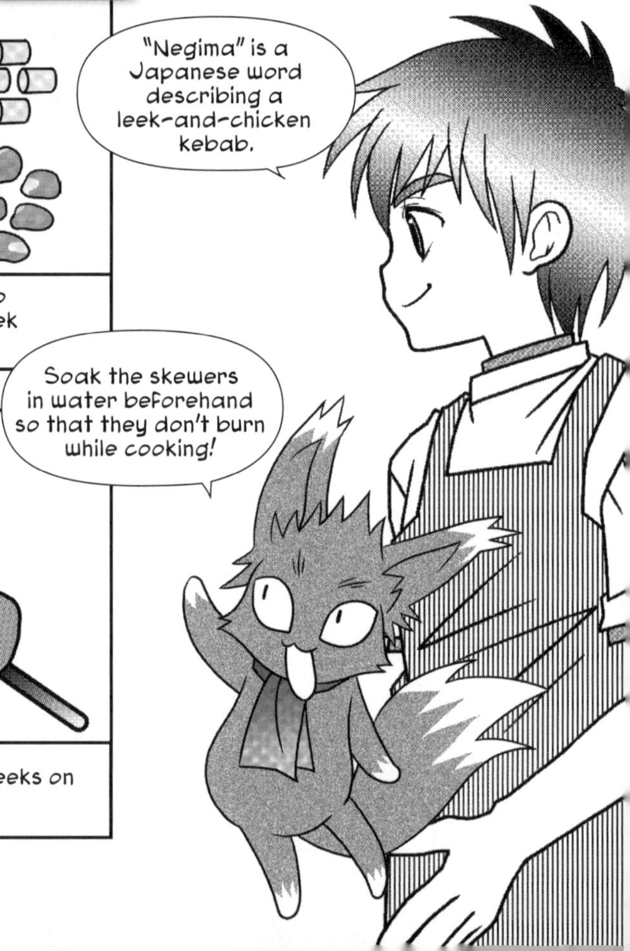
"Negima" is a Japanese word describing a leek-and-chicken kebab.
Soak the skewers in water beforehand so that they don't burn while cooking!

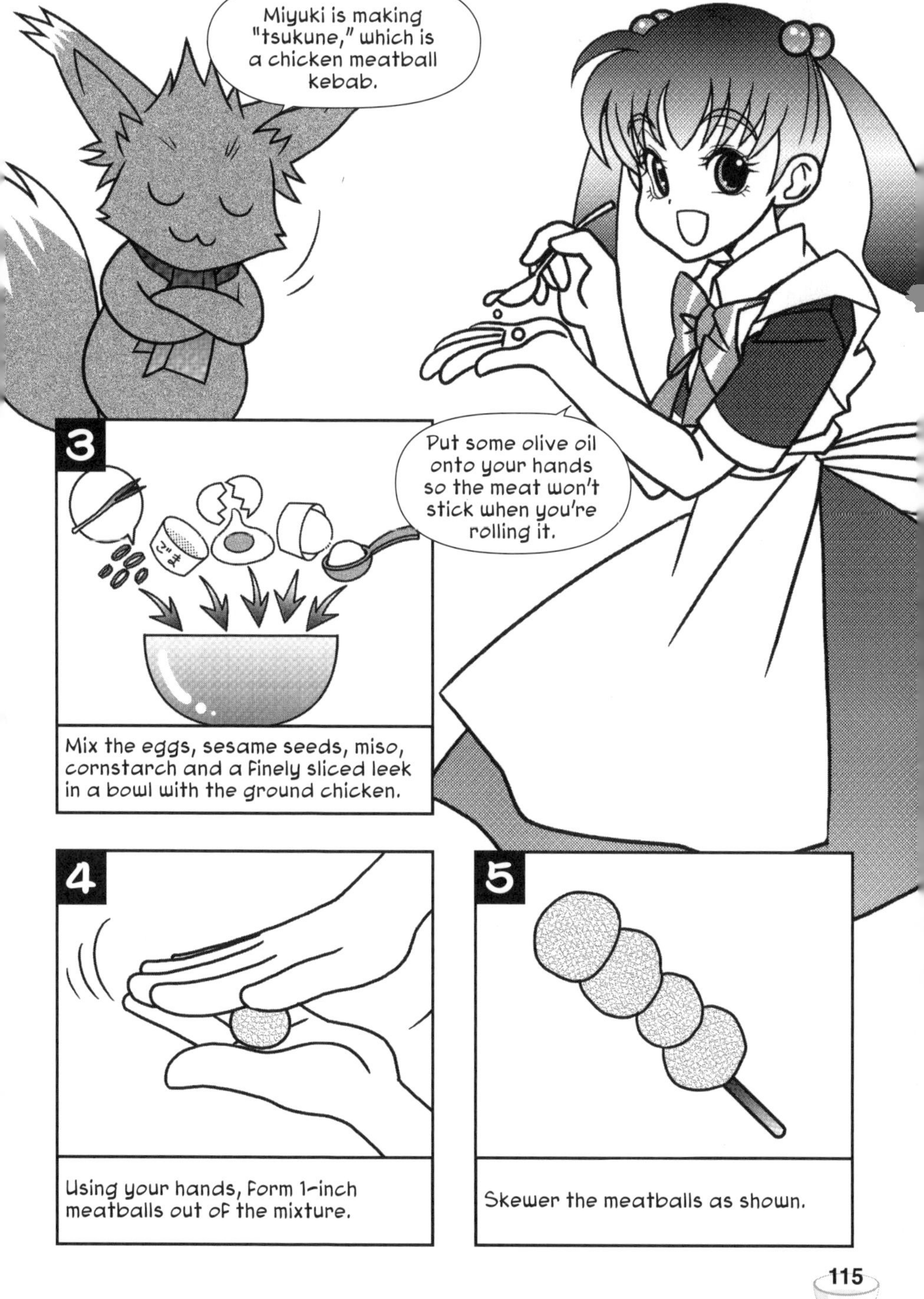
Miyuki is making "tsukune," which is a chicken meatball kebab.
3
Mix the eggs, sesame seeds, miso, cornstarch and a finely sliced leek in a bowl with the ground chicken.
Put some olive oil onto your hands so the meat won't stick when you're rolling it.
4
Using your hands, form 1-inch meatballs out of the mixture.
5
Skewer the meatballs as shown.

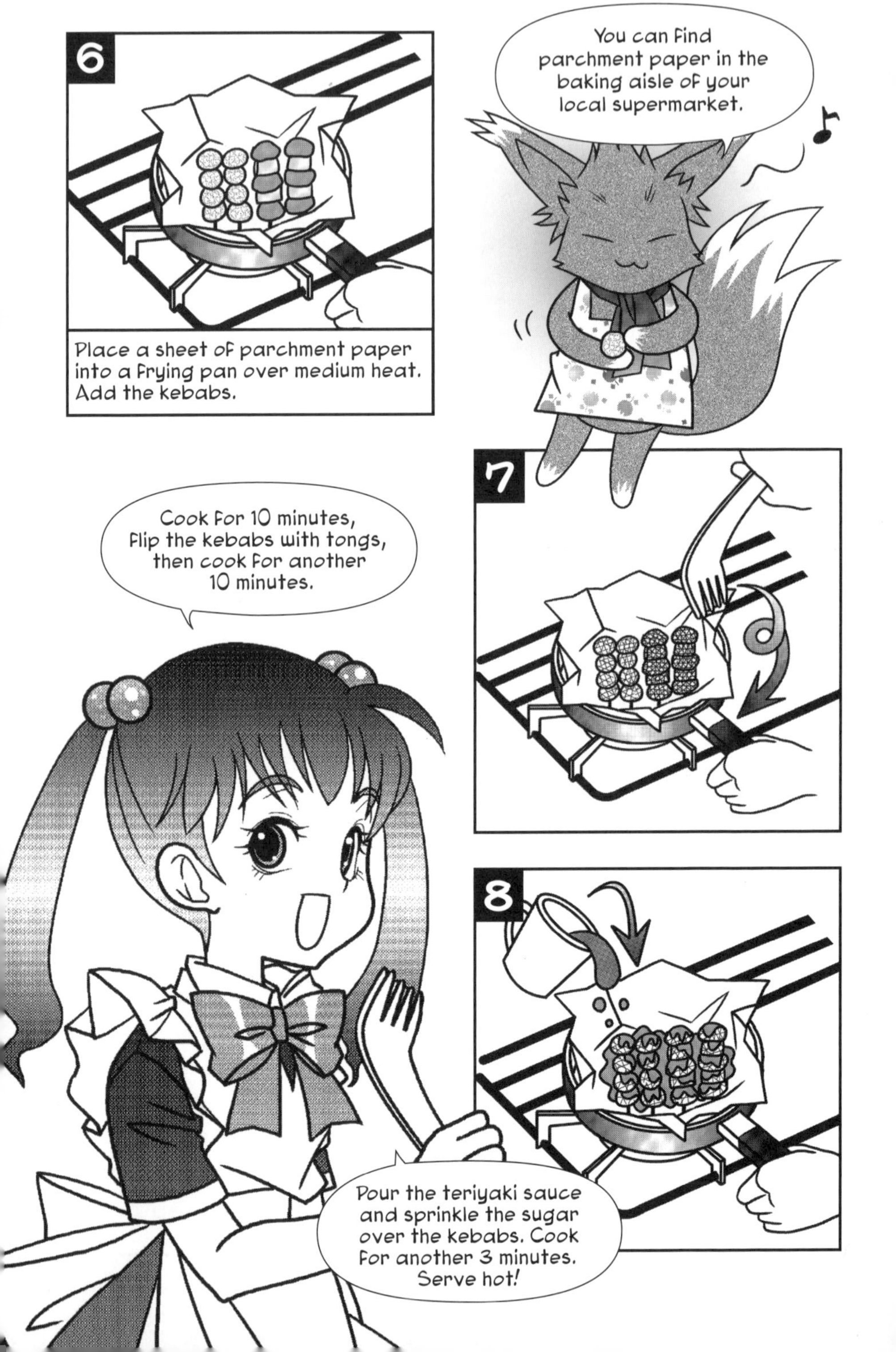
6
Place a sheet of parchment paper into a frying pan over medium heat. Add the kebabs.
You can find parchment paper in the baking aisle of your local supermarket.
Cook for 10 minutes, flip the kebabs with tongs, then cook for another 10 minutes.
7
8
Pour the teriyaki sauce and sprinkle the sugar over the kebabs. Cook for another 3 minutes. Serve hot!

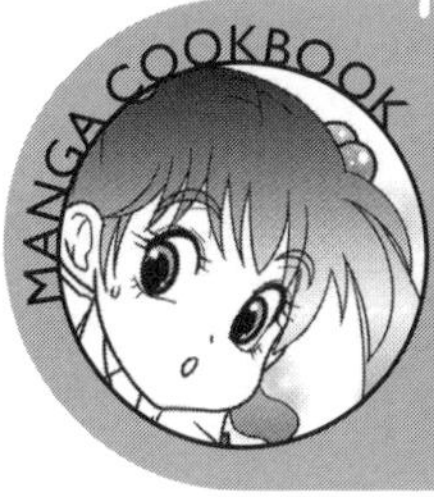
MANGA COOKBOOK

Gyudon 牛丼

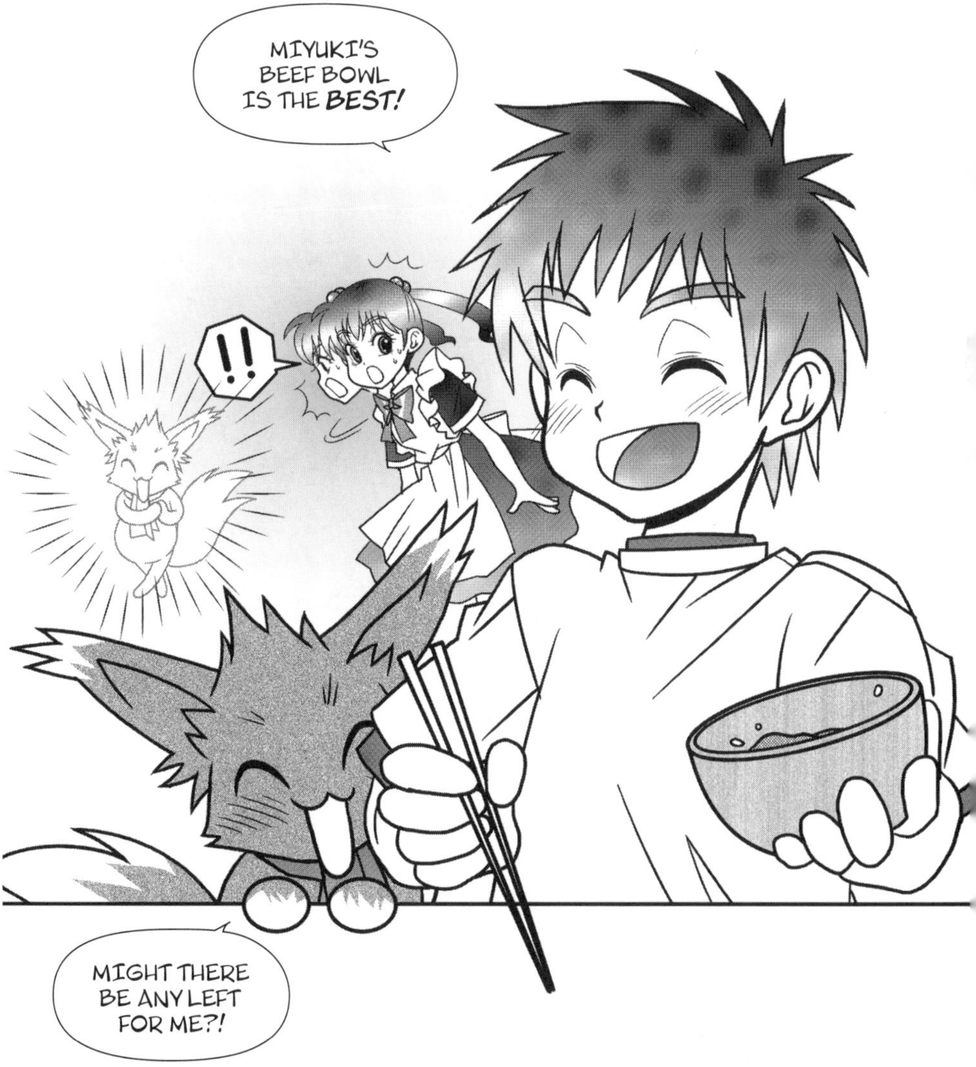
MIYUKI'S BEEF BOWL IS THE **BEST**!
!!
MIGHT THERE BE ANY LEFT FOR ME?!

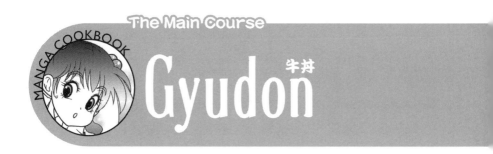

Gyudon (beef bowl)

945 calories (per serving)

⅔ pound thin-sliced beef

½ onion

½ cup teriyaki sauce (see page 109)

1 tablespoon sugar

¾ cup dashi (see page 20)

1 teaspoon vegetable oil

3 cups steamed rice

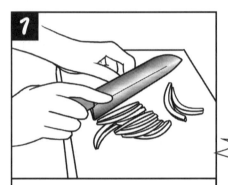

1

Slice the onion into thin strips and then set them aside.

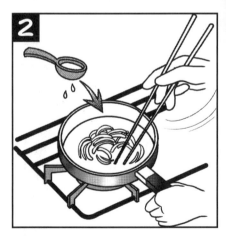

2

Fight back the tears when chopping onions by placing a damp paper towel next to your cutting area.

"Sweat" the onions by cooking them with oil in a pan until they release some of their moisture and are slightly translucent.

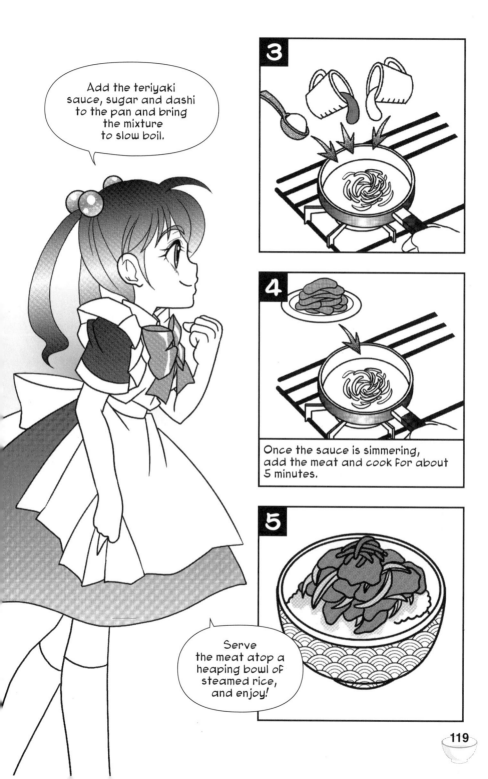

Add the teriyaki sauce, sugar and dashi to the pan and bring the mixture to slow boil.

3

4

Once the sauce is simmering, add the meat and cook for about 5 minutes.

5

Serve the meat atop a heaping bowl of steamed rice, and enjoy!

Miyuki's Notes on Gyudon

Whenever I make gyudon, I think of the first volume of the manga "Beck," when Koyuki's friend keeps trying to get him to go to "Yoshigyu," which is a pseudonym for Yoshinoya, a popular chain of gyudon restaurants in Japan.

Koyuki's friend obviously knows what I know – that eating gyudon is a great way to enjoy the taste of beef without going overboard. Because the meat is served atop plenty of healthy steamed rice, you'll leave the table feeling satisfied and full of energy!

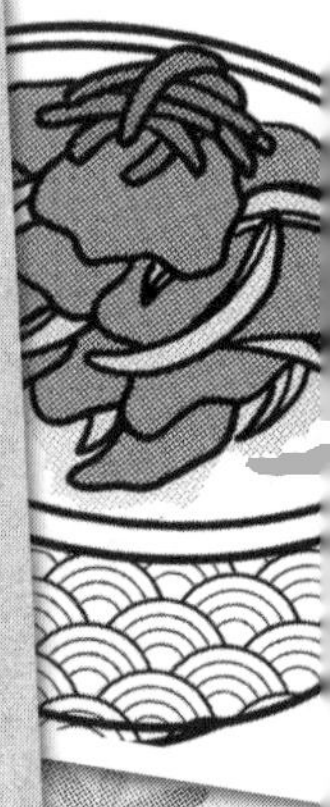

Gyudon is part of a category of Japanese cuisine known as "donburi," in which white rice is piled high with savory meats and vegetables. Popular donburi toppings include pork, chicken, shrimp tempura, sliced raw fish, and grilled eel. Because gyudon is relatively inexpensive and easy to to make, it has become one of Japan's most popular "fast foods," particularly among on-the-go office workers and students.

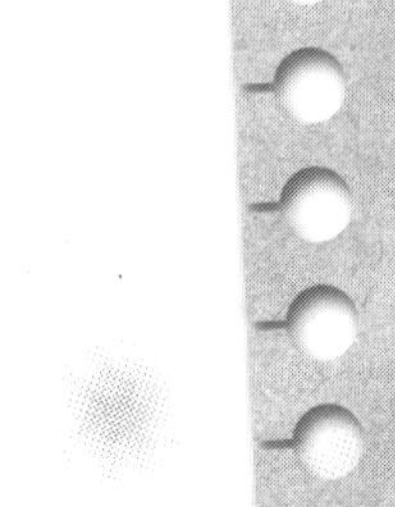

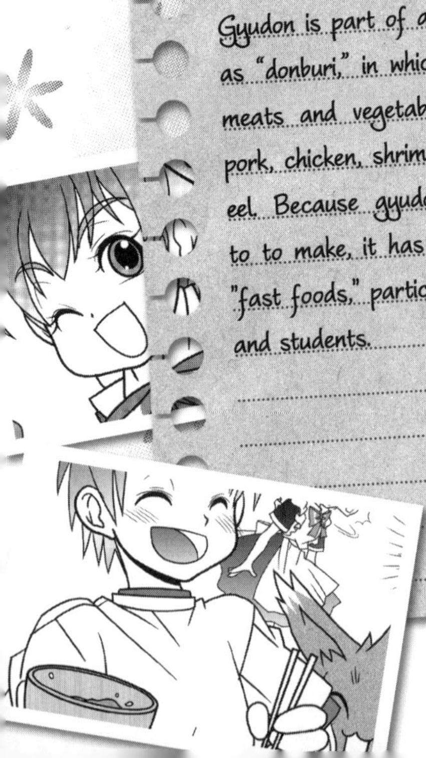

My Notes

My Notes

The Main Course

MANGA COOKBOOK

Okonomiyaki
お好み焼き

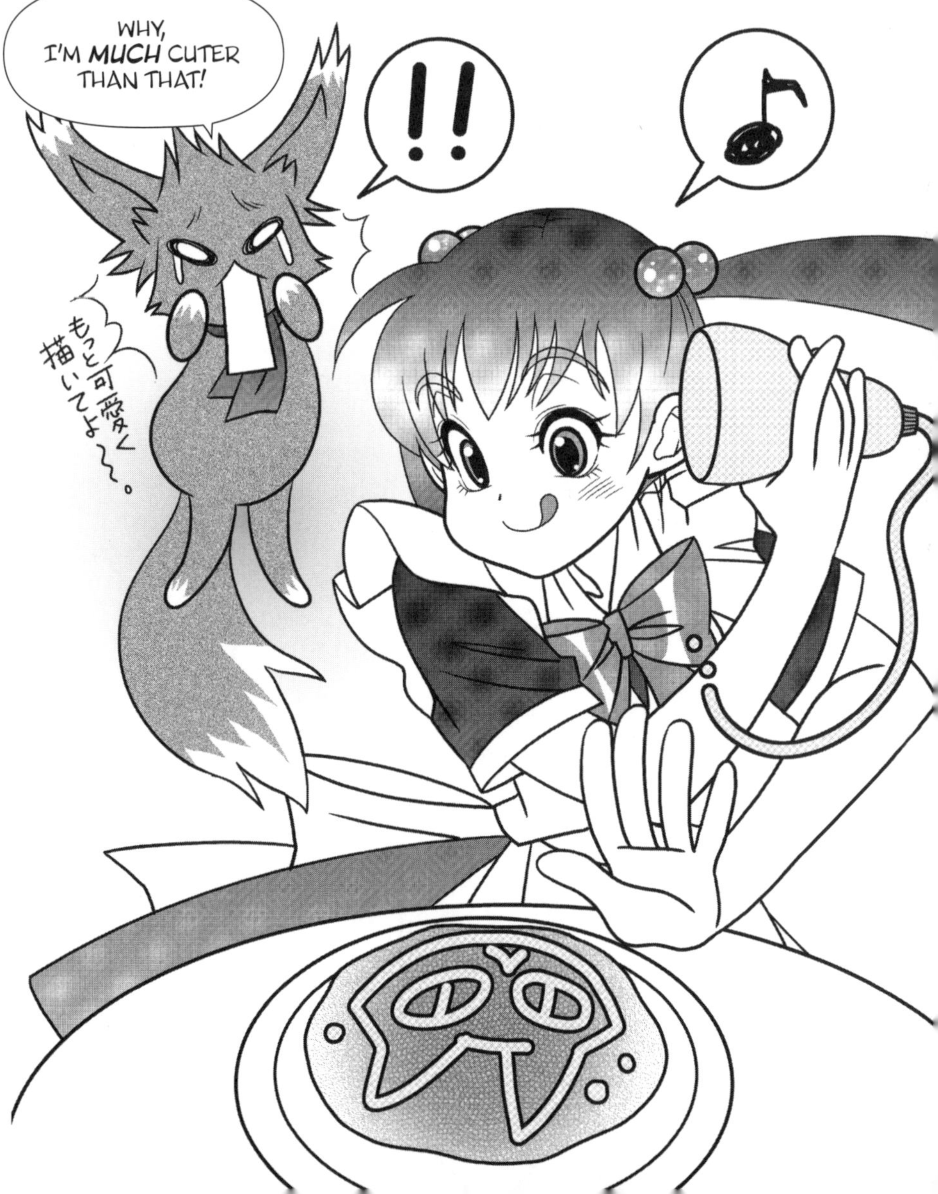
WHY, I'M **MUCH** CUTER THAN THAT!
!!
もっと可愛く描いてよ〜〜。

Okonomiyaki (Japanese-style pizza)

500 calories
(per serving)

- ½ pound cabbage
- ½ green onion
- 2 tablespoons milk
- ¾ cup dashi (see page 20)
- 1 cup flour
- 2 eggs
- 2 tablespoons mayonnaise
- 1 tablespoon butter
- ¼ teaspoon baking powder
- 1 tablespoon vegetable oil
- Okonomiyaki or Worcestershire sauce
- Dried bonito flakes (see page 20)
- 1 sheet of nori (see page 19)
- Extra mayonnaise for seasoning

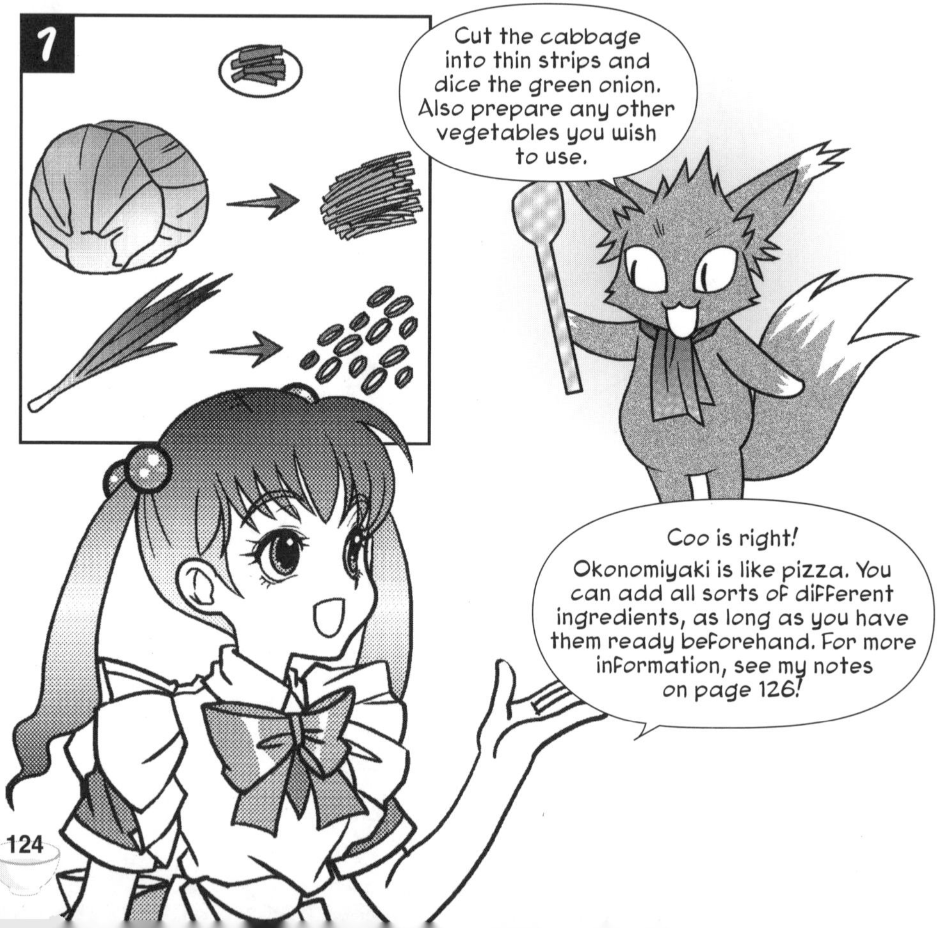
1
Cut the cabbage into thin strips and dice the green onion. Also prepare any other vegetables you wish to use.
Coo is right! Okonomiyaki is like pizza. You can add all sorts of different ingredients, as long as you have them ready beforehand. For more information, see my notes on page 126!

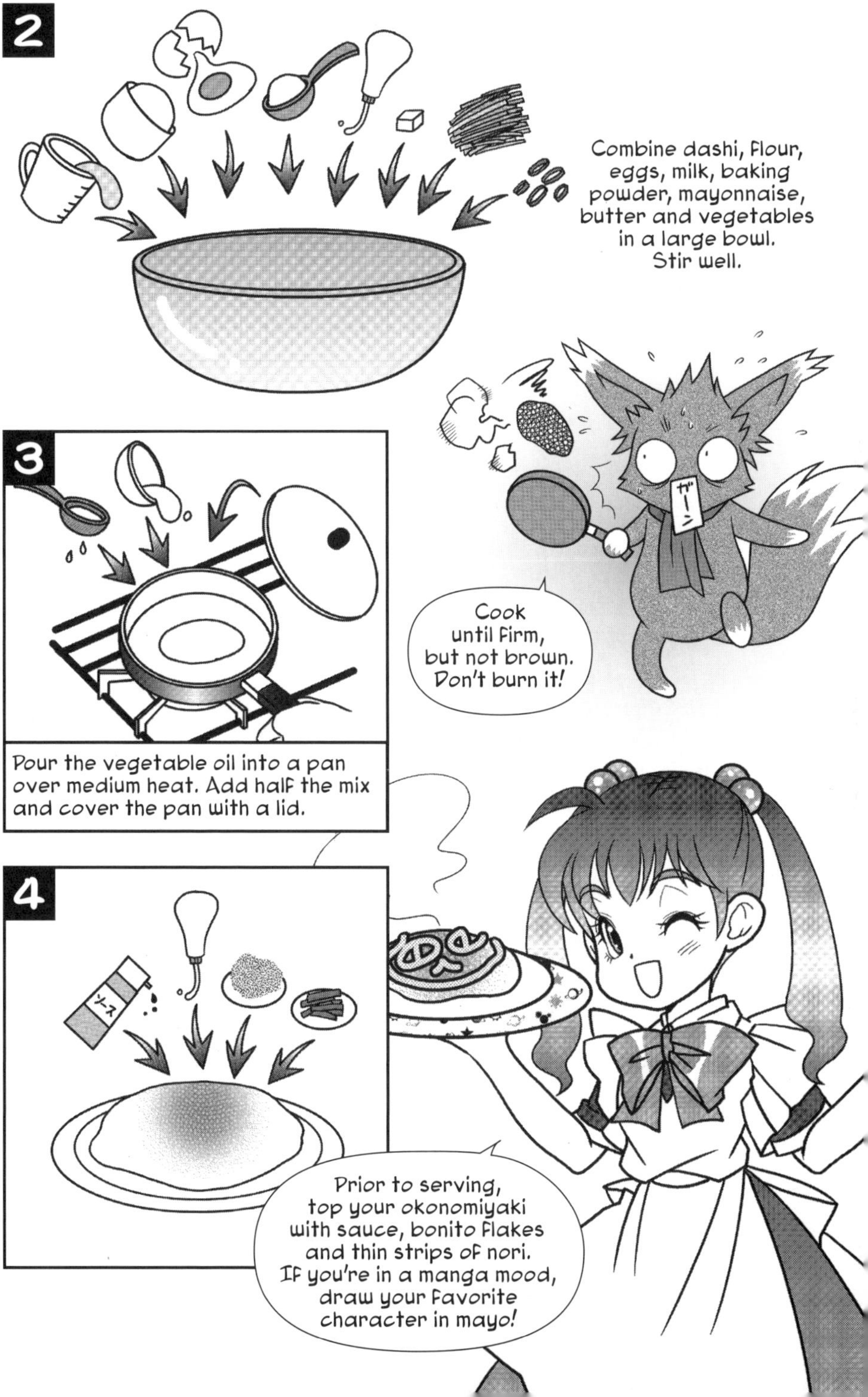
2
Combine dashi, flour, eggs, milk, baking powder, mayonnaise, butter and vegetables in a large bowl. Stir well.
3
Pour the vegetable oil into a pan over medium heat. Add half the mix and cover the pan with a lid.
ガーン
Cook until firm, but not brown. Don't burn it!
4
ソース
Prior to serving, top your okonomiyaki with sauce, bonito flakes and thin strips of nori. If you're in a manga mood, draw your favorite character in mayo!

Miyuki's Notes on Okonomiyaki

"Japanese pizza." "Japanese pancakes." You can call okonomiyaki whatever you want — just as long as you treat it with respect. Take, for instance, the scene in the second volume of Clamp's "Tsubasa: Reservoir Chronicle," where Kurogane commits an okonomiyaki faux pas by trying to flip the dish while it is still on the tabletop griddle. Not so fast, Kuro-kun! In Osaka (where okonomiyaki is said to have originated), that's the chef's job.

Enjoyed throughout Japan, okonomiyaki is a mixture of flour, eggs and dashi stock. Into that you can add just about anything you desire — pork, shrimp, cheese — it all depends on how creative you feel! Okonomiyaki is usually drizzled with sauce and mayonnaise, and topped with "katsuobushi" (bonito flakes; see dashi recipe on page 20).

The carbohydrates from the flour, fiber from the vegetables, and protein from the meat and eggs make it a nutritionally balanced dish. Japanese kids love okonomiyaki, and it's a staple at local matsuri (street festivals).

My Notes

My Notes

The Main Course

MANGA COOKBOOK

生うどん
Nama Udon

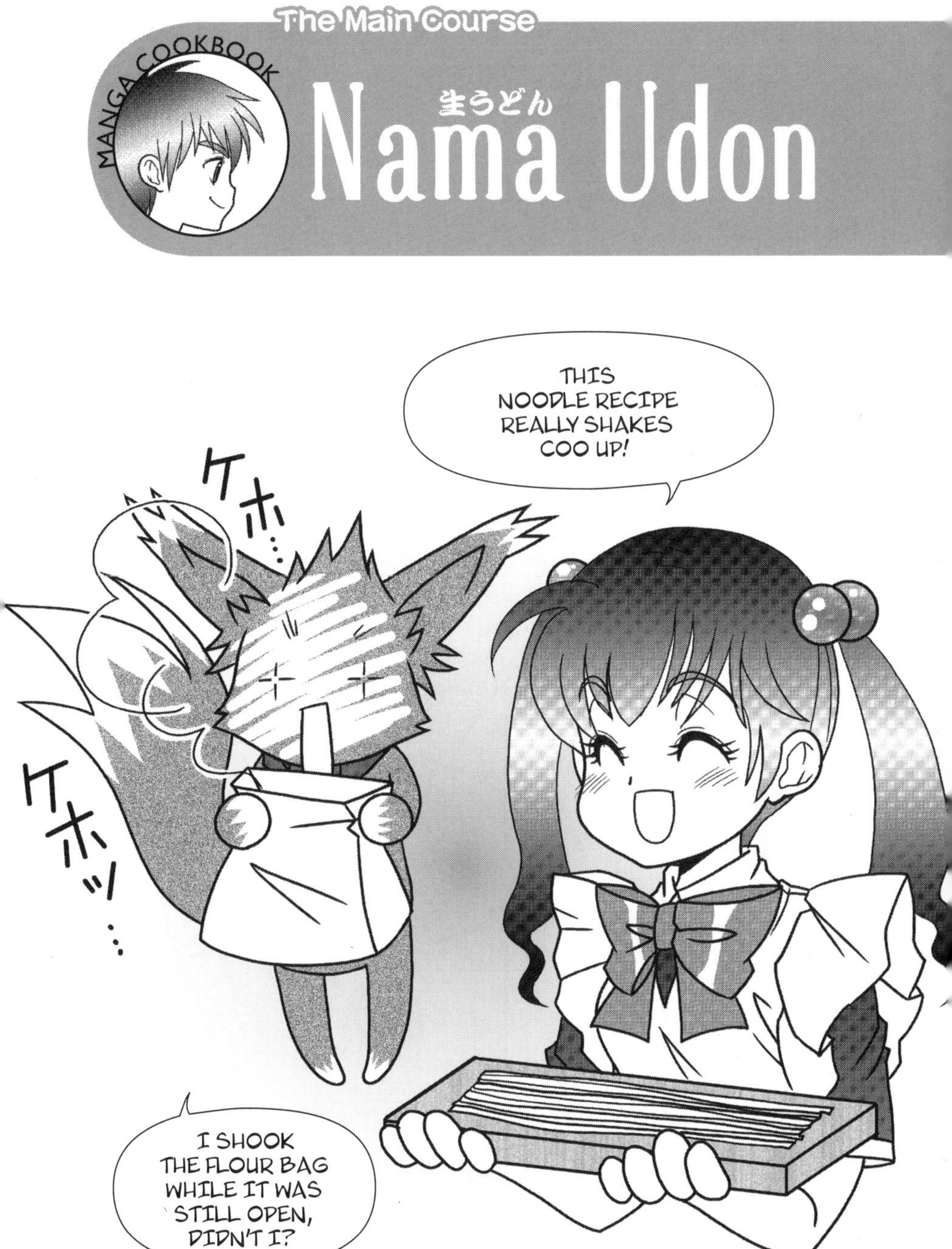
THIS NOODLE RECIPE REALLY SHAKES COO UP!
ケホ…
ケホッ…
I SHOOK THE FLOUR BAG WHILE IT WAS STILL OPEN, DIDN'T I?

Nama Udon (raw noodles)

1½ cups all-purpose flour

1½ cups bread flour

1 teaspoon salt

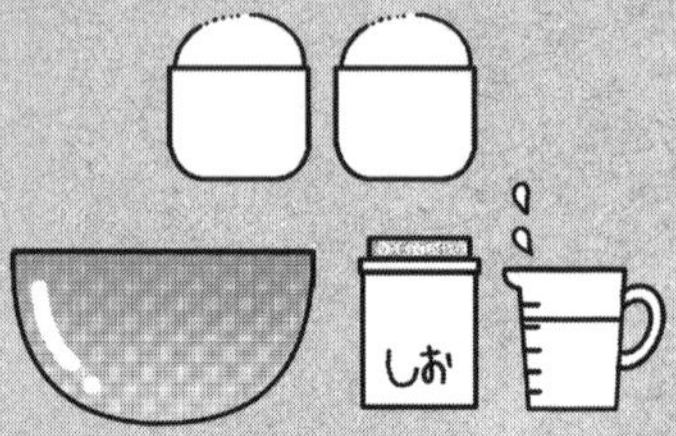
しお

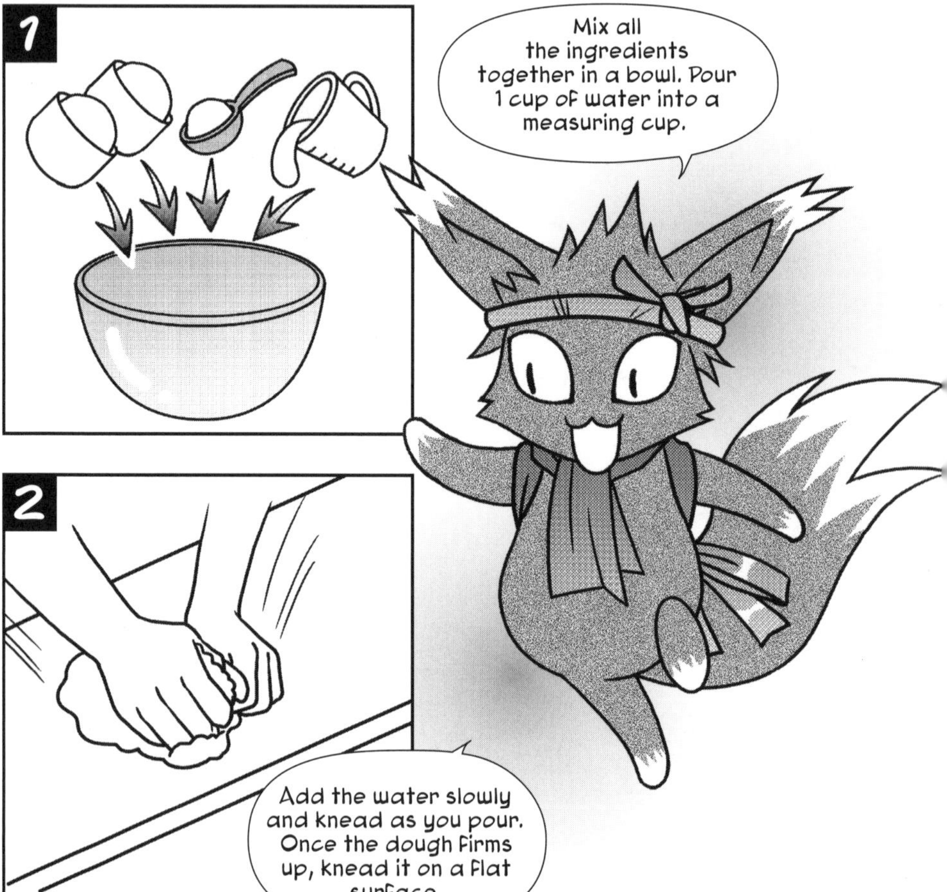
1
Mix all the ingredients together in a bowl. Pour 1 cup of water into a measuring cup.
2
Add the water slowly and knead as you pour. Once the dough firms up, knead it on a flat surface.

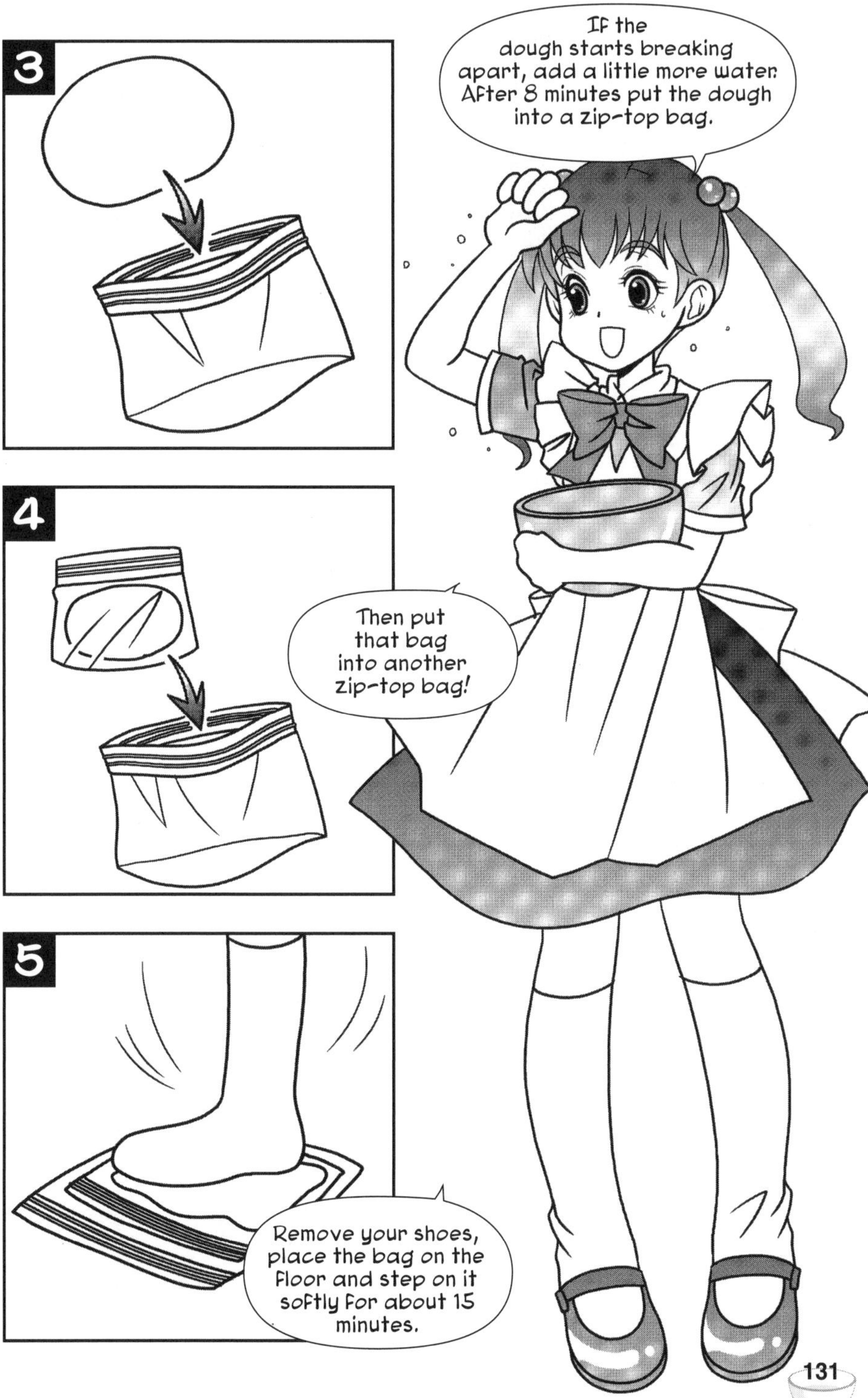
3
If the dough starts breaking apart, add a little more water. After 8 minutes put the dough into a zip-top bag.
4
Then put that bag into another zip-top bag!
5
Remove your shoes, place the bag on the floor and step on it softly for about 15 minutes.

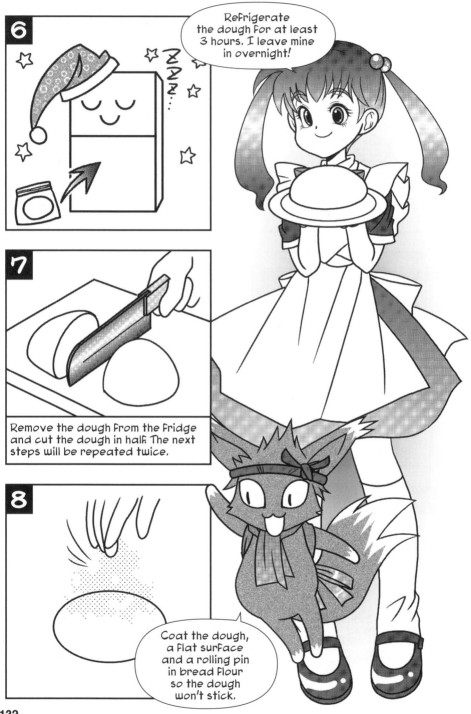

6

Refrigerate the dough for at least 3 hours. I leave mine in overnight!

ZZZ...

7

Remove the dough from the fridge and cut the dough in half. The next steps will be repeated twice.

8

Coat the dough, a flat surface and a rolling pin in bread flour so the dough won't stick.

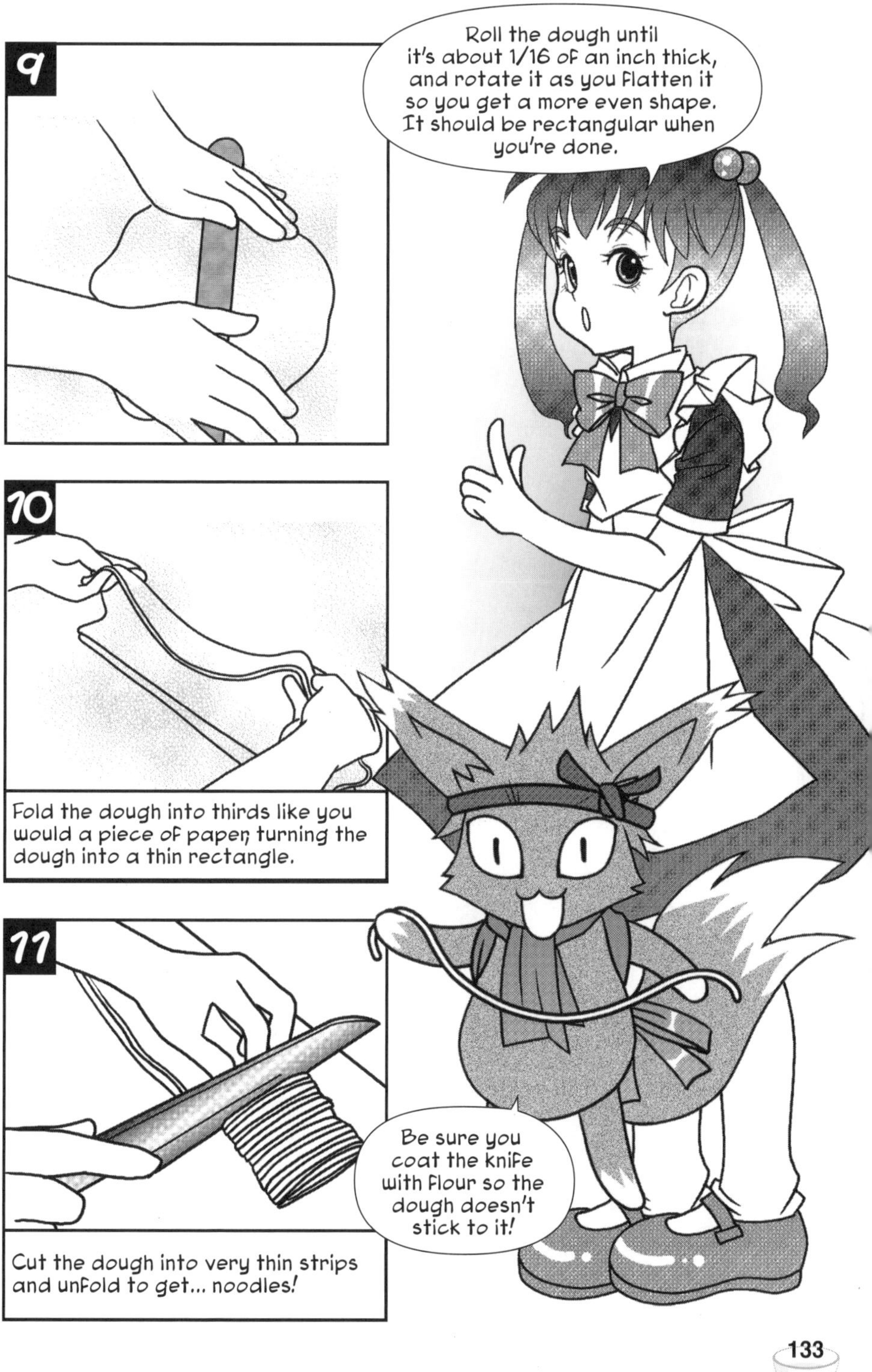
9
Roll the dough until it's about 1/16 of an inch thick, and rotate it as you flatten it so you get a more even shape. It should be rectangular when you're done.
10
Fold the dough into thirds like you would a piece of paper, turning the dough into a thin rectangle.
11
Cut the dough into very thin strips and unfold to get... noodles!
Be sure you coat the knife with flour so the dough doesn't stick to it!

Miyuki's Notes on Noodles

Did you know the world's first noodles were made in China nearly 4,000 years ago? It should come as no surprise, then, that Japan has also had a long-running love affair with ramen.

But it doesn't stop there. We also enjoy udon, buckwheat noodles called "soba," and thin "somen" noodles that are served chilled on hot summer days. All are relatively quick and easy to make, particularly if you're using instant noodles — just add water!

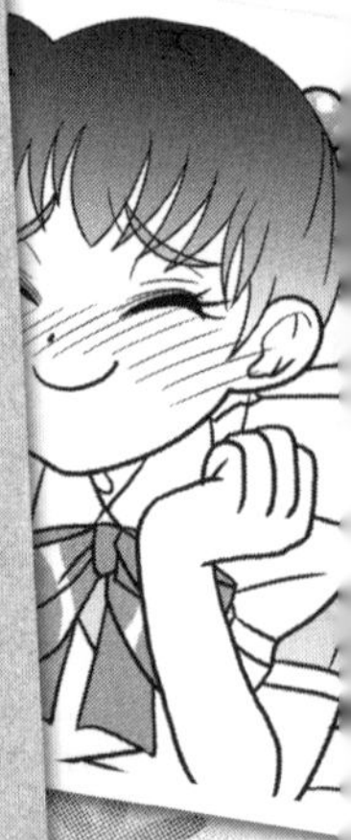

All this noodle talk may seem foreign to you, but udon actually has more in common with Western food than you might think. Udon dough is made out of pretty much the same ingredients as everyday bread. While bread dough uses yeast to make it rise, though, the only ingredients in udon are flour, water and salt.

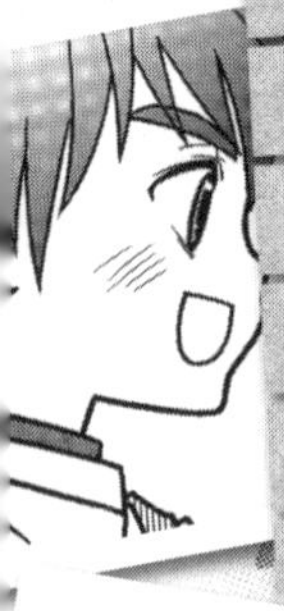

Make your own and see how easy it can be!

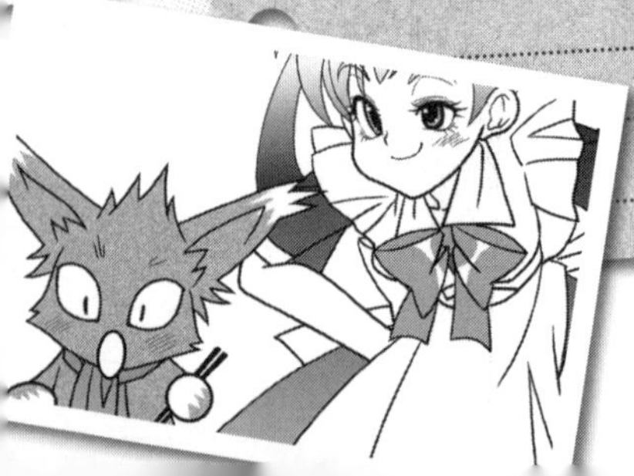

My Notes

My Notes

Cooked Udon うどん

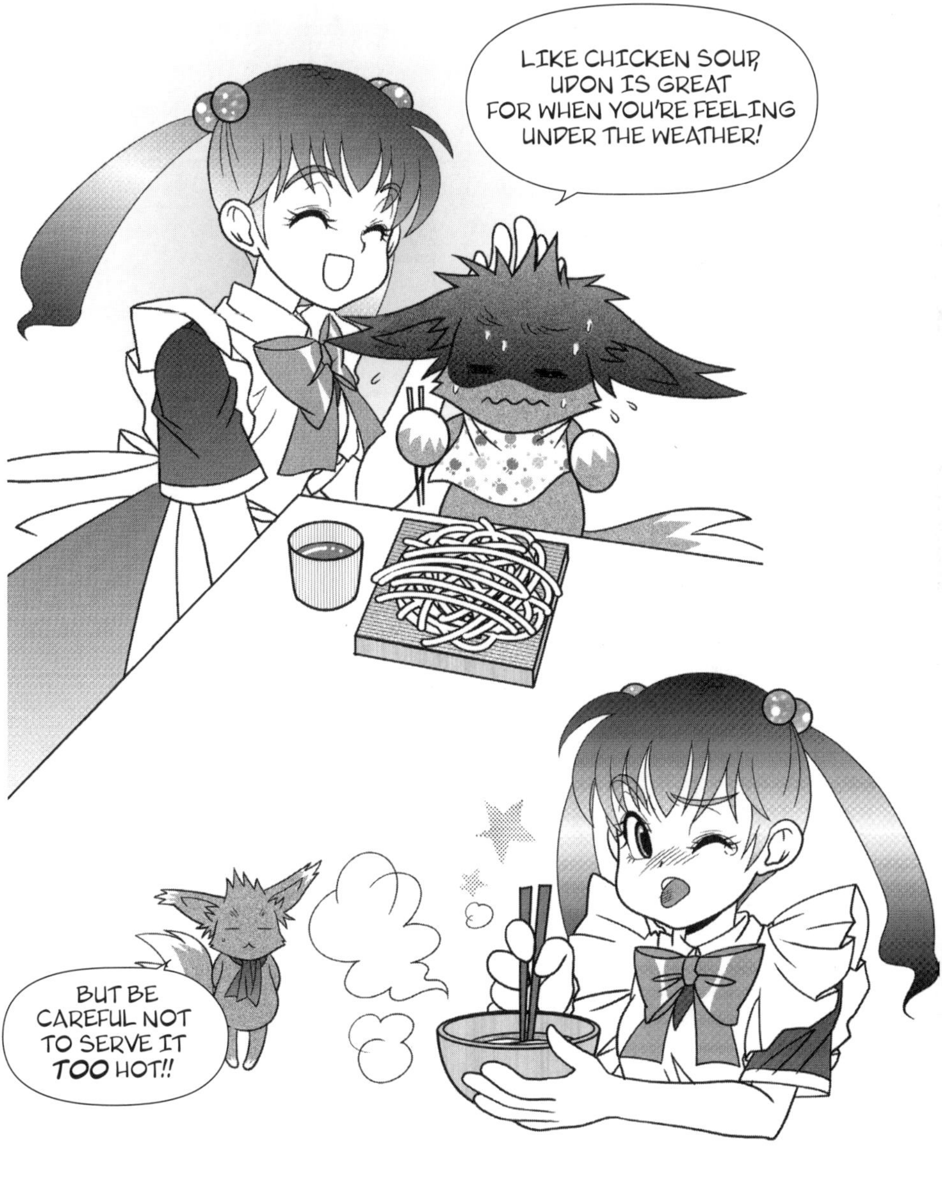
LIKE CHICKEN SOUP, UDON IS GREAT FOR WHEN YOU'RE FEELING UNDER THE WEATHER!
BUT BE CAREFUL NOT TO SERVE IT **TOO** HOT!!

Cold Udon

275 calories
(per serving)

1 teaspoon dashi stock (see page 20)

⅓ cup soy sauce

⅓ cup mirin (see page 19)

2 servings nama udon (see page 129)

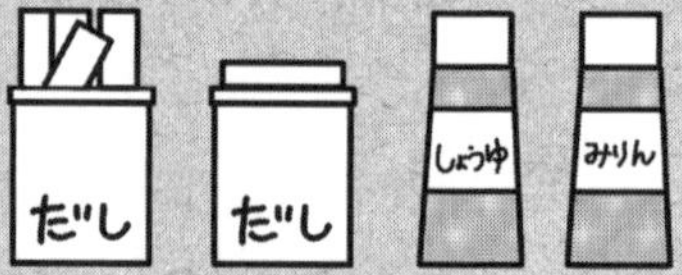
だし
だし
しょうゆ
みりん

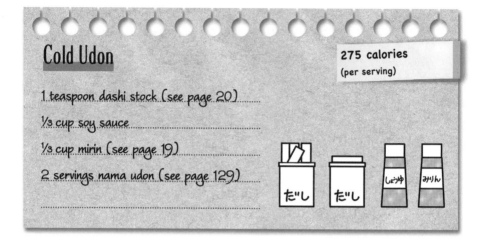

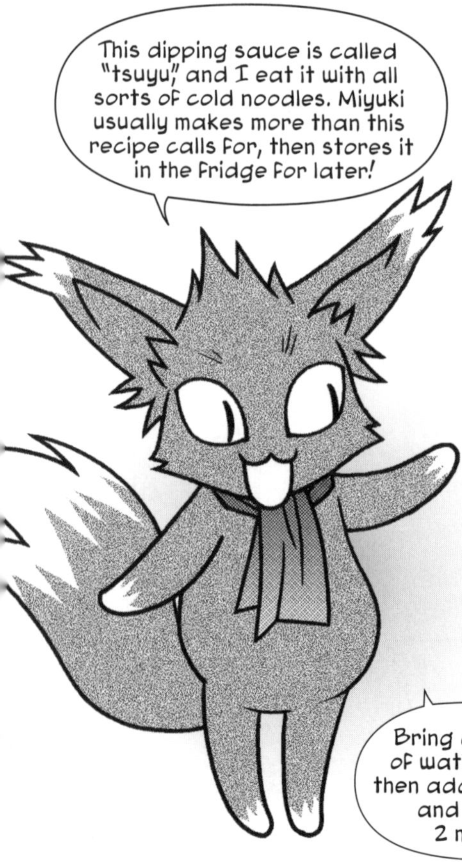
This dipping sauce is called "tsuyu," and I eat it with all sorts of cold noodles. Miyuki usually makes more than this recipe calls for, then stores it in the fridge for later!

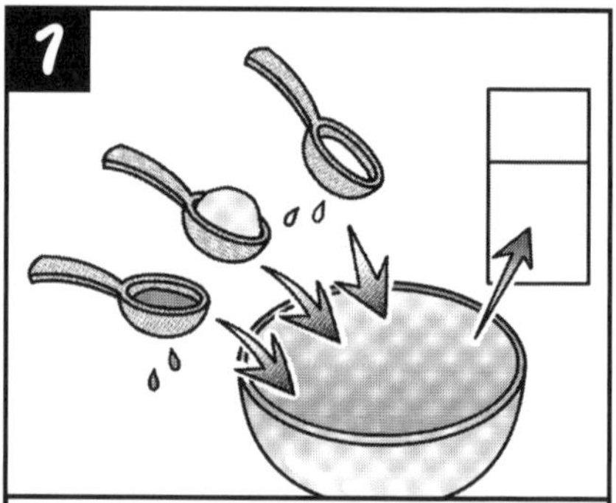
1

First, mix the dashi stock, soy sauce, mirin and a cup of cold water in a bowl. Set aside.

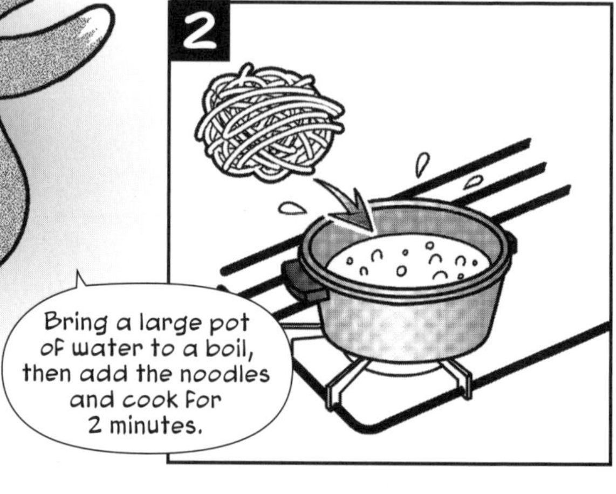
2
Bring a large pot of water to a boil, then add the noodles and cook for 2 minutes.

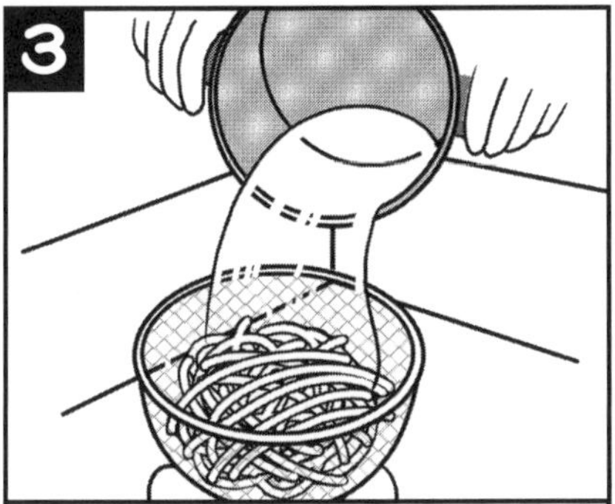

Carefully pour the udon into a colander in the sink and allow the noodles to drain.

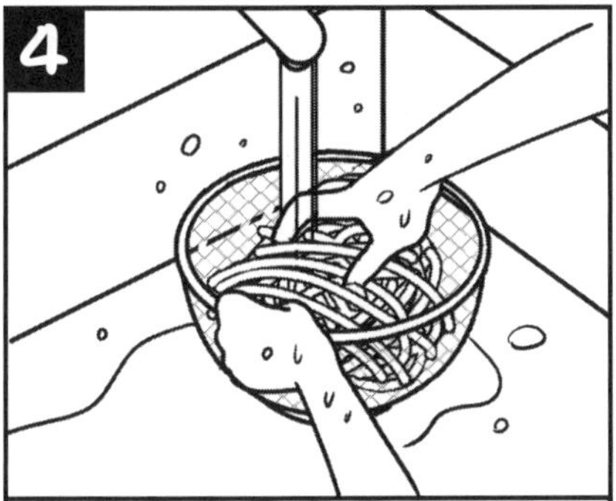

Rinse the noodles thoroughly, using your hands to stir them once they've cooled down.

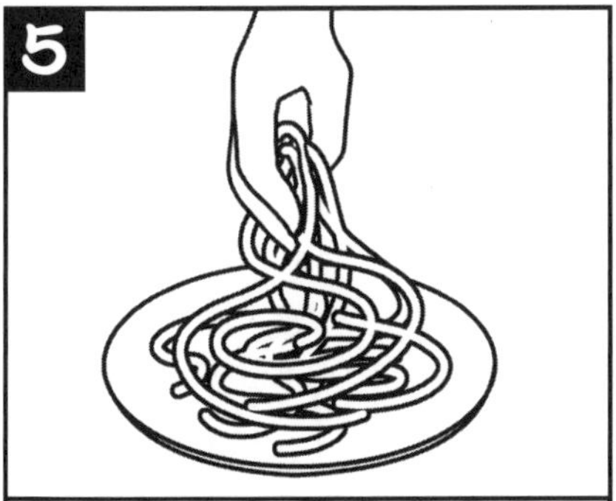

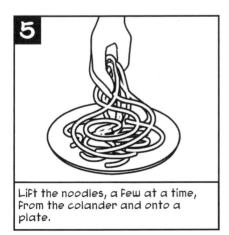

Lift the noodles, a few at a time, from the colander and onto a plate.

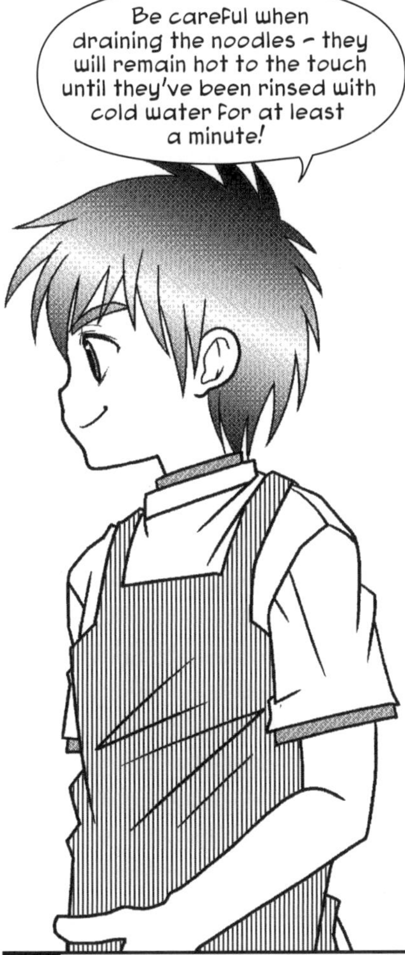
Be careful when draining the noodles – they will remain hot to the touch until they've been rinsed with cold water for at least a minute!

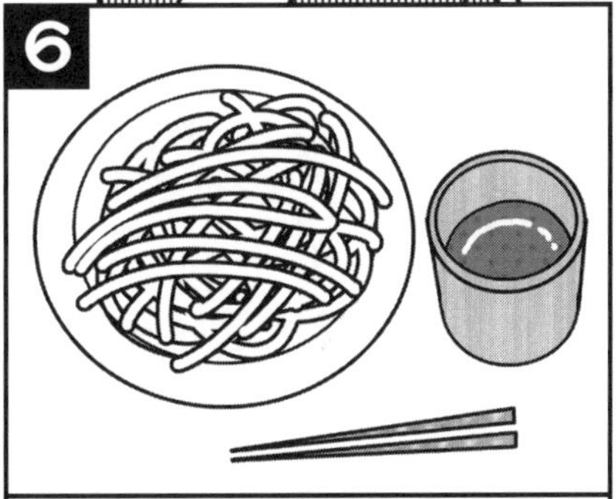

Pour some tsuyu into a small bowl and dip the noodles into the sauce as you eat!

Hot Udon

275 calories
(per serving)

2 tablespoons dashi stock (see page 20)

2 teaspoons salt

1 teaspoon soy sauce

2 green onions

2 servings nama udon (see page 129)

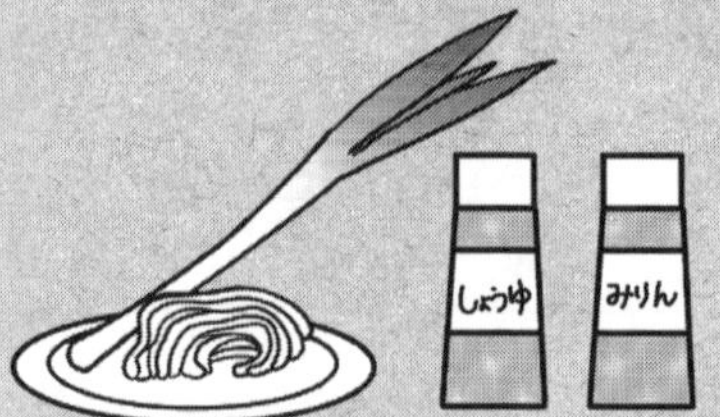
しょうゆ
みりん

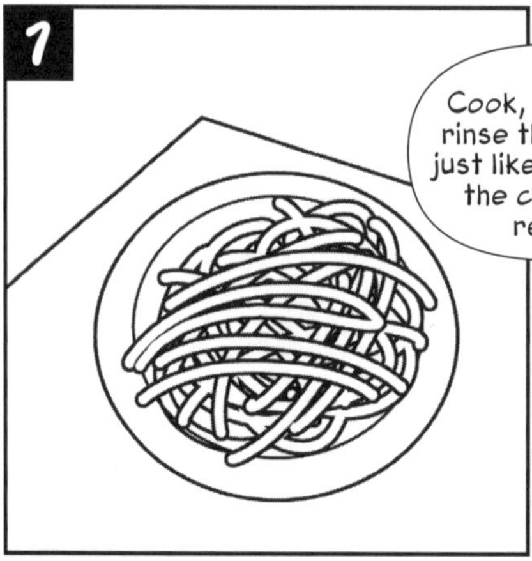

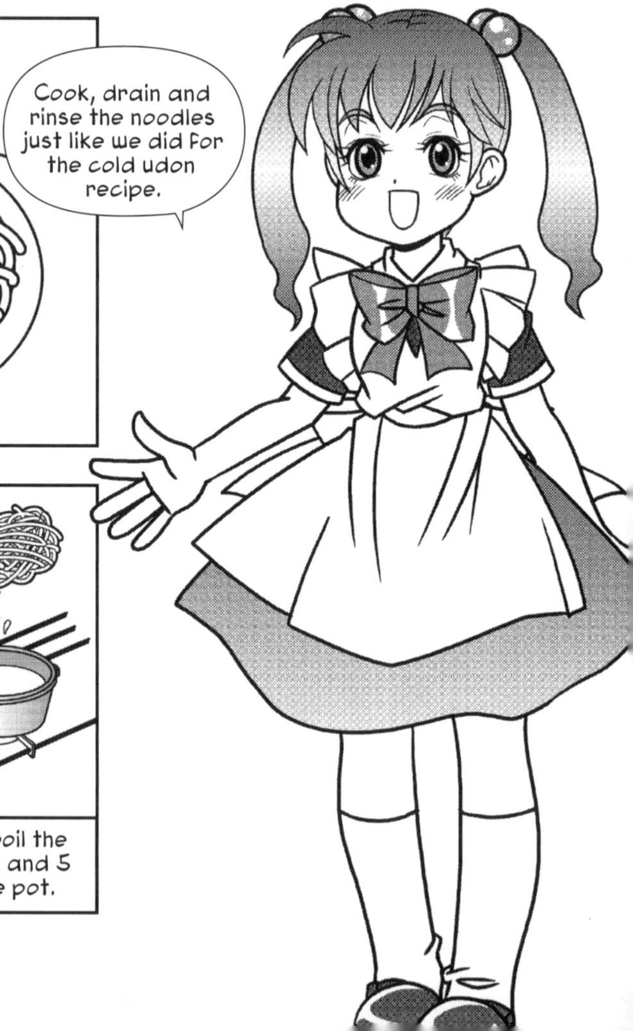
Cook, drain and rinse the noodles just like we did for the cold udon recipe.

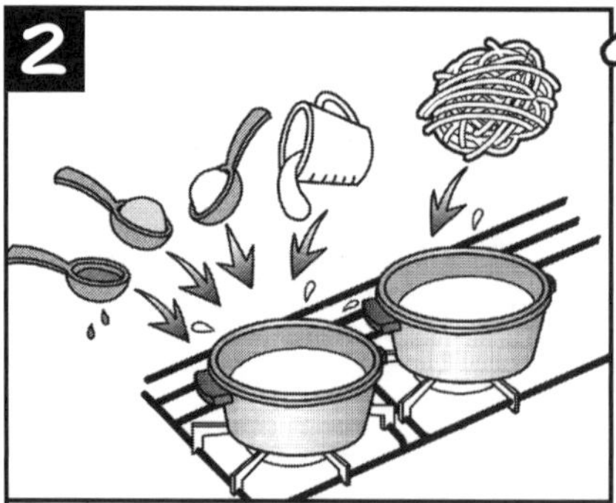

While cooking the noodles, boil the dashi stock, salt, soy sauce and 5 cups of water in a separate pot.

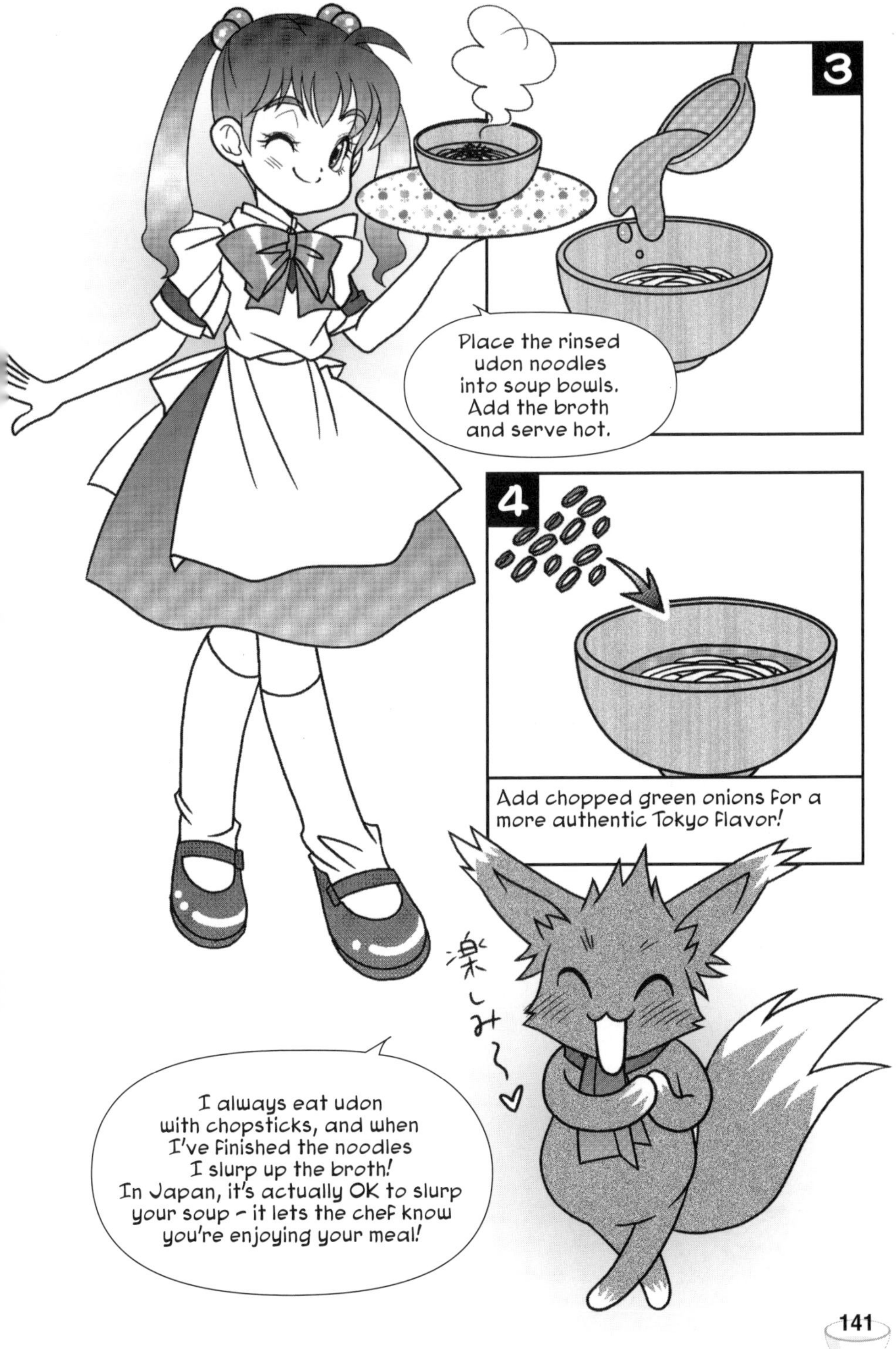
3
Place the rinsed udon noodles into soup bowls. Add the broth and serve hot.
4
Add chopped green onions for a more authentic Tokyo flavor!
楽しみ～
I always eat udon with chopsticks, and when I've finished the noodles I slurp up the broth! In Japan, it's actually OK to slurp your soup - it lets the chef know you're enjoying your meal!

Miyuki's Notes on Cooking Udon

When it comes to noodles, cooking them is half the fun. (The other half? Eating them, of course!) As I mentioned earlier, ramen, udon and somen are all popular in Japan.

Dry noodles can be purchased at any Japanese market and prepared in a flash, so people rarely make them by hand at home anymore. However, it's definitely more enjoyable when we do!

It's quite easy to make udon from scratch, and there are many regional varieties in Japan, all featuring their own cooking methods and flavors. Cold udon is refreshing on a humid summer afternoon, while hot udon loaded with fresh-cut veggies is perfect for wintry days or a late-night snack!

Nutritionists say udon helps with digestion, can be an effective cold remedy, and is a good source of quick energy before going out to play sports.

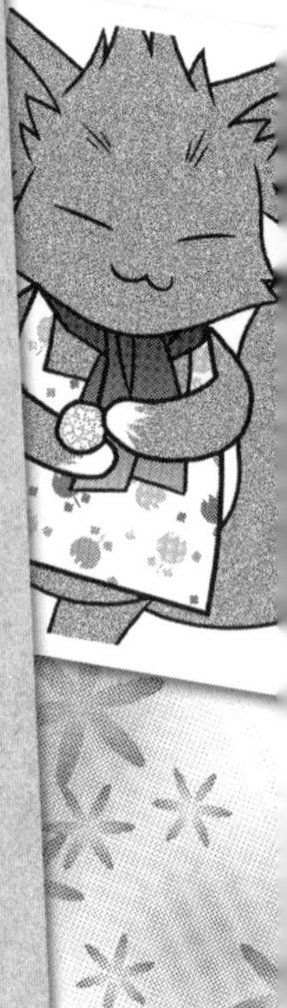

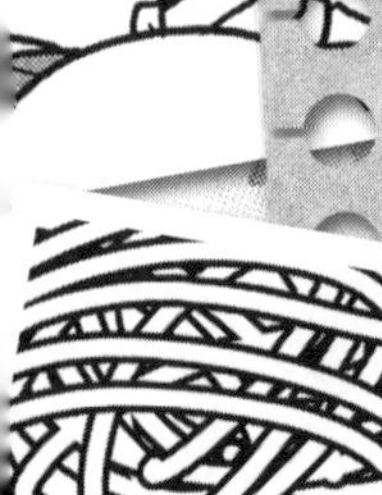

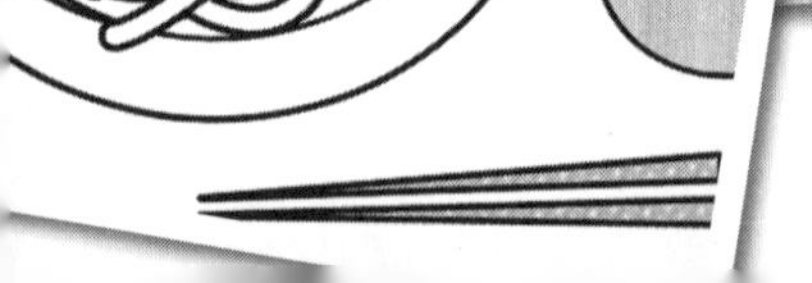

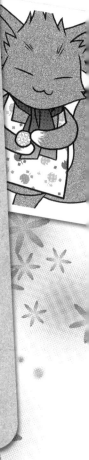

My Notes

My Notes

MANGA COOKBOOK

Welcome to Wagashi

3-Color Dango 三色団子

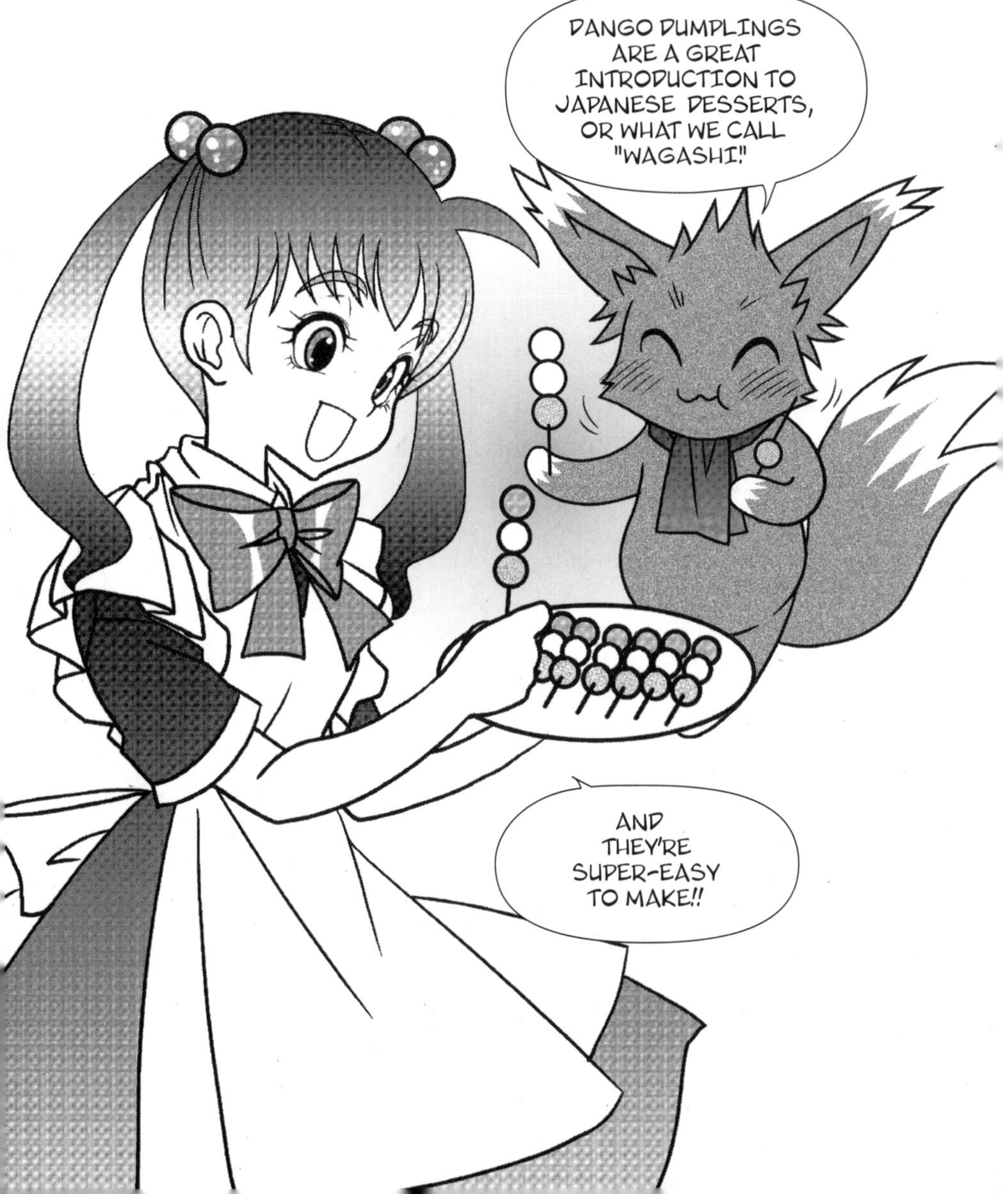
DANGO DUMPLINGS ARE A GREAT INTRODUCTION TO JAPANESE DESSERTS, OR WHAT WE CALL "WAGASHI."
AND THEY'RE SUPER-EASY TO MAKE!!

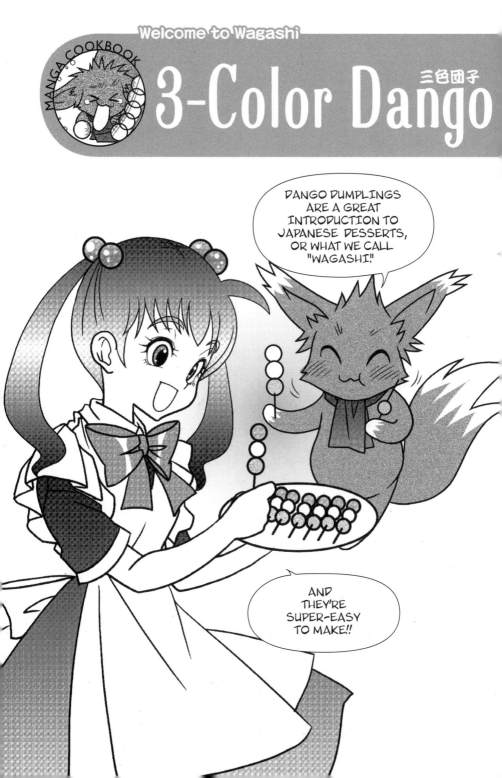

3-Color Dango (sweet dumplings)

About 30 calories
(per dango)

- 1 cup joshinko (see page 20)
- 2 tablespoons sugar
- ¼ cup shiratamako (see page 20)
- 1 drop red food coloring
- 2 teaspoons matcha powder (see page 20)

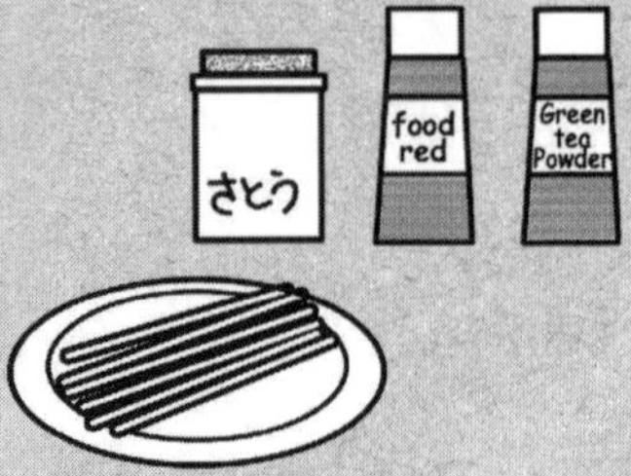

さとう
food red
Green tea Powder

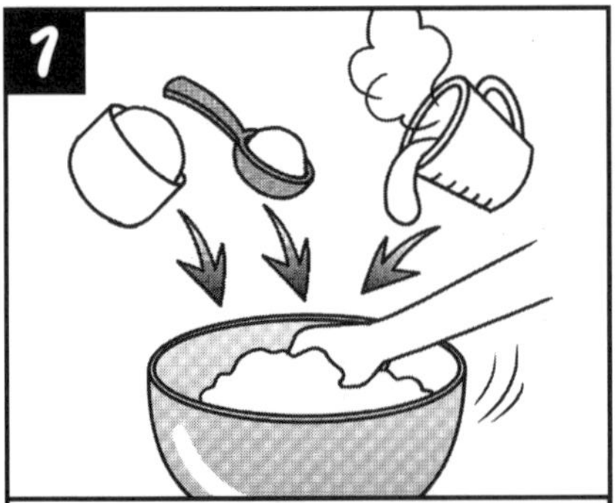

1 Pour the joshinko, sugar and 1/2 cup of hot water into a bowl, then mix and knead.

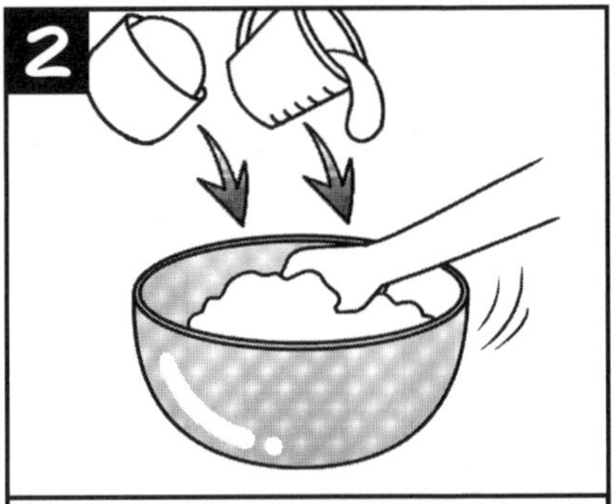

2 In another bowl, mix and knead the shiratamako with 2 tablespoons of cold water.

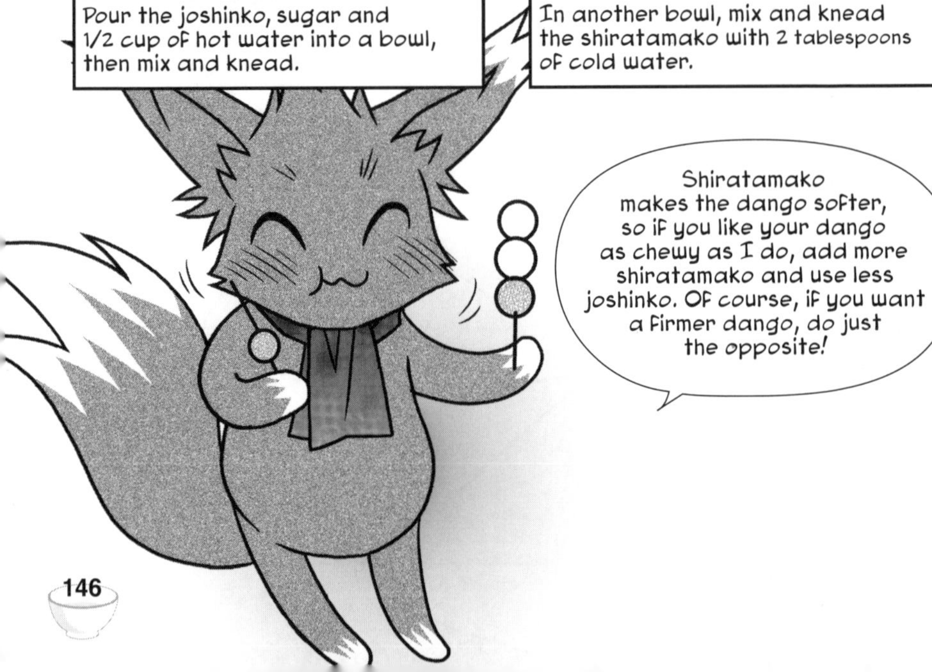

Shiratamako makes the dango softer, so if you like your dango as chewy as I do, add more shiratamako and use less joshinko. Of course, if you want a firmer dango, do just the opposite!

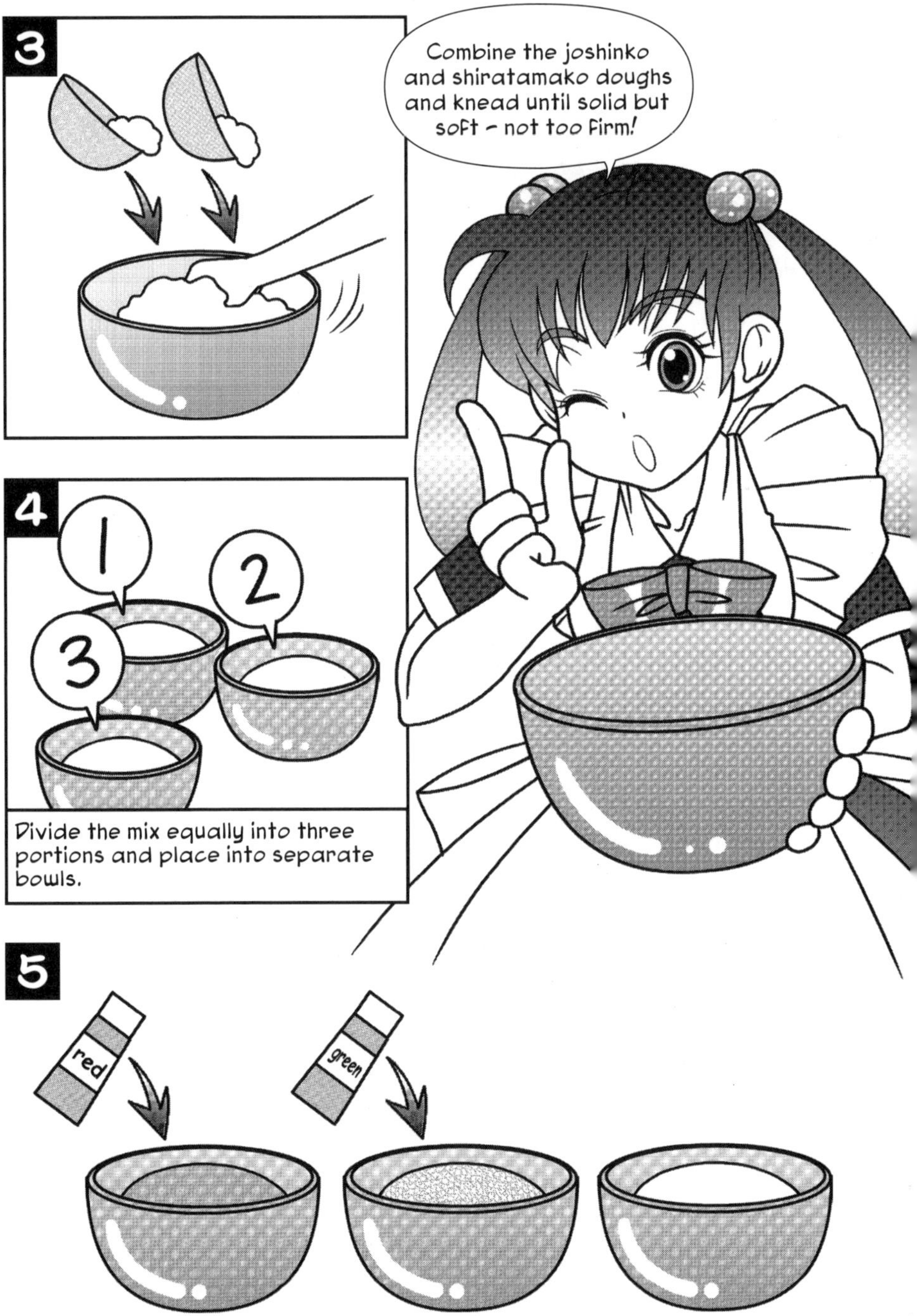
3
Combine the joshinko and shiratamako doughs and knead until solid but soft - not too firm!
4
1
2
3
Divide the mix equally into three portions and place into separate bowls.
5
red
green

Add 1 drop of red food coloring to the dough in one bowl,
and the matcha powder (which is green) to another.
Set the third bowl aside for white dango.

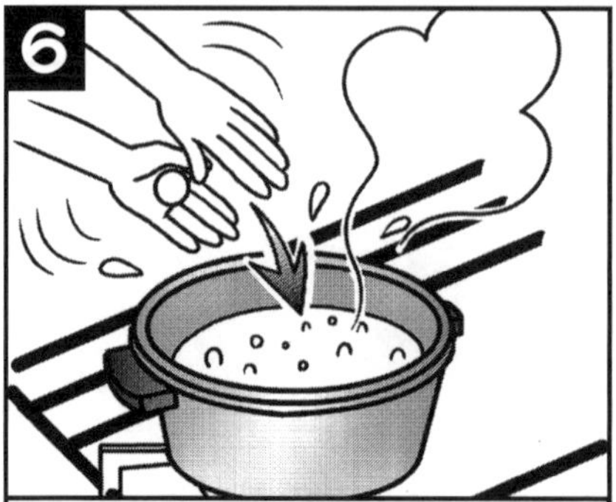

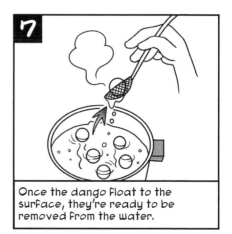

Roll the dough into bite-size balls and add to a pot of boiling water.

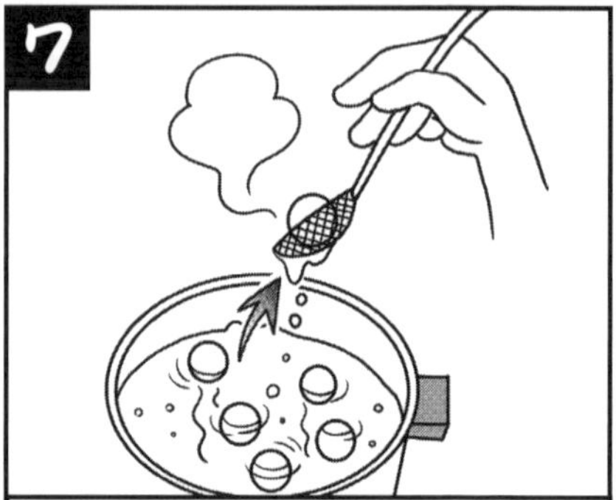

Once the dango float to the surface, they're ready to be removed from the water.

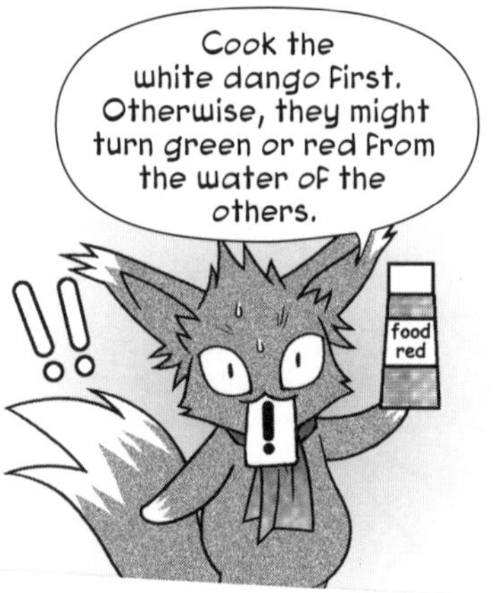
Cook the white dango first. Otherwise, they might turn green or red from the water of the others.
!!
food red
!

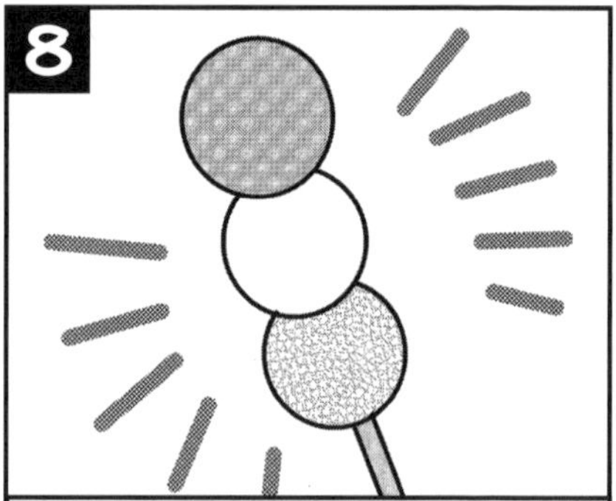

Place one of each color onto a skewer, as shown.

Miyuki's Notes on Dango

Dango are enjoyed year-round in Japan, and there are several varieties to choose from. Many of them are seasonal or regional, meaning there's always something new to try! My favorites are those covered with sweet, gooey sauces. Hiroshi prefers "mitarashi" dango, which are made with soy sauce, sugar and starch, and taste a bit salty.

Remember, if you can't find jyoshinko or shiratamako, you can substitute mochiko for both of them (see page 20).

Welcome to Wagashi

MANGA COOKBOOK

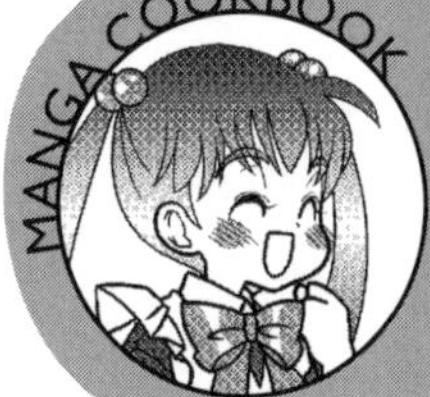

Anko Paste あんこ

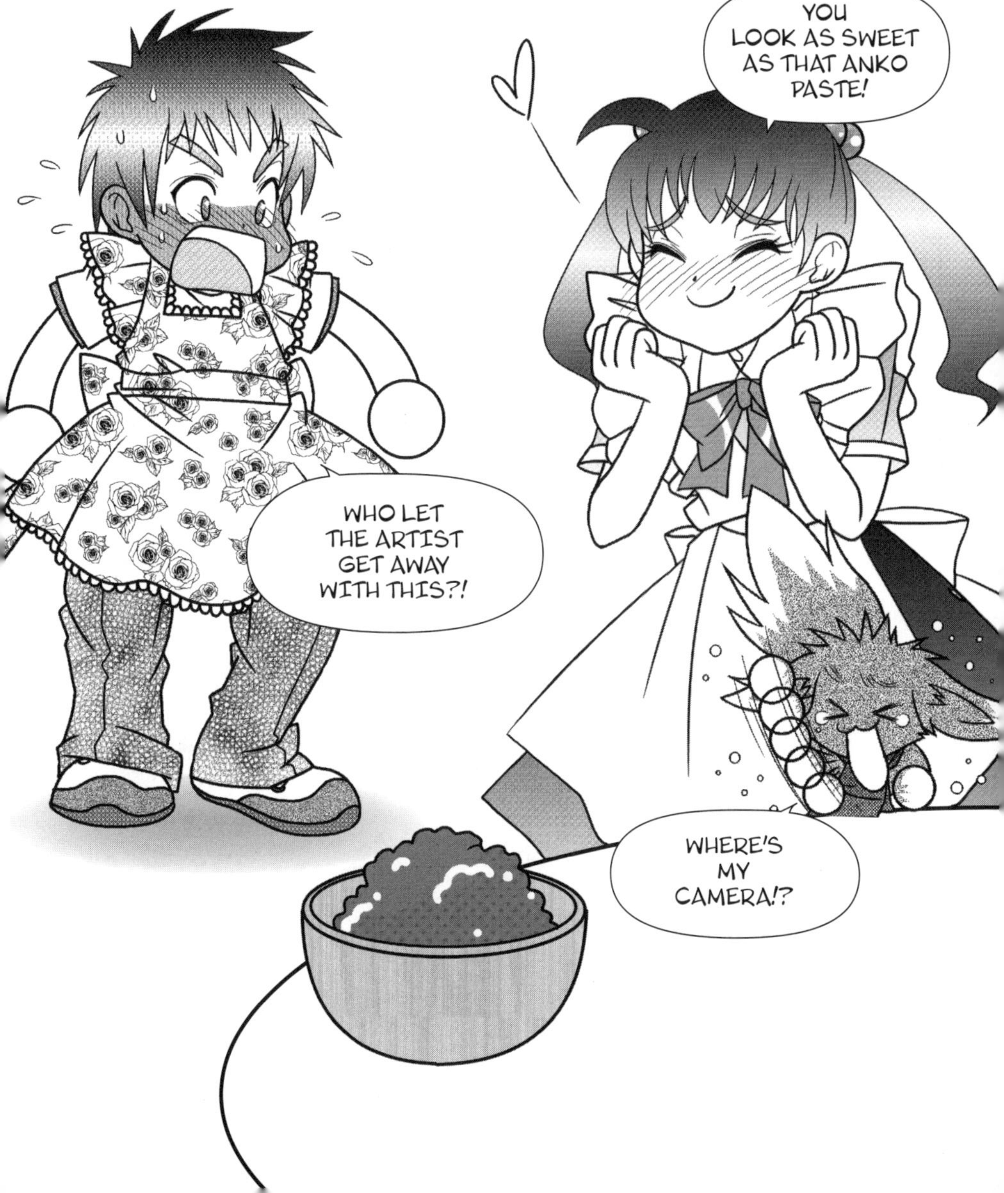
YOU LOOK AS SWEET AS THAT ANKO PASTE!
WHO LET THE ARTIST GET AWAY WITH THIS?!
WHERE'S MY CAMERA!?

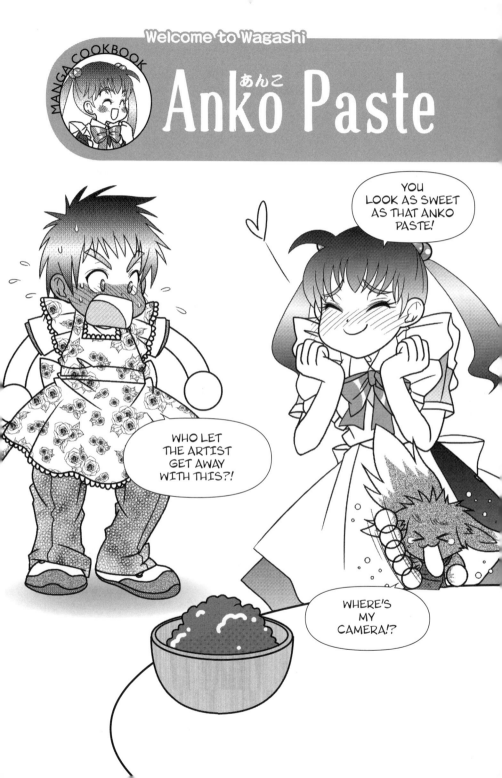

Anko Paste (sweet red bean paste)

- 2 cups adzuki beans (see page 20)
- 2 cups sugar
- 2 ½ teaspoons salt

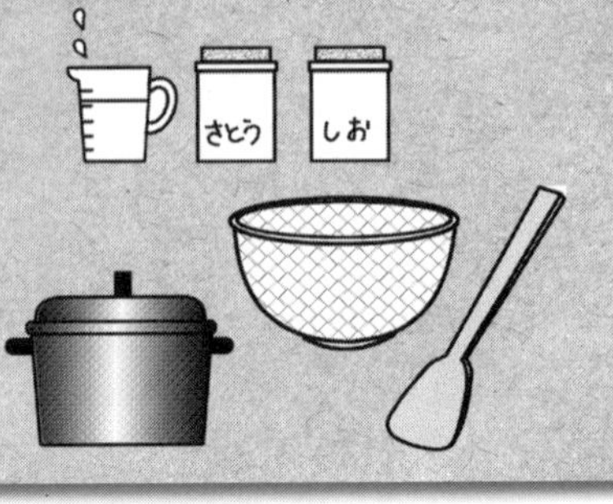

さとう
しお

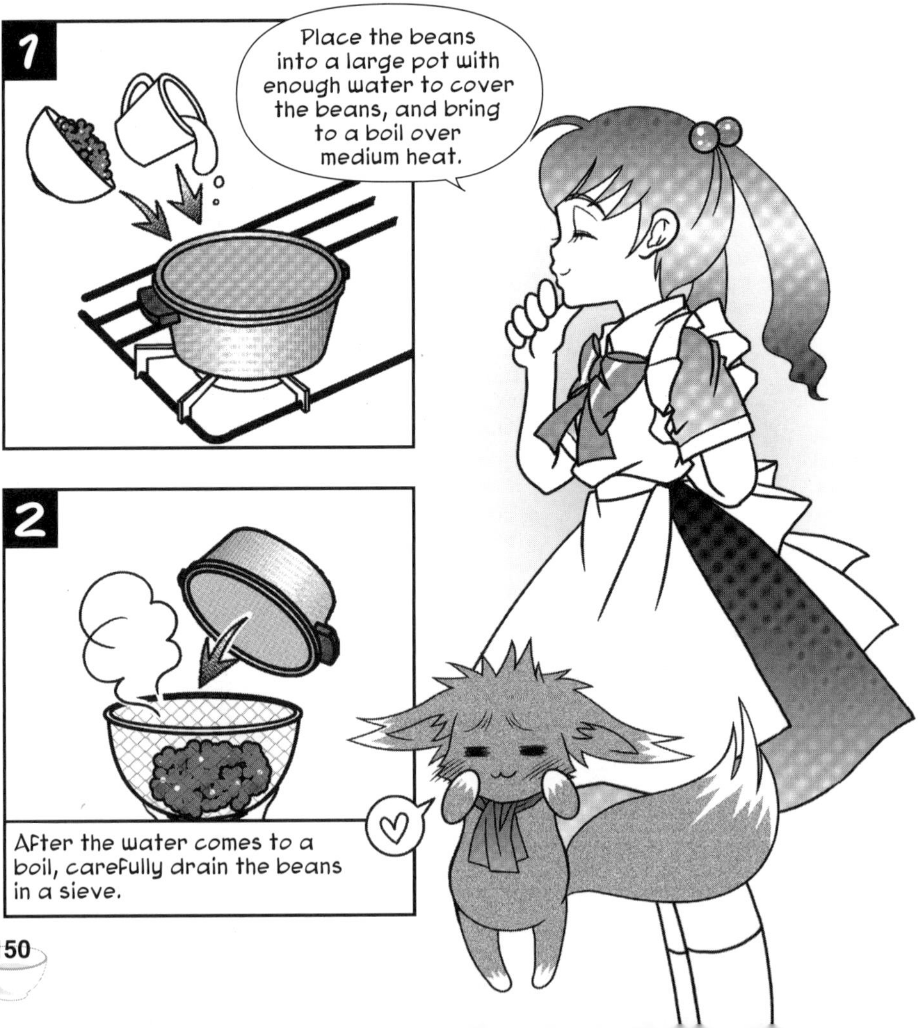

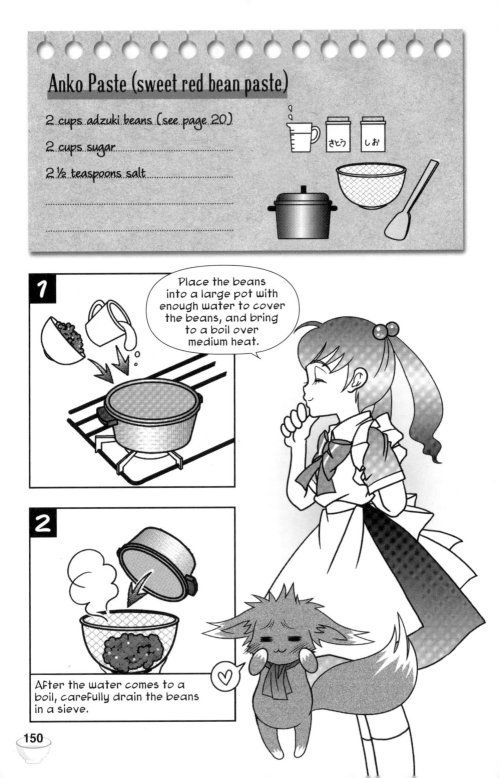

1
Place the beans into a large pot with enough water to cover the beans, and bring to a boil over medium heat.
2
After the water comes to a boil, carefully drain the beans in a sieve.

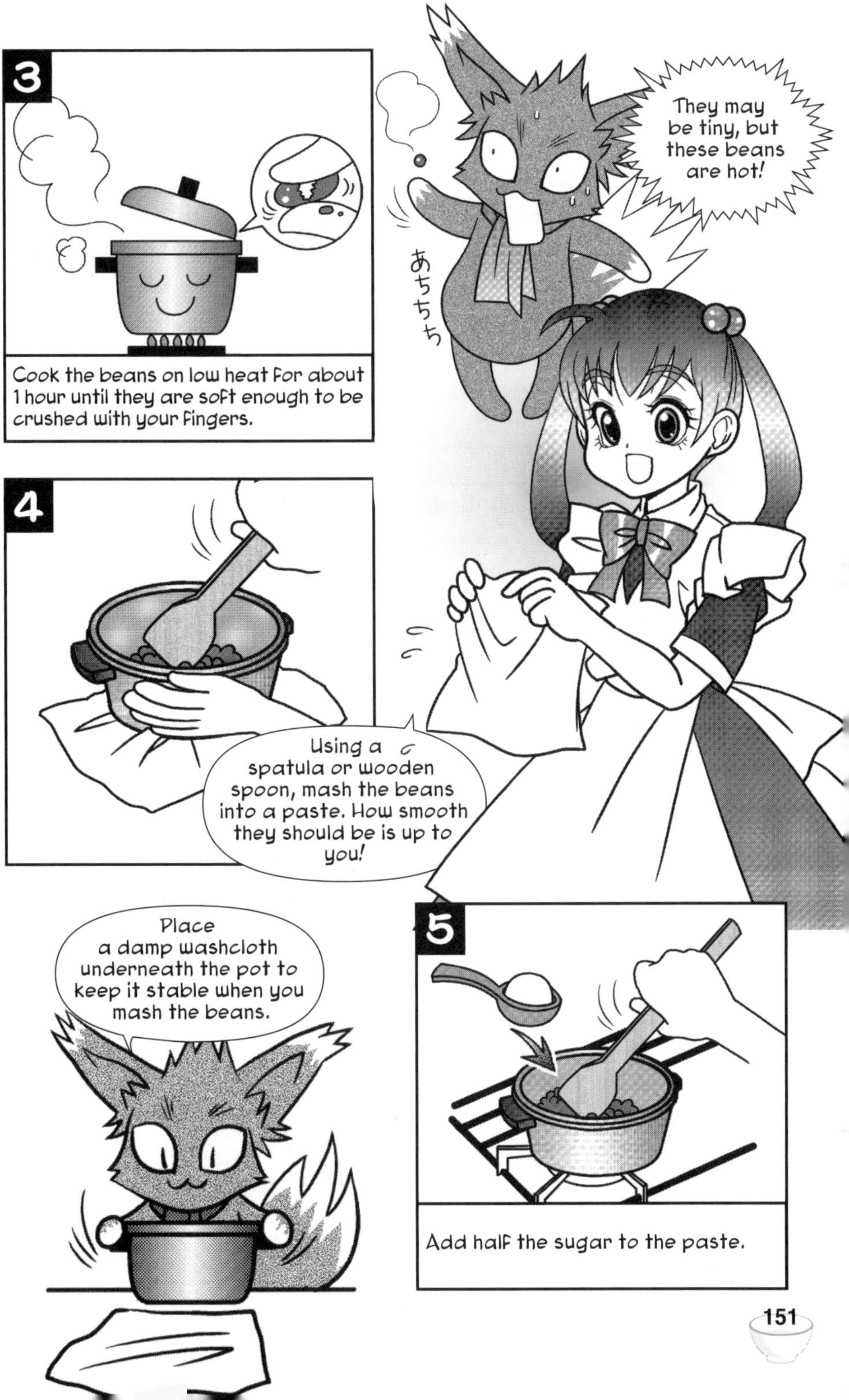
3
Cook the beans on low heat for about 1 hour until they are soft enough to be crushed with your fingers.
They may be tiny, but these beans are hot!
あちちち
4
Using a spatula or wooden spoon, mash the beans into a paste. How smooth they should be is up to you!
Place a damp washcloth underneath the pot to keep it stable when you mash the beans.
5
Add half the sugar to the paste.

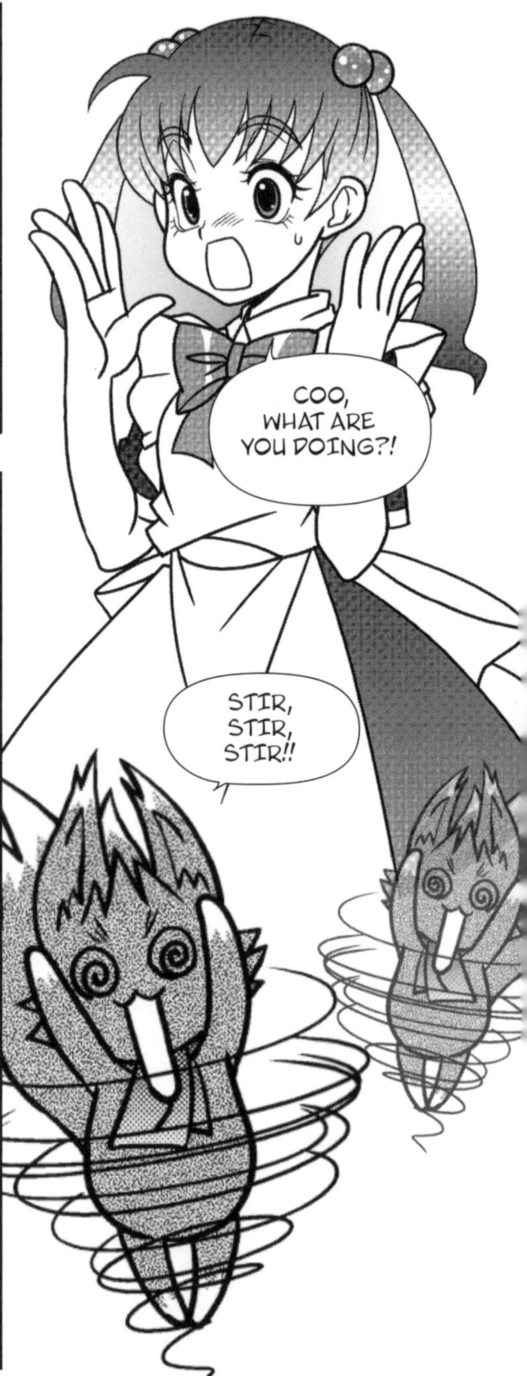
COO, WHAT ARE YOU DOING?!
STIR, STIR, STIR!!

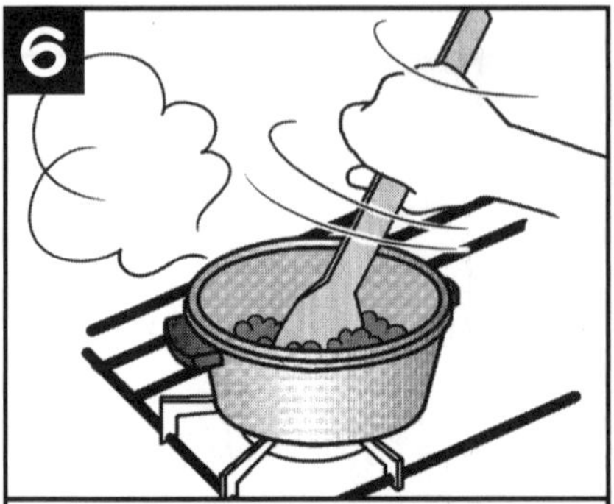
6

Warm over low heat and stir until the paste begins to thicken.

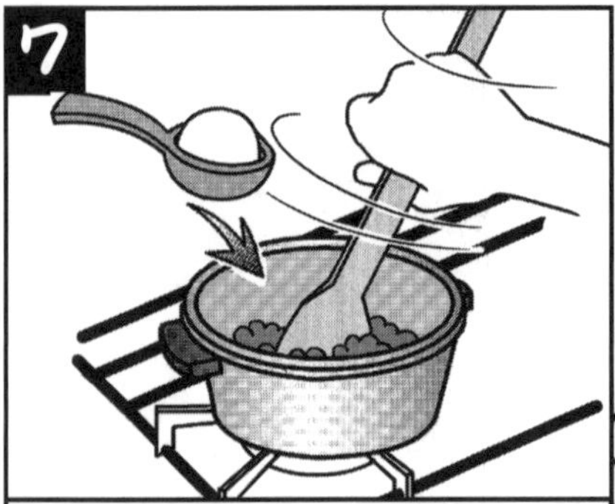
7

Stir in the other half of the sugar and continue to cook.

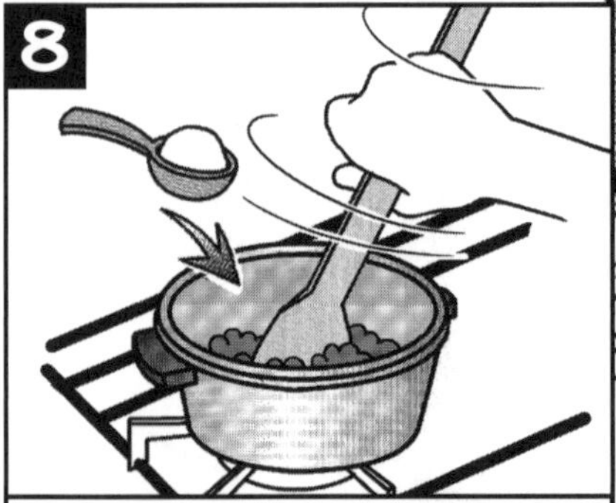
8

Stir in the salt and cook until the paste reaches the consistency of sticky mashed potatoes.

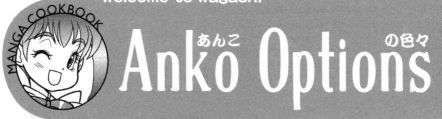

Welcome to Wagashi

Anko Options

あんこの色々

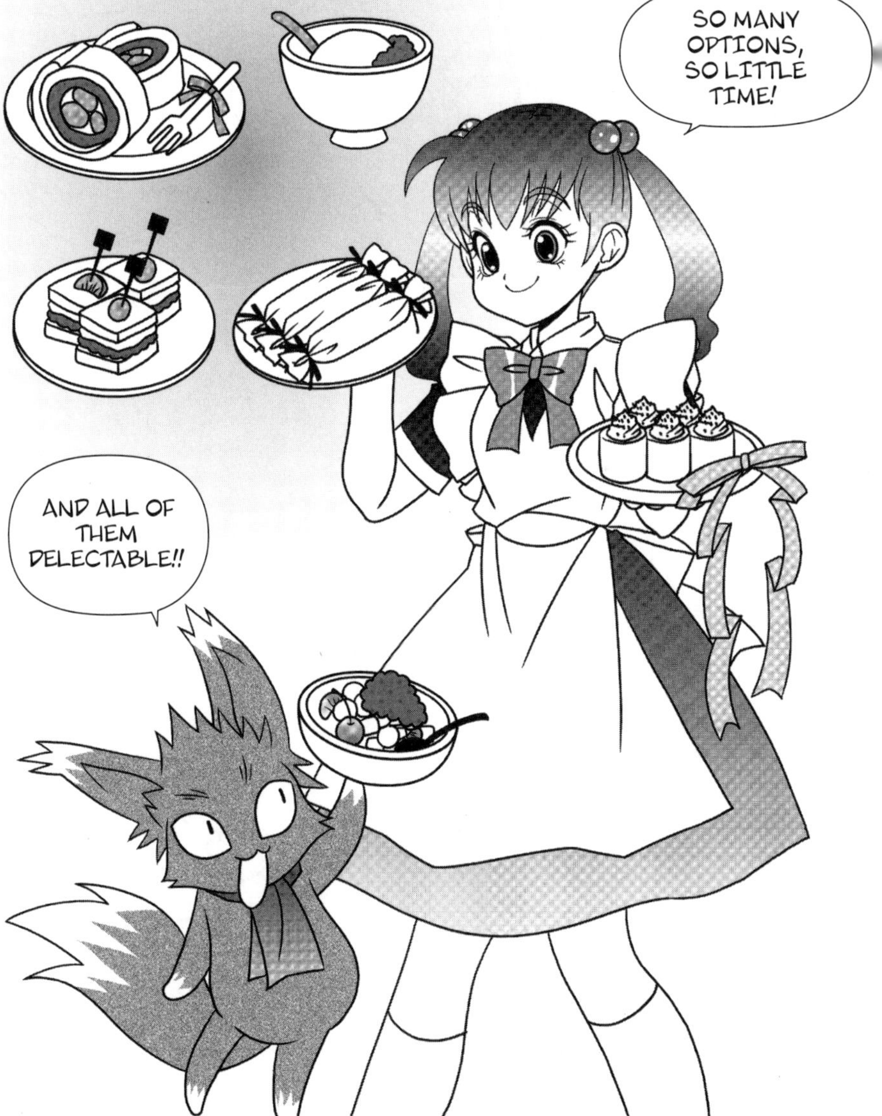
SO MANY OPTIONS, SO LITTLE TIME!
AND ALL OF THEM DELECTABLE!!

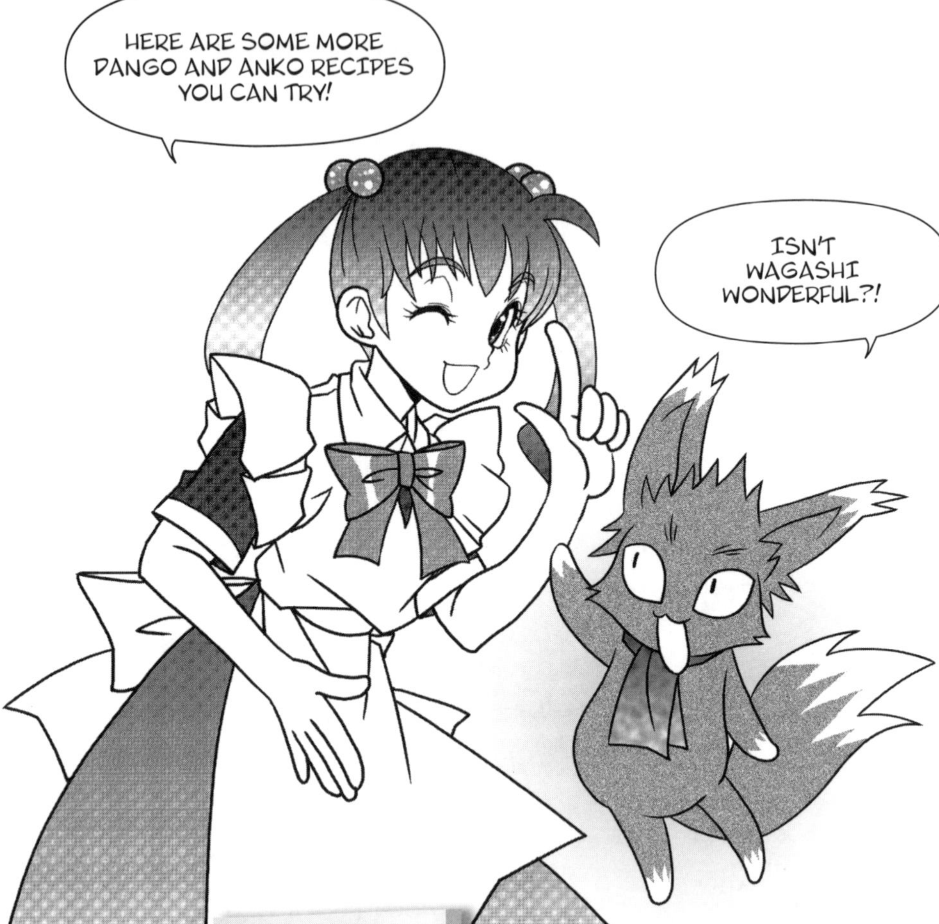
HERE ARE SOME MORE DANGO AND ANKO RECIPES YOU CAN TRY!
ISN'T WAGASHI WONDERFUL?!

Anko Dango

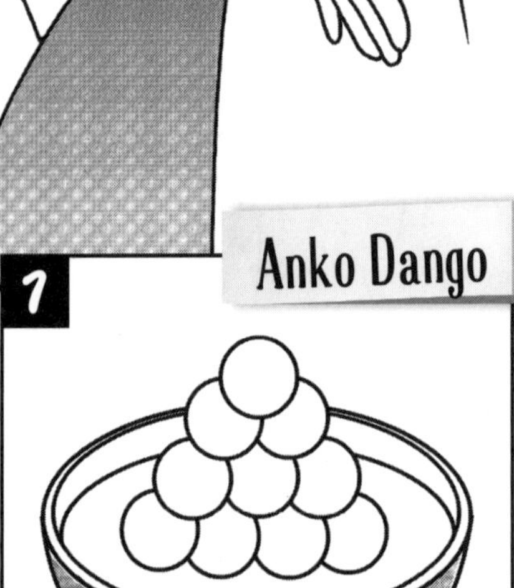
1

Begin with a pyramid of dango on a serving plate in a bowl.

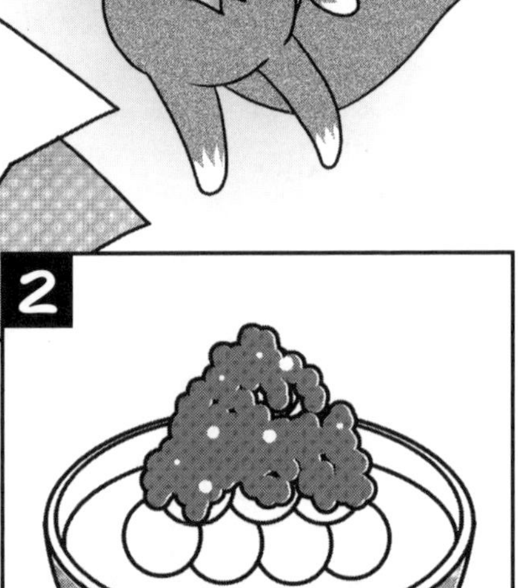
2

Top with a few large spoonfuls of anko paste. Serve and enjoy!

Anko Cake

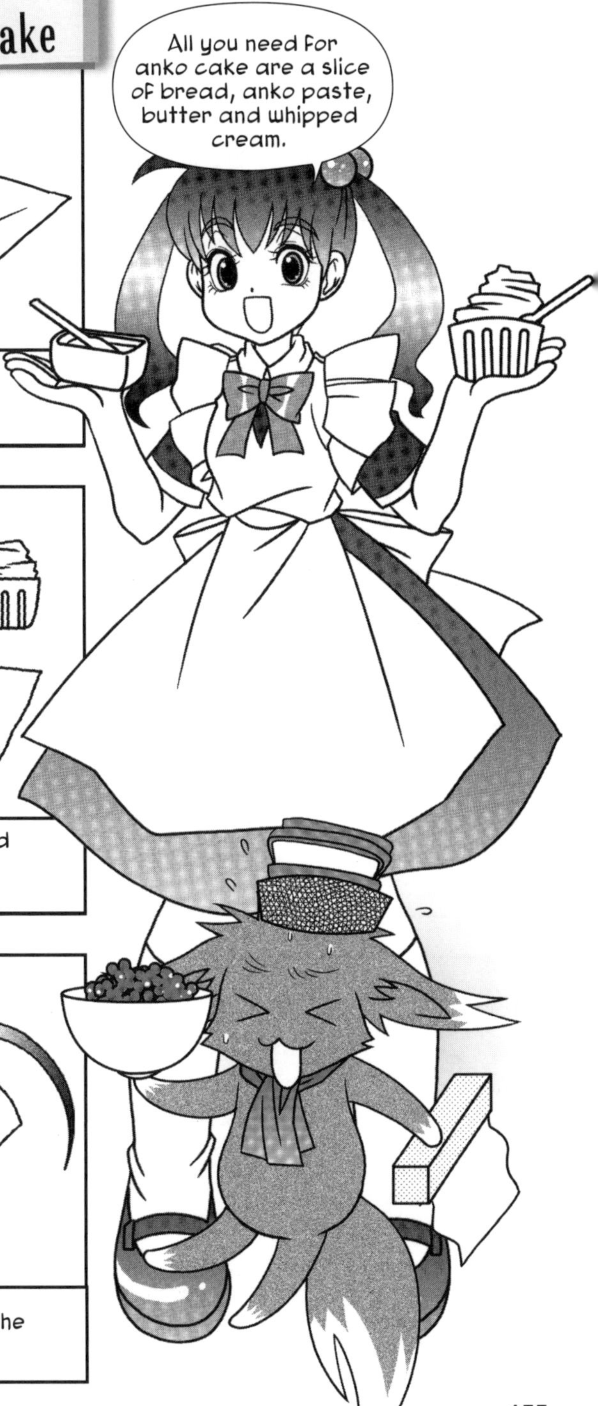
All you need for anko cake are a slice of bread, anko paste, butter and whipped cream.

1

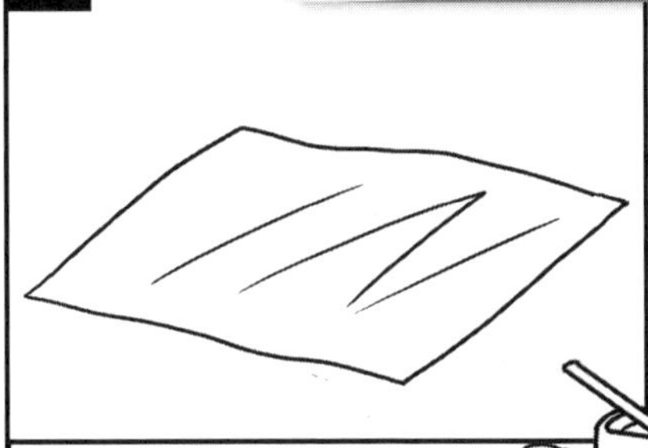

Start with a sheet of plastic wrap.

2

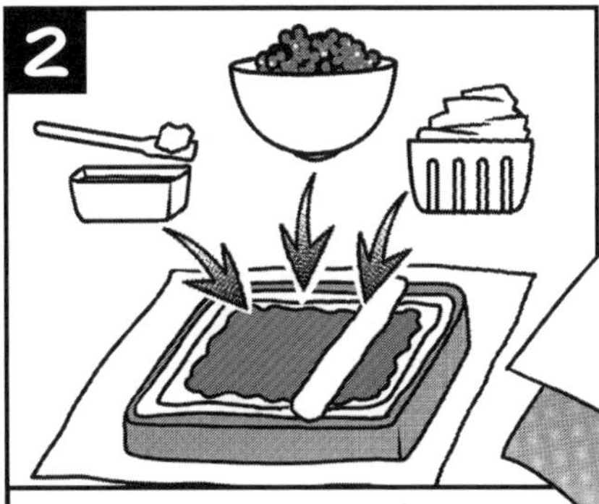

Spread some butter, whipped cream and anko paste onto a piece of bread.

3

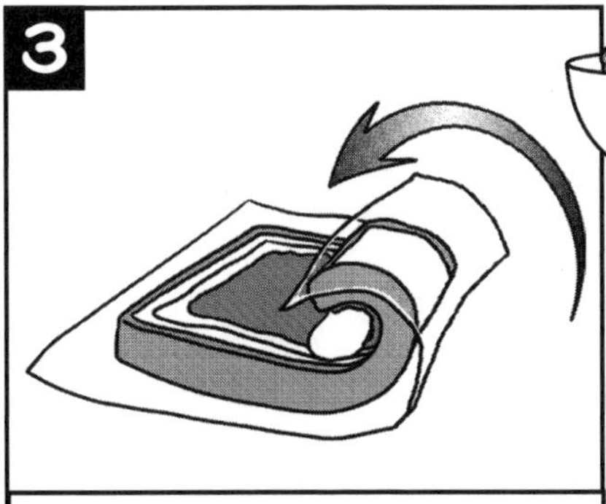

Use the plastic wrap to roll the bread into shape!

Anko Buns

1

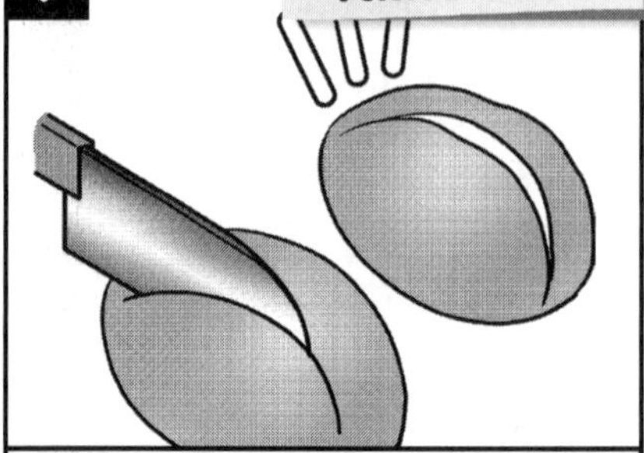

Slice a sweet roll or plain bun in half lengthwise.

2

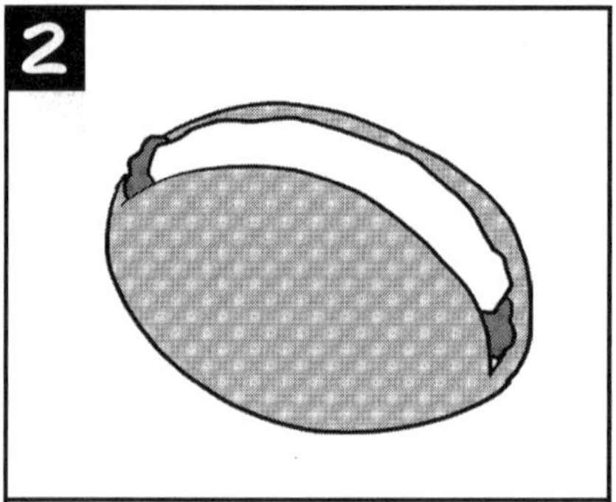

Fill the bun with anko paste and top with whipped cream.

3

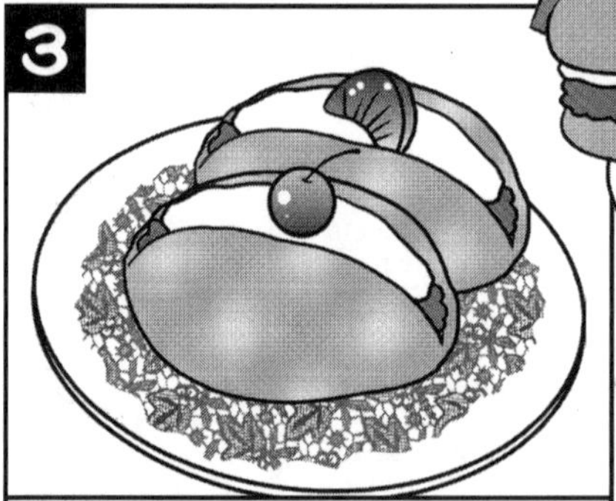

Decorate with orange slices or cherries.

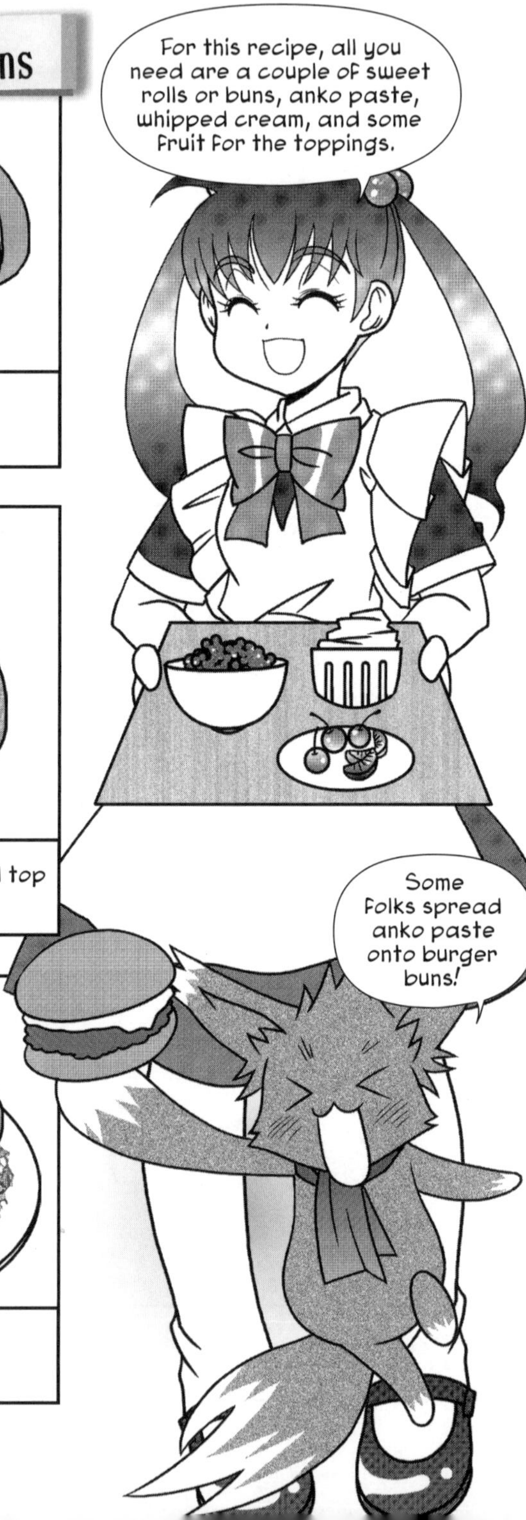
For this recipe, all you need are a couple of sweet rolls or buns, anko paste, whipped cream, and some fruit for the toppings.
Some folks spread anko paste onto burger buns!

Shiruko

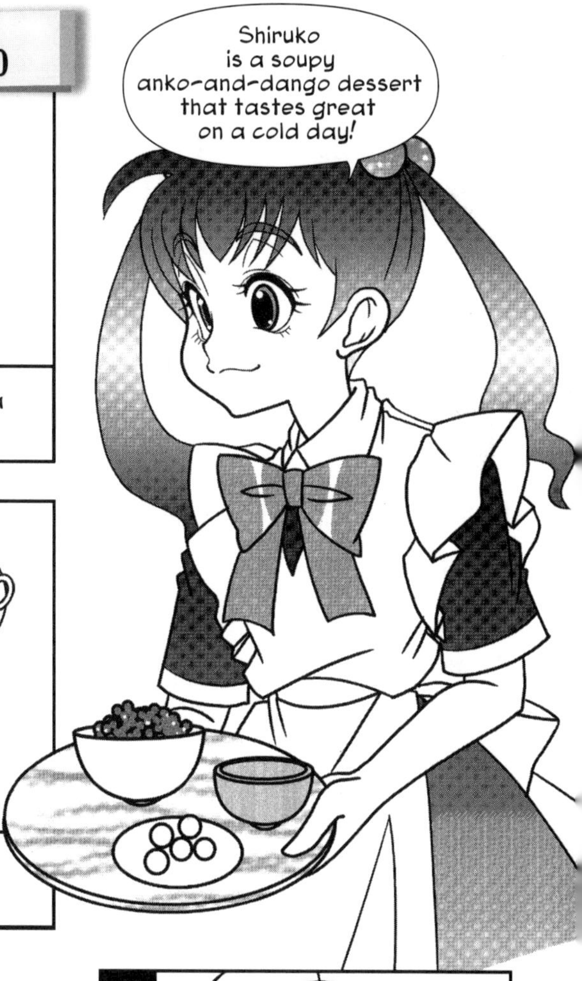
Shiruko is a soupy anko-and-dango dessert that tastes great on a cold day!

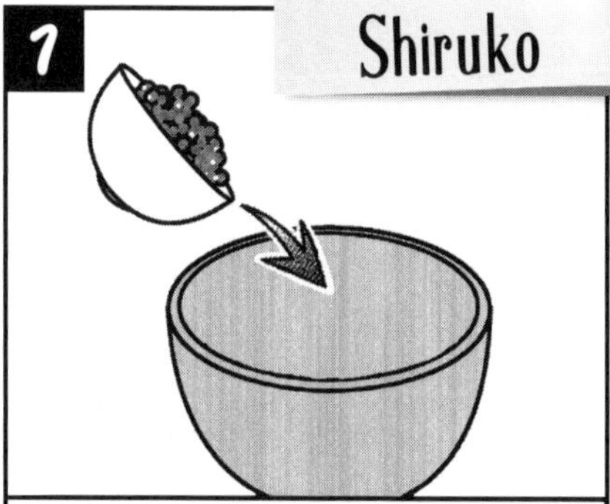
1

Place 1 cup of anko paste into a bowl.

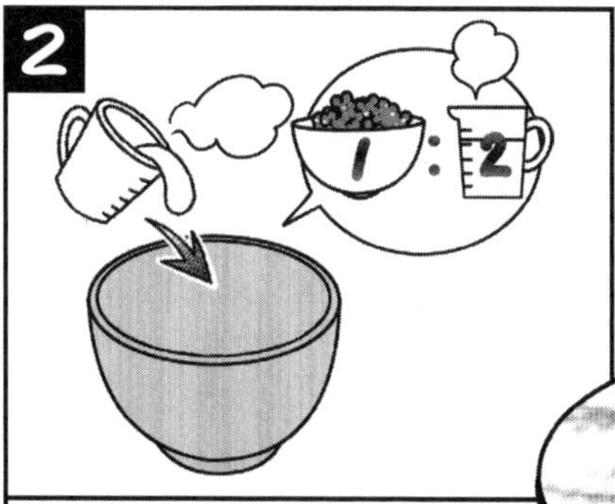
2
1 : 2

Add 2 cups of boiling water to the bowl.

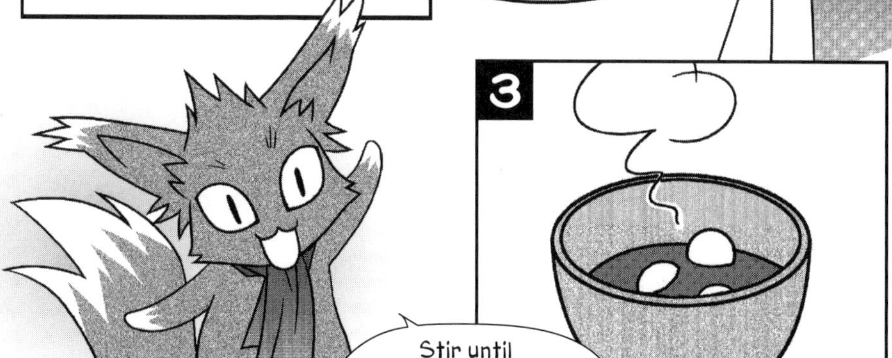
3
Stir until the paste is soupy, then add dango and serve hot! It's the perfect winter wagashi!

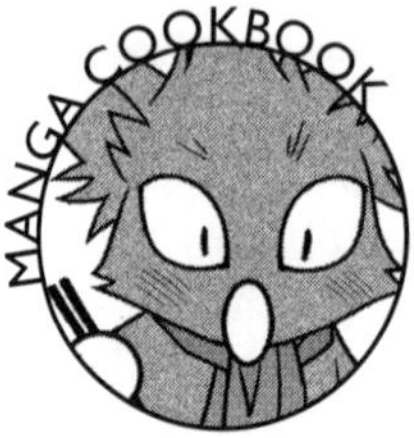
MANGA COOKBOOK

INDEX

RECIPES

MAIN INGREDIENTS

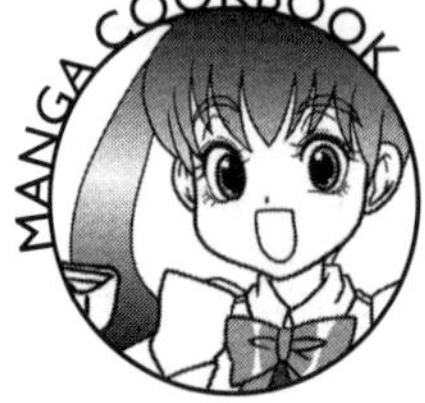
MANGA COOKBOOK

CREDITS

The Manga University Culinary Institute is:

YOKO ISHIHARA is a certified nutritionist and chef, having earned her degree from Japan's prestigious Kagawa Nutrition University. Ishihara-sensei contributed the recipes and notes to this book, and as a mother of three, knows nearly as much about manga as she does about cooking.

CHIHIRO HATTORI is best known as the artist whose delightful illustrations in Manga University's *Kanji de Manga* series have taught thousands of students how to read and write Japanese. An avid cook, she created some of the cute bento designs in this book, and has been known to sneak an Usagi Ringo or two into the lunch her husband carries to work.

Creative Director: Glenn Kardy
Project Coordinator: Mari Oyama
Translator: Naomi Rubin
Designers: Shinobu Sendai, Hiroko Takahashi, Naomi Rubin
Editorial Assistants: Eric Fischbach, Kelsey Brown
Asia-Pacific Logistics: Ron and Judy Hibbard

Special thanks to Edward Mazza